The BBC Shakespeare Plays

THE BBC SHAKESPEARE P·L·A·Y·S

Making the Televised Canon

SUSAN WILLIS

The University of North Carolina Press Chapel Hill *&* London

© 1991 The University of North
Carolina Press

Library of Congress Cataloging-in-
Publication Data
Willis, Susan, 1947–
    The BBC Shakespeare plays : making
the televised canon / by Susan Willis.
        p. cm.
    Includes bibliographical references
(p.   ) and index.
    ISBN 0-8078-1963-8 (cloth : alk.
paper)
    ISBN 0-8078-4317-2 (pbk. : alk.
paper)
    1. Shakespeare, William, 1564–
1616—Film and video adaptations.
2. BBC TV Shakespeare (Television
program) 3. Television
adaptations. I. Title.
PR3093.W55 1991
791.45'72—dc20 90-12899
                        CIP

The paper in this book meets the
guidelines for permanence and
durability of the Committee on
Production Guidelines for Book
Longevity of the Council on Library
Resources.

Manufactured in the United States of
America

95 94 93 92 91 5 4 3 2 1

Chapter 2 was published in somewhat
different form in *Shakespeare on
Television: An Anthology of Essays and
Reviews*, edited by J. C. Bulman and
H. R. Coursen. © 1988 by University
Press of New England. Used by
permission.

Portions of Chapter 5 were published in
somewhat different form in *Shakespeare
and the Arts: A Collection of Essays
from the Ohio Shakespeare Conference,
1981*, edited by Cecile Cary and Henry
Limouze. © 1982 by University Press of
America. Used by permission.

All quotations from the works of
Shakespeare are taken from *The BBC-
TV Shakespeare* scripts, which use the
Alexander text.

FOR BOB

who would have read it

Contents

Illustrations

Preface

The British Broadcasting Corporation (BBC) Shakespeare series, *The Shakespeare Plays*, the "First Folio of television" as it was called by some American television executives, began taping in 1978 and completed its 37-play cycle in 1985, marshaling the considerable resources of the BBC on behalf of England's premier playwright. The series thus affords ample scope for studying Shakespeare in production and also for studying television as a production medium for Renaissance drama.

The present study is a history of the BBC's production of Shakespeare's entire dramatic canon for television, a discussion of the producers and major directors who shaped the series, and a consideration of the technical elements of television that distinguish these productions from stage and film. Part 1 looks at the entire series itself as a phenomenon, its planning, various production decisions, outreach programs and materials, critical reception, and effect on both sides of the Atlantic. Part 2 examines the theories and procedures of the major directors and considers the stylistic choices that determine so much of the visual element in this visual medium. Part 3 provides a set of production diaries based on my observations at the BBC during the making of three Shakespeare productions; these offer a view of the creative process involved as well as insight into the exigencies of such television work.

Throughout this study, my focus is on primary materials and production experience as an aid to viewing, for knowledge of the production exigencies and overall circumstances of the series's history can enhance the critical response to the productions. This study, therefore, is intended as a history of the process and a descriptive basis for the analysis and evaluation of the BBC Shakespeare series.

Much of the research for this study was done during the making of the BBC Shakespeare series because I was granted the privilege of watching the BBC at work. As a researcher rather than a BBC insider, I have necessarily gone by what I experienced, what I learned, and what I was told. Throughout my observations and interviews, I have striven to establish an accurate account of events and procedures, and obviously without the help and cooperation of a great many people this study could not have been completed. Wherever possible I have cross-checked information, and I have tried to treat all my sources and subjects with respect and discretion, especially in the delicate area of production diaries, for rehearsal is necessarily the most private aspect of production, and taping and editing are intense activities.

The debts of thanks I owe are almost boundless, as is my gratitude for the help I was given and the kindness I was shown during my research on the BBC Shakespeare series, yet some specific debts must be paid. My colleague Bob Gaines, who dared me to find out what we both wanted to know, and Marvin Rosenberg and the National Endowment for the Humanities, who got me to England to study Shakespeare in production with a lively group of people, started far more than they know, for which I am grateful. To Jonathan Miller, whose openness and generosity made it all possible and thereby changed a decade of my life; to Henry Fenwick, *il miglior fabbro*, who shared his wisdom and insight and whose primary materials are essential for work on the series; to Fraser Lowden, who heaved only small sighs at all my interruptions and who was unfailingly helpful—words cannot express the depth of my thanks. I appreciate Shaun Sutton's allowing me to continue my work, James Cellan-Jones's willingness to let me observe, Jane Howell's and Elijah Moshinsky's taking time for interviews, and BBC staff members' and British and American corporate executives' talking with me and making materials available. Thanks are also due to Auburn University at Montgomery for adding the taped series to its collection and for a quarter leave and two research grants-in-aid to help with research; to the university's reference librarians; to Mary Maher for sharing interview material; to the Shakespeare Centre Library in Stratford-upon-Avon and its librarians; to Sandra Eisdorfer and the University of North Carolina Press for their encouragement; and of course to the BBC.

I am grateful to Marilee Mallory for her generous help putting the manuscript on computer; to Chet Palmer for being computer guru; to Ray Dooley for reading the manuscript; to Franz Michel for sharing his rehearsal photographs; and to Judith Paterson, Cindi Sutherland, Cheryl McKiearnan, and Donald Nobles for hospitality or for help during my research forays. To Sal Brinton, Patricia Preece, and Karen Edwards, whose friendships made a real difference; to Nancy and Rick Anderson and George Browning, the long-suffering friends who over the years maintained the home-front for me; to Brian and Karen Hynes for cheerfully offering friendship and a home away from home; and to my family for endless cat-sitting and moral support, many thanks are not enough.

If there are errors or oversights in this work, despite my best efforts at accuracy, they are entirely my responsibility.

Susan Willis
Montgomery, Alabama

One

A History of the BBC

Shakespeare Series

Therefore let every man now task his thought
That this fair action may on foot be brought.
—Henry V

Let's follow to see the end of this ado.
—The Taming of the Shrew

1 The BBC and

The Shakespeare Plays

One fine summer day in Scotland the BBC Shakespeare series was conceived out of whimsy. Surveying the grounds at Glamis Castle in 1975 while directing James Barrie's *The Little Minister* on location there, BBC producer Cedric Messina observed that the park would be the perfect setting for an *As You Like It*, and the BBC Shakespeare series originated. Of course, it was not the Shakespeare series then, that massive cultural and educational phenomenon, for only as Messina pursued his idea about *As You Like It* did he expand it to include the entire Shakespeare canon. But that original moment of inspiration generated the sequence of events that evolved the televised series.

As Messina officially recounts it in the preface to the series's scripts,

> The autumn of 1975 gave birth to the idea of recording the complete canon of the thirty-seven plays of the national playwright. . . . The first memo on the subject of televising all the plays emanated from my office on 3 November 1975, and was addressed to Alasdair Milne, then Director of Programmes, and now Managing Director, Television. We were asking for his blessing on the project. His reply was immediate and enthusiastic, as was that of the present Director-General, Ian Trethowan. This warm response to the idea stimulated us in the Plays Department to explore the possibility of making the plan a reality—six plays per year for six years, with one odd man out. It has been called the greatest project the BBC has ever undertaken.[1]

It all sounds rather jolly and effortless. But, in fact, not everyone in the Drama division and the BBC favored Messina or the project, and he had to labor to gather the support he needed.

Messina first had to sell the idea of a Shakespeare series to his own colleagues in the BBC's Drama/Plays group, who proved his most difficult challenge. Their doubts were both aesthetic and economic, the horns on which any production proposal is apt to be caught. Those in charge of Drama gave little support to Messina's first proposal, saying no one had really discovered how to do Shakespeare on television yet, and moreover it was an absurd idea: there were, after all, *thirty-seven* plays by Shakespeare and no compelling reason to do them all. There would be no support from BBC Enterprises, the sales and services branch of the organization, they argued, nor would there be overseas sales. (In that, of course, due to careful marketing, the series ultimately surprised them.) Advocates of the series pointed out its educational value, especially in America. One such proponent was Alan Shallcross, Messina's script editor, who continued that role into the Shakespeare series until he became a producer himself; he had taught at New York's City College for a year and testified that American students often knew comparatively little about drama. The BBC could have a first with the entire canon on television, an opportunity that perhaps it alone had the organizational capability to achieve; furthermore, Shakespeare was not just the world's greatest dramatist but also a native English playwright. Why not do the series, they urged.

Whatever reasons backed the idea, opposition was firm, and it appeared for a time that the proposal would die in the Drama group. Then Messina benefited from some organizational strategy and a bit of luck. Rather than be denied, he forwarded the proposal over their heads, to the administration at the BBC—the Director of Programmes and the Director-General—seeking their good wishes. Once beyond the divisional politics and power brokering of the Drama group, Messina's public relations ability had greater effect; more people were exposed to the idea, the educational division offered to plan introductory programs, and at length he won the support of Alasdair Milne and Ian Trethowan, who intervened in the Drama group's planning on behalf of the Shakespeare series idea. The Drama section at last acquiesced, though those involved did not forget. So the proposal went into planning. It is likely that the very scope of the endeavor finally became more asset than liability during these considerations, appealing to the "charge of the light brigade" values that built the British Empire—it was a grand project, no one else could do it, no one else would do it, but it ought to be done. Thus, in the moral equation of gallantry, duty transformed into desire, and the scheme was sanctioned because, as Henry Fenwick observed, it seemed "gloriously British and gloriously BBC."[2]

Almost simultaneously the proposed series met with some unlooked-for good fortune. Before the series was officially under way, Alan Shallcross's cousin Denham Challender, then executive officer of Morgan Guaranty Trust Company of New York's Tokyo office and aware that Morgan Bank was interested in underwriting a public arts endeavor, suggested to his superiors the Shakespeare series as a project to support. Morgan Bank then contacted the BBC to discuss possibilities. With coproduction money springing up and the blessings of the upper echelons at the BBC, Messina embarked on the long, slow process of arranging the infinite details to make the proposal a reality. A large, dynamic South African, a wheeler-dealer who can be both pompous and appealing, a man long involved with drama productions at the BBC, Messina had the credentials and the organizational drive to spend several years pushing for the project, gaining commitments, pursuing financial backers, and arranging funding. He was a man with a cause, and Messina can be very effective when working for a cause, but he was also at the right place at the right time.

Messina marshaled some strong arguments on behalf of the series. As he had pointed out, of the entire television industry, the BBC was uniquely prepared to undertake such an endeavor, for drama was already a regular and significant component of BBC television production, with an accepted and important place in the BBC's overall mission to inform, to educate, and to entertain. In 1975 when Messina proposed the series, the division of the BBC known as Drama/Plays was producing as many as 120 plays a year, which in terms of viewing is roughly two per week, a figure that does not include serialized productions, which fall into a separate BBC drama group, Series and Serials.

Since the mid-1950s the finest contemporary dramatists had provided original television scripts to the BBC and Britain's commercial television companies, playwrights the likes of Tom Stoppard, Harold Pinter, Samuel Beckett, John Osborne, Trevor Griffiths, Howard Brenton, Alan Bennett, David Hare, Simon Gray, and Michael Frayn, among others.[3] For over twenty years drama had had a vital artistic forum on British television. As the Shakespeare series began, London television critic Sean Day-Lewis claimed that "no broadcasting organisation and no theatre has produced half so many good new plays as BBC television has managed in this decade."[4] And in addition to new plays, traditionally scheduled on BBC 1, the classics also figured prominently in BBC drama, works by Sophocles and Shaw, Ibsen and Chekhov, and of course Shakespeare, usually shown on BBC 2. It was high tide for television drama, which taken at the flood as it was by Messina led to the good fortune of the Shakespeare series. Such a proposal would have been impossible had it appeared even a few years later, for then the tide was ebbing, not only due to budget constraints but to a progressive withdrawal of former coproduction sources and an Americanization of programming priorities away from single dramas. The Shakespeare series may well be the last expression of the exuberant British commitment to drama on television, if the current trend continues.

A look at the years during which the Shakespeare series was produced is instructive of the place of drama within the BBC. While such drama productions accounted for only about 5 percent of the BBC's actual on-the-air hours per week in 1983, for instance, the BBC allocated more than 20 percent of its network production budget to drama, an area that also used 41 percent of its design and scenic services, almost as much as all other areas combined, at a cost averaging £200,000 per hour produced, by far the most expensive of the BBC's program areas.[5] Long-standing regular drama slots in BBC television scheduling included *Play for Today*, *Play of the Month*, *60-Minute Playhouse*, *45-/50-Minute Playhouse*, and *Theatre Night*. For 1984–85 *Play for Today* had seventeen productions; *Play of the Month* six; *60-Minute Playhouse* six; *45-/50-Minute Playhouse* eight; and *Theatre Night* on BBC 2 four, not counting the Shakespeare plays. But the effect of changing times shows in the number of plays produced. Unlike the 120 plays produced annually a decade before, in 1983–84 the BBC produced approximately 45 single plays in addition to the serials, with 2 or 3 contemporary plays for every classic. By 1986–87 the total for production had declined to 28 plays, and some of those already taped had not yet been scheduled for broadcast. Thus, it is not just that Drama/Plays at the BBC was accustomed to producing drama for television, but that Messina approached the BBC at a propitious time for a large drama project.

For years Messina himself had produced the *Play of the Month*, and when citing the BBC's credentials for televising the Shakespeare series he proudly points to these broadcasts specifically:

> The BBC has presented during the last ten years, at peak viewing time on BBC 1 on every fourth Sunday night, *Play of the Month*, a series of classical productions ranging from all the major plays of Chekhov to a number of Shavian masterpieces. Aeschylus has been produced in the series, and so have many of the plays of William Shakespeare. So not only in the presentation of Shakespeare, but also in the translation to the screen of the great dramatic statements of all ages and countries has the BBC demonstrated that it is fully equipped to meet the enormous challenge of *The BBC Television Shakespeare*.[6]

Messina's point about the BBC's production experience is well taken, for the BBC began producing individual Shakespeare plays for television early in 1937. Since that initial production of scenes from *As You Like It*, in fact, the BBC has televised thirty-two of the thirty-seven plays. After an outburst of entire productions of or scenes from thirteen different Shakespeare plays in 1937 and five more productions in 1938–39, the BBC has fairly steadily produced several plays a year since 1946. *Julius Caesar*, *A Midsummer Night's Dream*, and *Macbeth* have been most frequently produced in part or whole (eight to ten times each), with *Twelfth Night*, *Henry V*, and *Othello* following (five to seven renditions each).

Before the Shakespeare series, all the other plays in the canon had had at least one and sometimes up to four BBC televised productions except *Henry VIII*, *Pericles*, *Timon of Athens*, *Titus Andronicus*, and *The Two Gentlemen of Verona*, none of which the BBC had televised.[7] While the BBC occasionally taped theatrical productions, such as the Royal Shakespeare Company's (RSC) *Wars of the Roses* (1965), the National Youth Theatre's *Troilus and Cressida* (1966), and Franco Zeffirelli's National Theatre production of *Much Ado About Nothing* (1967), among others, the vast majority of the productions were made by the BBC specifically for television, most of them in the studio with about 10 percent outside broadcasts (location work), such as the 1974 *Twelfth Night* filmed at Castle Howard with Janet Suzman as Viola. There was no established house style for Shakespeare at the BBC because the productions were spread over so many years with different directors and were often made for different purposes and audiences. Since 1957, for instance, some have been specially made as Plays for Schools, that is, streamlined versions of the plays emphasizing major scenes produced with students in mind and broadcast during school hours in installments.

Yet televising most of the canon over a forty-year span differs significantly from planning to produce the entire canon in six years, an endeavor requiring special organization and special funding. Messina focused his efforts on getting financial backing for his plan and after three years of wooing and maneuvering was able to combine £1.5 million ($3.6 million) of American backing in coproduction with Time/Life, based on grants from Exxon Corporation, Metropolitan Life Insurance Company, and Morgan Guaranty Trust Company of New York, with £5.5 million in British funds to come up with the £7 million ($13.5 million) 37-play production budget he needed[8]—a huge investment that many questioned. But the series belied worries that it would not sell. By 1982, the series had paid for itself and was even making a profit due to foreign sales; according to a press report, Brian Wenham, Controller of BBC 2, "claimed . . . that Shakespeare is the *only* series of programmes whose sales have completely covered their costs in this way."[9]

Garnering the American money proved more difficult than the early interest had implied due to the politics of modern artistic endeavor. The general credits for the series in America suggest the complexity of the arrangements: "The series is made possible by grants from Exxon, Metropolitan Life, and Morgan Bank. It is a BBC-TV and Time/Life television co-production, presented for the Public Broadcasting Service by WNET/Thirteen, New York." Each of the groups credited played a vital role in establishing the series. Morgan Bank was interested in beginning public service outreach such as arts funding but found the $3.6 million the series needed a bit steep for an initial venture. Meanwhile, Exxon heard of the series and approached Morgan Bank to suggest a joint underwriting, but Exxon only wanted to offer one-third of the capital. WNET, the New York City Public Broadcasting Service (PBS) station long associated with the BBC, and Time/Life, which as the BBC's American distributor and agent at the time was coproducer of this venture involving American money, realized they needed a third funder when late in 1976 the Corporation for Public Broadcasting (CPB) got involved in the discussion.[10] Because the CPB used public funds, its interest in the series aroused the attention of American labor unions and theatre professionals, who saw American money going to subsidize British productions at the cost of American jobs as an explicit slight to American artistry. The American Federation of Television and Radio Artists (AFTRA), joined by the American Federation of Labor and Congress of Industrial Organizations (AFL-CIO), pressured the CPB's board of directors to withdraw its commitment. A furor was building, but before it forced a decision, early in 1978 another underwriter appeared, Metropolitan Life Insurance Company.

In fact, the first *Much Ado* and *Romeo and Juliet* had already been taped by February 1978, so the resolution of the American financial support was timely. All the money was budgeted with an inflation rate of about 5 percent, and the American funds were contracted at a set rate of exchange, $1.80/£,[11] so that by 1980 when the pound was worth nearly $2.50 those overseeing the money in Drama/Plays at the BBC said "it was hardly worth it."

The dollar slowly strengthened and by series's end in 1984–85 was briefly almost $1/£, but the advantage came too late to help much of the financing.

Though it provided only a part of the money necessary for the series, such a coalition to underwrite arts programming is remarkable for American corporations; firms usually want sole credit for any endeavor. Jac Venza, WNET's Executive Producer for Performance Programs, observed, "It was one of the few times that we got three separate corporate funders to agree to funding something six years into the future. That was in itself a kind of extraordinary feat."[12] Yet each American firm chose to underwrite the BBC Shakespeare series for a different reason. According to Sheila Walker of McCaffrey-McCall, Exxon's advertising agency, Exxon was already the biggest single supporter of the arts in the United States[13] and had been one of the five or six major underwriters of PBS programs, such as the *Great Performances* series, the slot in which the Shakespeare series was eventually broadcast. For both Morgan Bank and Metropolitan Life, the appeal of the Shakespeare series was the permanence of the achievement, the fact of doing the entire canon, and "quality identification" with Shakespeare and the BBC.[14]

Working out the knotted skein of financial and distribution details took time and patience, but Messina was unrelenting in his efforts. In fact, there would have been no BBC Shakespeare series without Cedric Messina and his fund-raising. His dedication, tenacity, and persuasiveness pulled together agreements, both technical and financial, that let the series occur. He was forthright about his abilities and priorities regarding the series; he stated flatly that he was no Shakespeare scholar, "and I don't mind saying that. But I sure know how to get his plays produced. That's what's really important, isn't it? . . . There's a certain philosophy behind any project, but the main thought is to get the show on the road. And that was perhaps the hardest part of the task."[15] Others involved had more worries about the philosophy behind the project, though. Concerned lest the productions get too wild or experimental, the American underwriters sanctioned Messina's stated goal, which was to make solid, basic televised versions of Shakespeare's plays to reach a wide television audience and to enhance the teaching of Shakespeare. They used their promised financial contributions for aesthetic leverage and wrote into the contract a brief description as guideline for the productions: the plays were to be set in Shakespeare's own time or in the historical period of the events (such as ancient Rome for *Julius Caesar*, around 1400 for *Richard II*), they were to be no more than 2½ hours long, and they were to have "maximum acceptability to the widest possible audience."

Though this brief, as it came to be known, governed the entire series's approach to the plays, it posed no initial problem, for it merely stated Messina's intentions. But the brief does raise several questions, all of which demonstrate that far more concern was spent on financial matters than on interpretive or aesthetic issues in planning the series. To insist on period setting may seem mild enough, but period fidelity is no guarantee of success. Shakespeare's own company used contemporary rather than historical dress, and while much can be gained by setting a Shakespeare play in its own era, that is not the only useful approach to production. Modern-dress productions have been some of the strongest contemporary successes, for instance, the Royal Shakespeare Company's 1965 *Hamlet* with David Warner or Richard Burton's "rehearsal clothes" *Hamlet*. The RSC, like other companies, has in recent years also quite effectively used Victorian and Edwardian settings for Shakespeare's plays, and Peter Brook's *A Midsummer Night's Dream* with trapezes in a white box was hardly a Renaissance "period" production. No wonder some critics saw the series as tame and conservative, but the decision was based on financial caution rather than aesthetics.

More disturbing than a restriction of setting is the limit on running time, a purely practical consideration of those in the television business. Alan Shallcross, script editor of the first two seasons, pointed out the accepted television belief that "if you ask someone to sit for more than two hours you're in trouble."[16] Based on this tenet, the staff and underwriters decided no play should run over 2½ hours. (Messina's original proposal may actually have been for two-hour productions based on the *Play of the Month* model, an idea that expanded in the early discussions.) The 2½-hour limit generously allows Shakespeare's "two hours' traffic" for the few plays short enough to be so presented, but not all the plays can be performed within that span. Some cutting naturally occurs with almost every Shakespeare text in production, but the possibility of losing well over an hour of *Hamlet* makes some difficulty for anyone valuing a fairly full text. Facing that possibility before it arose, the BBC early on decided "in principle" to run the longer major plays such as *Hamlet* and *King Lear* with nearly full texts, perhaps by broadcasting them over two nights.[17] Of course, the idea that all Shakespeare's plays should fit the same time slot like water taking the shape of its container underestimates the various structures and diverse rhythms of the plays. Even Shallcross later said the time limit had been determined by their *Play of the Month* experience and that the move toward playing a more complete text was the right one. Nonetheless, the first plays of the Shakespeare series were trimmed to fit the slot; fortunately, most of them were shorter plays and posed less editorial challenge than did *Romeo and Juliet*, the longest of the first season's plays. Yet the decision about length was practical and, as in many of the arts today, at its root financial.

Moreover, "acceptability" is a contemporary normative term for production, with a range of possible meanings from "inoffensive" or "innocuous" to "high quality" and "exciting," depending on what one considers acceptable and to whom regarding Shakespeare in performance. In practice, these criteria for production apparently set no very stringent standard; the underwriters simply proposed to disseminate the plays widely for cultural and educational benefit. Many people, they hoped, might see Shakespeare performed for the first time in the televised series, a point Messina emphasized repeatedly; others would doubtless recite the lines along with the actors, as Winston Churchill is reported to have done in the theatre. Consequently, expectations and criteria for judgment would either be virtually nonexistent or quite high. The terms Messina himself used in publicizing the series were "accessible" and "entertainment."[18] Did it matter how good the productions were so long as they were "acceptable" by some standards—audience share, critical reception, or overseas sales? Being acceptable is not always synonymous with being good, however, and initially the goal seems to have been the former, with a few forays into the latter.

PRODUCING THE SERIES

Messina did try to shepherd the series to success as he saw it, and he soon realized it was a far more complicated venture than *Play of the Month*. He arranged for a literary advisor to the series, Professor John Wilders of Oxford's Worcester College. Wilders would have liked to have done a new edition of the plays for the BBC Shakespeares, but he joined the project too close to actual production time and so advised that the series use the Alexander text (the *Complete Works* edited by Peter Alexander, 1951), the British standard. Wilders was quite involved during the Messina years, making weekly trips to London to answer questions at rehearsals, though once Jonathan Miller took over as producer fewer questions remained unanswered, and somewhat against his liking Wilders became more a token figure. Early on, though, he was a vital part of the intricate planning.

One of the first decisions involved the production order of the plays. Some held out for chronological order of composition, but as Messina pointed out, that "would have meant the series opening with the comparatively unknown *Henry VI Parts 1, 2, and 3*. This idea was hastily abandoned. A judicious mixture of comedy, tragedy and history seemed the best answer."[19] In other words, Messina and Shallcross thought a varied season would have more appeal, and the first season was stacked with familiar, appealing shows—*Much Ado, Romeo and Juliet, Julius Caesar, As You Like It*—with *Measure for Measure* for diversity and *Richard II* to begin the two tetralogies of history plays, which, it had been decided, would be produced in historical order, *Richard II* through *Richard III*. When *Much Ado* went by the way, *Henry VIII*—a play seldom produced but with great historical appeal, especially when done on location in Tudor castles—was planned as next in line and joined the first season. While the well-known plays were supposed to be the draw, everyone quickly realized the lesser known plays might prove the greater successes when given attention in this medium, a point Messina began purveying as the series was launched in America.[20]

Of course, not all of the decisions affecting production style were Messina's alone. One proposal the BBC considered for its Shakespeare series was forming an ensemble company such as the RSC's to perform the plays. The RSC, naturally, saw itself as the only trained and experienced production vehicle to perform the canon in any medium and disdained the BBC's plans, just as Joseph Papp of the New York Shakespeare Festival was incensed at American money backing a British series when American television could have done its own series (though at three times the cost). But the major hurdle to the ensemble proposal was Equity, the British actors' union, which rejected the idea, preferring that as many of its members be involved in the project as possible. Equity did grant special terms concerning fees for repeat broadcasts, extending the usual two-year grace period to six years for these Shakespeare productions, an option the BBC left almost unused.

British Equity remained wary of the implications or possible compromises implicit in American coproduction money, however, and, in order to forestall the importation of American stars, wrote into its contract a clause that only British actors could be used in the series. This stand was put to the test early in Messina's tenure as producer amid talk of hiring James Earl Jones to play Othello. As the issue became copy for the press on both sides of the Atlantic in early 1979, Messina and Shaun Sutton, then head of BBC Drama, insisted that they wanted Jones for his ability and eminence; Equity argued they were overlooking capable black British actors, vetoed the offer of the part to Jones, and refused to budge, even threatening a walkout. The problem was for a time subverted rather than resolved by postponing *Othello* to a later season, though subversion proved to be resolution once Jonathan Miller got hold of *Othello* and decided it was not a play about race at all so did not cast a black actor of any nationality in the role. Perhaps in response, Jones again performed *Othello* on stage in America in 1981. Some, however, continued to regret the BBC's inability to use Jones and considered it the biggest mistake of the series.

As this incident attests, going into production increased the political elements and conflicts between unions and the BBC; politics and conflicts also increased within the BBC itself as the series began. During Messina's long involvement with the BBC he had acquired both friends and fierce antagonists because the internal politics of television are highly charged, at the BBC as everywhere else. Messina went about running the Shakespeare series in much the same way he had produced *Play of the Month* for eight years. *Play of the Month* involved productions of classic plays, usually featuring a star from film or a television series just as in American miniseries, and for the first Shakespeare series's production planned, *Much Ado*, the casting reflected this approach. Michael York was cast as Benedick, and Beatrice was to be played by Penelope Keith, star of the popular British sitcom *The Good Life* and an actress without any major experience in Shakespeare (though her performance in *Much Ado* was reported to be quite good).

This *Much Ado* was rehearsed, taped, edited, given publicity (several articles included production shots), but never released, a decision that prompted much ado indeed. Stories of this production have undoubtedly magnified over the years—how unfortunate the "chemistry" and the casting were, how unacceptable the final product. The BBC will quietly let one conclude that aesthetic concerns necessitated its cancellation. The first press report rumored it would be held until 1980 to retape parts to avoid someone's "heavy accent,"[21] then "because it is not considered good enough for transmission."[22] But some of those involved with the production later said that while this *Much Ado* may not have been great, the production was certainly on a level with some others in the series, and from a visual standpoint the show with its large romantic set was quite lovely.

The actual cause of the problem apparently stemmed from internal politics, an internecine struggle focused on Messina rather than on the show, its director, or the performers, a struggle that left lasting scars. While Messina was the man to plan the series, it seemed he was not the man to produce it. He was part of too many power struggles; too many directors would not work for him; he proceeded with too many of the traditional production habits. The battle over *Much Ado* was actually a battle over power and the producership; once Messina lost and the show was cancelled his tenure as producer was jeopardized. When a reporter later asked about the need to change producers, Shaun Sutton simply commented, "I thought the approach was a little ordinary and that we could do better."[23]

Weathering the cancellation of *Much Ado* did not end the series's problems. Instead of opening with *Much Ado*, the show groomed to lead off the series, it opened with *Romeo and Juliet*, a well-known play frequently studied in schools and even more familiar since Zeffirelli's film. As the play was aired, with much touting of the casting—especially the fact that unknown Rebecca Saire had just turned fifteen while playing Juliet—the actress used her press interviews to attack the director's treatment of her and his interpretation of Juliet's role as too childlike and asexual. Director Alvin Rakoff and the BBC hierarchy defended his approach, and years later those involved from the Drama area would regret the incident and what they considered the young actress's unbecoming, unprofessional behavior.

While this series of flaps over specific productions kept the British press occupied, the American press and American Shakespeareans focused on the public relations campaign for the series as a whole, a point to which the British press returned. Messina, in his voluble, grand manner, had apparently said that the BBC series would be the "definitive" productions of Shakespeare's plays, thereby raising the hackles of scholars and production professionals alike. Alan Shallcross later commented that he and Messina insisted from the beginning that the series would not be definitive; though they anticipated the criticism, he said American publicity ignored them and made the claim anyway.[24] "Definitive" when used of production implies perfect, ideal, flawless—a benchmark for the age. No one believed that television productions, even British television productions, could fulfill that claim. Given the comparative rarity of even great theatrical productions, to assert before the series began that these renditions would be definitive seems foolhardy at best.

In Britain the claims were many times seen as press puffs, just so much publicity rhetoric, but they were sometimes taken seriously and were almost always taken seriously in the United States out of a variety of impulses, some of them vindictive. Years later that battle cry "definitive" would be flung back at the BBC in attacks on the productions in print or at scholarly conferences. For example, take an article in *Critical Quarterly* by Martin Banham, "BBC Television's Dull Shakespeares," wherein he castigates the BBC for dry and disappointing productions that emphasize visual "prettiness" and diminish dramatic effects. He takes exception to a BBC publicity handout that says "there has been no attempt at stylisation; there are no gimmicks; no embellishments to confuse the student"; he observes that the best, most interesting recent Shakespeare productions have been very "gimmicky" in the sense of "adventurous," a trait he finds sadly lacking in the meek, unimaginative style of the series' first two seasons.[25] Whereas Cedric Messina saw "straightforward productions" as an asset,[26] many scholars and critics advocated daring, and later in the series when the productions got daring, they then, perhaps predictably, clamored for more traditional approaches.

Though the publicity designed to arouse widespread public interest also aroused specialists' ire, it probably led some viewers to see Shakespeare in performance for the first time. What they saw if they tuned in during the first two seasons was, as Messina said, "straightforward," for while he focused on planning the series, Messina did not plan the productions. He may have thought they needed no planning; they would be done as such productions had always been done at the BBC. His outlook was later waggishly characterized as "let's do some rather good Shakespeares." The differences in the productions are the differences in the directors, for, as Messina acknowledged, "the directors are responsible for the interpretations we shall see."[27] The producer selects the director and evokes an attitude toward production as a whole, provides a stimulating creative environment for the work, discusses production concepts, and is active in cast selection (Messina was willing to cast major roles independently well in advance of the productions; for example, as Henry Fenwick reports, Messina had already penciled in Robert Shaw to play Lear before that actor's sudden death in August 1978).[28] The director, who may have been hired a year in advance for the ten-week production period, plans the production, selects the cast, gives conceptual guidelines to designers, and with the production staff sees the production through. The producer makes some appearances at rehearsals, oversees the taping (to various degrees depending on the director and the producer), and may pop in during editing. One of the producer's most influential decisions about production, therefore, is his choice of director. Or at least, choice is the beginning of the process, depending on the director's availability, salary expectations, and willingness to work on the series.

Messina used six directors for the first season of six shows (actually seven, if one counts *Much Ado*) and added two more the second season, John Gorrie, who did *Twelfth Night* and *The Tempest*, and Rodney Bennett, who did *Hamlet*, with David Giles returning to finish the *Henry IV–Henry V* sequence begun the previous year with *Richard II*. All were experienced television directors, but not all were experienced Shakespeare directors. Messina had worked with Alvin Rakoff, Basil Coleman, Gorrie, and Giles previously, while Herbert Wise, who did *Julius Caesar*, was well known for his work on *I, Claudius*. Of the rest, neither Desmond Davis nor Rodney Bennett had directed Shakespeare before. Hiring a diversity of directors and especially giving some good directors a first experience with Shakespeare proved to be one of Messina's best contributions to the series in production.

While having a number of different directors might suggest a variety of approaches, the presence of two plays filmed on location in the first season's schedule affected and unified the style used for the other shows. Messina and many of the directors spoke of television as an exceptionally realistic medium. With the directors of *As You Like It* and *Henry VIII* working on location, the others wanted to be more realistic, too, and avoid an extreme stylization they considered more difficult for this medium and its audience. John Gorrie's productions during the second season expanded the effort at realism with his geographic sense of interior and exterior at Olivia's house in *Twelfth Night* and the 360-degree setting of cliff face, woods, and shore in *The Tempest*. In finishing the historical tetralogy, however, Giles sensed a great shift in style between the *Henry IV* plays and *Henry V*, the first two being focused on the domestic, on rooms, but the third involving public action and large spaces, for which he wanted a far more stylized environment and panoramic action.[29] The plan for *Henry V* was to have much open space and a more presentational approach; in taping, however, the stylized settings came across as a shade more realistic than the designer intended.[30] Bennett's *Hamlet* was the first fully stylized production of the series. Though initially *Hamlet* was considered for location shooting, that changed when it was decreed that all subsequent plays were to be produced in the studio. Bennett was unperturbed: "Though on the face of it *Hamlet* would seem to be a great naturalistic play, it isn't really. . . . It has reality but it is essentially a theatrical reality."[31] Thus only at the end of the second season does the series begin to explore a greater range of approaches to Shakespeare's plays for television, from natural or realistic to stylized in harmony with the play's subject and mood and the director's inclinations.

Given his production principles, Messina was always, of necessity, looking ahead in casting. For instance, he contracted Derek Jacobi to play Hamlet almost as the actor agreed to do Richard II,[32] a decision in keeping with the series's overall objective of trying to get respected actors experienced in the parts to play Shakespeare's major roles, especially the tragic leads. Messina had seen Jacobi's Hamlet in a 1977 West End production that subsequently toured the United Kingdom and the Far East for nearly two years; as a result the BBC production dates for *Hamlet* had to be postponed pending Jacobi's return.

Not all the BBC's efforts to land famous actors for the great roles succeeded, however. For example, series's literary advisor John Wilders reported in an interview that *Measure*'s director Desmond Davis sought Sir Alec Guinness to play the Duke, but that actor declined. In fact, Kenneth Colley who took the role was the thirty-second actor asked,[33] a tribute to the number of talented actors in Britain and a testimony to the casting efforts that recurred in the series. Elijah Moshinsky said he could never fathom why some parts posed problems; in his experience with the series the hardest to cast were Theseus in *Dream* and the King of Navarre in *Love's Labour's Lost*. Yet even when the actor was amenable, problems could occur. During the opening season, for instance, Messina wisely included Sir John Gielgud in the series's first two shows, as Chorus in *Romeo and Juliet* and John of Gaunt in *Richard II*. Though the roles were small, his performances were predictably fine, and his name made for good press. In the second season Messina also wanted him to play Prospero, one of the many Shakespeare roles for which he is famous, as a means of preserving one of his great stage performances. But contractual problems arose, and by the time Messina maneuvered a solution, Gielgud had made other professional commitments. So Michael Hordern, who had just completed an acclaimed rendition of Prospero with the RSC in Stratford, was engaged to play the role instead. Such is the story of production—the plays presented and the dreams or insubstantial pageants of what might have been. Similar casting circumstances occurred annually during the series's production, but the effort over Prospero is probably the most memorable.

Messina's tenure as producer was not without its high points, even though from a production standpoint the series began as a special adaptation of *Play of the Month* attitudes and techniques. Nonetheless, the political tensions within the Drama section, submerged during planning, began to reappear once the series was actually in production. The forces against Messina grew more powerful, and the BBC suddenly had a new problem, that of replacing Messina on the series he fostered. (That it was an inside matter and not a result of critical reception is evident from the critics' comments when the change was announced; the *Times* [London] critic, for instance, evinced much surprise and for some time thereafter remarked, "I thought Mr. Messina was doing a fine job.") The BBC solved the problem by dividing the series into three two-year segments and, as if they had always intended it, proposing a separate producer for each. No insiders could take over from Messina without extending the tensions, so they looked for an able outsider to produce the next group of plays. But an insider could conclude the series, especially an insider long associated with the administration of the Drama area who, as that administration changed, was inter-

Cedric Messina, producer of The Shakespeare Plays *from 1978 to 1980, during the filming of* As You Like It. © *BBC*

ested in associating himself with the Shakespeare series before he retired.

So the series ended up with three producers, Cedric Messina, Jonathan Miller, and Shaun Sutton, each chosen for specific reasons and specific tasks. Although it was patchwork, the plan

Jonathan Miller, producer of The Shakespeare Plays *from 1980 to 1982, on the set of* Antony and Cleopatra. © *BBC*

Shaun Sutton, producer of The Shakespeare Plays *from 1982 to 1985.*
© *BBC*

achieved its purposes remarkably well: its symmetry covered the political tensions beneath it, Miller was famous and talented enough to draw new interest to the series, and Sutton could bring the work to a peaceful end. They salvaged appearances and the producership, but what the initial Messina years cost the series in tensions, alienations, and lack of fresh thought or vigorous technical/aesthetic planning it would never recover. That we have the televised Shakespeare series at all is entirely due to Messina; that we have the Shakespeare series we have and not perhaps a better, more exciting one is also in large part due to Messina. What the series could have been may be a moot point, but the topic surfaces occasionally with those involved with the productions, especially with Jonathan Miller, who had the singular task of redeeming the effort that was already somewhat tainted in the eyes of the profession. The degree to which he succeeded attests his creativity, his intelligence, and his enthusiastic, contagious energy in approaching the project.

Miller had a great deal to overcome despite some triumphs in the first season—the highly acclaimed *Richard II*, the award-winning *Measure for Measure*, and the very popular *Henry VIII*. As he began to work on the Shakespeare series, however, the entire atmosphere changed. Miller did not have the assumptions of one long associated with the BBC nor had he worked with an established production slot so that he naturally transferred its methods to the series. Instead of doing what the BBC usually did, Miller saw the series as a means of examining the limits of televised drama, of seeing what the medium could do; it was an imaginative, creative venture. Knowing what the situation had been, he tried to interest the finest directors he could in the project—such directors as Peter Brook, John Dexter, William Gaskill, even Ingmar Bergman—efforts that some saw as presumptuous since they came to naught but that others took as a sign that times had changed.

And changed they had. Even the secretaries commented how different the atmosphere was, how interested in and excited about the series people now were due to Jonathan Miller. With a playful mind and kinetic thought process, with strong opinions and a yen for experimentation, Miller shook the series loose, introduced a new set of directors, and fostered their diverse interests and abilities as well as demonstrating his own. Not everyone agreed with his interpretations, but everyone was interested in seeing what he was doing. Trained as a physician specializing in neurology, Miller had first made his name in theatre in the Edinburgh Festival fringe production *Beyond the Fringe* that he helped to write and perform along with Dudley Moore, Alan Bennett, and Peter Cook, a satirical revue that transferred to London's West End and to Broadway. He had subsequently directed many notable theatrical productions, working regionally at the Nottingham Playhouse and Greenwich Theatre, among others, and extensively in London for the newly formed National Theatre at the Old Vic under Sir Laurence Olivier. He had also directed for television at the BBC despite having left one of its television directing courses during its first week. Whatever he did seemed to be startling, worth talking about. But from the beginning of his producership, rather than focus on himself as inspiration, he simply went about being inspiring, fostering the sense that everyone was vitally involved, that the productions were collaborative, a team effort.[34] That was how he worked—attracting the best people he could and then using the best of everyone's abilities to the fullest.

For Miller there is a limit to the naturalism one can achieve putting Shakespeare on television, a limit determined by the language and by the fact that the plays come from the past,[35] each of which he considers a richness for production. Others have shared such a view; Herbert Wise, who directed *Julius Caesar*, had commented, "I don't think Shakespeare is ideally suited to television, and in my view no one in the past has really cracked it."[36] Perhaps not, but during his years with the Shakespeare series Miller encouraged everyone to try.

The directors Miller brought to the series were as much an artistic contribution as the productions he directed: Jane Howell, serious and symbolic in approach; Jack Gold, with a "vigorous and efficient and interesting imagination,"[37] who had never before done Shakespeare; and Elijah Moshinsky, the bright young director of operas and plays whom Miller introduced to television. In characterizing the three, Miller said they shared "vigour, common sense, lack of sentimentality, a modernity without gimmickry, a muscular vigour of imagination,"[38] qualities Miller obviously wanted to foster for the productions themselves—life and freshness and intelligence. Miller's choice of directors proved as successful as he had hoped or foreseen; Howell and Moshinsky proceeded to direct many more plays under Miller's and Sutton's producerships, and Gold returned for *Macbeth*.

The fourth director Miller hired for season three proved to be the exception, however. To direct *Timon* Miller contracted Michael Bogdanov, a talented director who was then with the National Theatre. Bogdanov joined the staff but overlooked the production guidelines, insisting instead on a modern-dress Oriental rendition. A crisis was inevitable, for regardless of Miller's own sympathies with updated productions, the constraints stemming from coproduction money and the brief made Bogdanov's *Timon* unproducible in the series, so Miller finally took over the casting and planning of the production himself just before rehearsals started. In light of this occurrence, Bogdanov's later comments on the BBC Shakespeare series, which he condemned as "the greatest disservice to Shakespeare in the last 25 years," and his use of *Timon* as the prime example of Shakespeare's modernity make a catty kind of sense.[39] Small wonder Miller divided his second season as producer among the proven and sympathetically creative directors he had found—Howell, Moshinsky, and himself. Moreover, having decided to do the four-play Wars of the Roses sequence with one director left only three other directorial slots that next season.

Miller's interest in suggestivity recurs in the work of Howell and Gold, and his allusions to art reappear in Moshinsky's productions, though these plays are at opposite ends of the presentational spectrum—Howell's and Gold's stylized, and Moshinsky's very detailed, like a painting come to life. Miller himself mixed styles—in *The Taming of the Shrew* the rich, honestly domestic and Vermeer-like interior of Baptista's house against the more stylized Paduan street and the open space and shadows forming Petruchio's house or the geometric precision of Troy in *Troilus and Cressida* contrasting the tatty clutter of the Greek camp—as he pursued his goal of discovering the possibilities of televising Shakespeare.

Far more strongly than either of the other two producers, Miller had a vision of Shakespeare as an Elizabethan/Jacobean play-wright, as a man of his time in social, historical, and philosophical outlook. The productions Miller himself directed reflect this belief most clearly, of course, but he also evoked such an awareness in the other directors. If there was not to be a single stylistic "signature" to the plays under Miller's producership, there was more nearly an attitudinal one. Everything was reflexive for the Renaissance artist, Miller felt, most especially historical references, and so Antony of Rome, Cleopatra of Egypt, and both Timon and Theseus of Athens take on a familiar late sixteenth- and early seventeenth-century manner and look.

The tone of the fourth season, Miller's second and last, was affected by the nature of the plays being produced and by the impending end of Miller's tenure with the series. Once started, he would have liked to see the whole project through, but the BBC had already hired a third producer before Miller began; there was no changing that. Miller agreed to direct one more play under Shaun Sutton's producership, and during the editing of *Troilus and Cressida* he speculated which play to choose of those tragedies left, *Coriolanus*, *Lear*, or *Macbeth*. He had never done a *Macbeth* but had done a televised *Lear* for the BBC in 1975, a two-hour version of the play for *Play of the Month* that he and others at the BBC were quite pleased with, as well as a stage *Lear* before that. He had not changed his mind about that play, he said, so there might be less point to doing it again, but it was nonetheless an enticing and challenging prospect, not easily turned down. He kept turning over ideas for *Macbeth*, but subsequently the lure of *Lear* won out. Though Sutton initially offered Miller *Love's Labour's Lost*, Miller requested *Lear*.[40]

Throughout the series's fourth season the attitude that the productions were *interpretations* strengthened among the directors. Miller had always thought so and fostered that idea with Moshinsky and Howell, who agreed. Moshinsky's *Dream*, with what Moshinsky called a style of "romantic realism," was darker in its vision, grimmer in its reality than is usual for that woodland romp. Howell faced the opposite challenge of producing the seldom seen *Henry VI* series, and she used her natural inclination to treat an acting company as a family to establish a repertory company of actors for the plays and a second company of actor-fighters to complement them in portraying the battles of the Wars of the Roses. The spare, nonrealistic unit set contrasted the intensely detailed and referential period sets of other shows and let the action reach theatrically toward the modern world.

While he was directing, Miller rather enjoyed working on the Shakespeare series; the problems, the tensions, the frustrations left him annoyed but largely undaunted. Because he was a strong director, however, he had more problems being a producer for other plays, and many times he hated the job. The paperwork alone was not intriguing because it occupied too little of his energy, so he left some of the daily caretaking of the producer's office to others. As producer there was almost no opportunity for his own creativity because a producer should be "benign and facilitating," he said; "Your only *real* contribution is your choice of director."[41] Miller's own virtues and beliefs caused his problems as producer, for he produced by the Golden Rule: since as a director he liked to be left alone to get on with a production, that is how he treated the directors he hired. He was available for discussion and suggested possibilities, but he respected his directors' artistic independence: "The job of the producer is to make conditions as favourable and friendly as they possibly can be, so that *their* [the directors'] imagination is given the best possible chance to work."[42]

As producer, he found there were continual liabilities in his self-imposed gag rule; if he disagreed with an interpretation or saw a better, different way of playing a scene, he would find rehearsals or taping quite torturous, and so he tended to check in sporadically rather than sit through whole days in the control room. Playing the producer's role, he always tried to be supportive, and he would genuinely exult in production choices that excited him. Watching the studio taping of *All's Well That Ends Well* from the producer's box, he reveled in the sets, the look of the actors, the period detail, and pleased with Moshinsky's accomplishment, he would bound out to praise these bits during breaks. His own work benefited from the other directors' styles and discoveries, especially from Moshinsky's; there was a sense of growth and dialogue on all sides as the series progressed. But unless he was actively engaged in directing a play, these years were by and large not a happy experience for Miller.

Miller knew he disliked producing when he took the job, "but," he said, "this seemed rather important to do, to take this series and put it right—do the plays correctly." And because his bitter split with Peter Hall at the National Theatre had cost him his base of operation, he added, "I wanted a chance to direct. I need a home in the theatre, a place to work on classical plays. . . . The place to go was television."[43] Producing took its toll, however, and he found no other immediate theatrical home after the series. It was during this time that Miller again decided to leave the theatre and return to medicine, accepting a research fellowship in neuropsychology at the University of Sussex after he left the BBC, and while that decision (which, fortunately for theatre, was only temporary) resulted from a variety of influences, his experience as producer contributed to it.

The transition between Miller's producership and Sutton's proved less perceptible because Miller directed another show in the series and because the changeover occurred halfway through the *Henry VI–Richard III* sequence, rehearsals and taping for which encompassed September 1981 through early April 1982. With the new year Sutton took over the series, though Miller was on staff as director of *Lear* through early April. Because the six-plays-a-year-for-six-years schedule began lagging during the middle years, Sutton was left with fourteen plays to produce, and production of the last two seasons spread over three years and into a fourth. Working around directors' other commitments caused some of the delay, for Moshinsky was busy with operas in England and Australia, while David Jones, whom Sutton added to the directorial pool, had film work on *Betrayal* under way. Sutton got Moshinsky to do a production a year, *Cymbeline* in 1982, *Coriolanus* in 1983, and *Love's Labour's Lost* in 1984. Along with Jack Gold's *Macbeth*, Miller's *Lear*, and the end of Howell's history sequence, Moshinsky's work and David Jones's *The Merry Wives of Windsor* rounded out Sutton's first year with only one director who had not previously worked in the series.

Sutton's second year of producing proved different, however, for as Moshinsky and David Jones moved into new productions, Sutton added Don Taylor and James Cellan-Jones, both BBC directors of long experience. With only a few shows remaining to complete the series, the time frame expanded rather than contracted. Sutton asked David Giles, who had directed the *Richard II–Henry IV and V* sequence, to return for *King John*, Howell was to follow with *Titus Andronicus* in the spring of 1984, Moshinsky agreed to do *Love's Labour's Lost* in the summer, and it looked as though the series would end with the show it was originally planned to open with in 1978, *Much Ado*, a most ironic symmetry. In anticipating that last "mini-season," as he called the smaller groups of plays, Sutton considered asking one of the directors already working with the series to direct *Much Ado* but eventually sought veteran director Stuart Burge to take it.

With completion of the series in sight, the plan ran into the perhaps inevitable but unanticipated delay of a labor dispute: as *Titus Andronicus* was about to go into the studio, the scene shifters' union went out on strike, and because of the intricacy of BBC production planning and the lead time involved, the show could not immediately be rescheduled in the studio. Then the actors had other commitments, and Howell wanted to keep as many of the original cast as possible. When a fall studio date was proposed, the RSC refused to let Trevor Peacock, who was the BBC's Titus, off for the evening studio work, so the production was finally planned for February 1985, almost a year after its original taping date and six months after the rest of the series was completed.

With so many more directors working under Sutton, the range of individual production styles was more varied than under Miller. Greater stylization, stark curtains and boards, and Elizabethan verisimilitude each found expression in various productions, as did a concern for period and for timelessness. Diverse attitudes about the nature of studio production also burgeoned at the series's close. From a pre-Norman invasion *Macbeth* the plays' settings spanned to an eighteenth-century *Love's Labour's Lost*, the only setting in the series to exceed rather than simply stretch the original directive about productions set in Shakespeare's time or the historical time of the action. The *Macbeth* focused on a psychological portrayal; the *Lear*, too, made the characters loom large against a simple background. Battle scenes were vicious in the Wars of the Roses plays, operatic and erotic in *Coriolanus*. The comic homeyness of *Merry Wives* contrasted with the gilded cupids and formal romantic conventions in *Two Gentlemen*. Where Miller focused intently on a matrix of production concerns (such as the television "picture" as painting or the period and historical veracity), Sutton was amenable to the diverse interests and suggestions of his many directors.

Sutton's attitude toward the productions and their styles had a professional pragmatism: "Three things really matter in all drama . . . : there is the script, the director, and the cast. If you've got those three right it doesn't matter if you do it on cardboard sets, or moderately lit—it doesn't even matter in television sometimes if it is badly shot. . . . Scripts are the foundation of the whole thing, rather than the way you present them. Writers, directors, actors: if those three are good, you can do it on the back of a cart."[44] While Sutton advocated formalized settings, he proved wary of gimmicky productions: "If you decide to stylize, I think you have to ask yourself, *have you made the play any better?* Further, I think it should be done by clever men, geniuses like Miller and Brook."[45] More than ideas, Sutton emphasized the technical demands of the televised plays: "The director also has to understand how to use cameras to *pace* the production. Unique to television is the multicamera. So the television director has to get to be a technician on top of everything else. Pictures, he's got to understand pictures—how to use the cameras." Hence, Sutton sought proven television directors for the productions, and his only reservation about Miller's work with the series was on the basis of training, that "he'd done none of the routine series."[46]

The difference in these two men's backgrounds noticeably affected their approach to the Shakespeare plays. Yet if Sutton was not the dynamic center of intellectual and energetic force Miller had been, perhaps he did not have to be. He had years of experience with the BBC, which he joined in 1952 after fifteen years in the theatre, directing and writing for some of the BBC's most popular early series such as *Z Cars* and *Sherlock Holmes*, and later serving as head of Serials in *The Forsyte Saga* era, then as head of the Drama group. Having helped shape the BBC's traditions, he was less interested in challenging them, and he also inherited the renewed momentum of the series. With his characteristic "all in a day's work" tone, Sutton reflected on the series: "It's all been enormous fun. . . . Never solemn, full of giggles, not self-possessed and gloomy, not too immersed in the intellectual content. It's the end of a great era, a great incident in the life of television."[47] This hale-and-hearty attitude is in some ways like Messina's, the insider's assumption that after all these years the BBC knows how to televise drama and need not think about it.

BROADCASTING THE SERIES

Without doubt, the delayed, seemingly piecemeal production schedule at the end of the series dissipated some of the power of the televised canon as a broadcast phenomenon. Even in the planning stages, everyone had known it was not going to be easy to capture or hold an audience for thirty-seven Shakespeare plays over more than six years. Most television programming works on the principle of addiction: it is patterned on a weekly basis so viewers look for specific programs regularly. That was not possible with the expansive Shakespeare series. Consequently, both the BBC and PBS initially took care in scheduling the productions and began with another pattern for programming.[48] On BBC 2 the Shakespeare series was planned for transmission as "seasons"; the shows for each season were to be broadcast in two groups, one in the late fall, one in winter, a method designed to focus publicity efforts. In the first season, 1978–79, there was model programming: three shows broadcast at weekly intervals in December, the other three at weekly intervals in February, all on Sunday evenings starting about eight o'clock, with an interval of five minutes halfway through, during which the BBC showed *News on 2* and a weather report. The second season, 1979–80, began smoothly, but the winter season got a bit diffused by the late production of *Hamlet* (having waited for Jacobi, it was in the studio as the others were being broadcast), which was shown in May, and by *The Tempest*'s being shown in a Wednesday evening slot.

For the next two years, 1980 and 1981, there was no apparent pattern to the scheduling. Half the productions were broadcast on Sunday evenings, now starting at 7:15 because they ran longer, and the rest were scattered on Wednesday, Thursday, Friday, or Saturday. Apparently Miller worried less about uniform scheduling—it may have been less important to him—for BBC insiders Messina and Sutton somehow achieved a more consistent pattern of programming for the plays. During this period, however, the BBC also broadcast its only repeats of the entire series, *Henry V* for St. George's Day (which is also Shakespeare's birthday) 1980 and *Henry VIII* and *Twelfth Night* in June 1981.

In 1982, the end of the Miller-era transmissions, there was no winter season; *King Lear* did not appear until the following September, followed by *Merry Wives* on a Tuesday in December. Only the *Henry VIs* regularized scheduling throughout January 1983. Most of these were shown on Sunday evenings at 7:15, a last effort to renew the earlier pattern. The November–December 1983 scheduling shifted the productions to Saturday evenings, and from *Macbeth* on, the last nine Shakespeares were Saturday evening broadcasts, except for *Two Gentlemen*, which went out the Tuesday after Christmas in 1983. By late 1984, when it became apparent that the programmers meant to leave the Shakespeares on Saturday, the BBC decided to make a virtue of the shift, and since the plays were scheduled opposite *Dynasty* on BBC 1, they billed an entire set of BBC 2 arts programming on Saturday evenings as "The Saturday Alternative" and presented opera, ballet, and drama in this slot. Four Shakespeares went out at two-week intervals, a reprise of the "season" concept, and *Titus* completed the series three months later.

In America, PBS programming had somewhat more order in its over six years of broadcasting the Shakespeare series. The first two seasons were shown in an 8:00 Wednesday evening slot during the spring of 1979 and 1980, the plays appearing at two-week intervals. *Hamlet* trailed on a Monday evening in November of

1980, and for the next three years (*Shrew*, January 1981, through *Pericles*, June 1984) the Shakespeare plays appeared on Monday evenings with the exception of the *Henry VIs*, which were relegated to Sundays at noon. In 1980 and 1982 came the only repeats of the American Shakespeare broadcasts, *Richard II* and *Hamlet* respectively. *Much Ado* was given a Tuesday evening broadcast in October 1984; then the last three shown in America—*King John*, *Titus*, and *Love's Labour's Lost*—moved to Friday evening. Or at least this was the master plan, but since PBS is not a network and its programming times are not mandated for the local stations, stations are free to hold a show, rescheduling it as they feel is appropriate for their viewing public. Thus not all the Shakespeares were seen nationwide at the time WNET, the producing station in New York, showed them.

As the taping and broadcast schedules got more complicated, some of the productions were transmitted in America before they were seen in Britain. This was the case with *Antony and Cleopatra*, *Cymbeline*, *Macbeth*, *Coriolanus*, *Pericles*, *Much Ado*, and *Titus*. Most of these were broadcast within the same month on both sides of the Atlantic, but in America *Cymbeline* was aired seven months earlier and *Pericles* six months earlier than in Britain. *Julius Caesar* was seen during the same week in both countries, as was *Othello* later. Yet since very little attention was paid to the reception of the productions on the opposite sides of the ocean for press purposes, almost nothing mutually beneficial came of this scheduling.

To lure the viewers to these scheduled broadcasts, a major public relations effort was mounted in Britain and in America. Both public relations campaigns with the press followed the accepted methods: parties, previews, press materials, and parleys with the stars. In Britain, however, every aspect of the public relations program was planned and executed by a division of the BBC itself. As a monolithic and virtually self-sufficient organization, it has its own publicity departments, educational programming, and even its own publishing house, all of which got involved with the Shakespeare series.

Because the general approach used to publicize the Shakespeare productions in Britain centered on press previews in a seventh-floor suite at BBC Television Centre, some people felt in retrospect that the BBC had not promoted the series as it might have. The sheer mass of the effort may have been against them; they did try a bit of variety. Because there were thirty-seven Shakespeare productions and because the effect of thirty-seven identical previews and receptions would pale, the publicity for the series at times offered special season openers, showing preview clips from the productions and making a number of stars available to the press. These occasionally went beyond a reception at Television Centre. The launch party for the third season, Miller's first, was held at the George Inn in Southwark, near the site of the Globe Theatre.[49] The press preview for the sixth season (1983–84), perhaps the grandest, took the press to Glamis Castle in Scotland for the day in honor of the Scottish tragedy, the season's opening production. Stars from the sixth season's shows were flown in to be available for interviews— Ian Hogg (Banquo) of *Macbeth*, Alan Howard (Coriolanus) and Joss Ackland (Menenius) of *Coriolanus*, Tyler Butterworth (Proteus) of *Two Gentlemen*, Wendy Hiller (Aemilia) and Cyril Cusack (Aegeon) from *The Comedy of Errors*, and Patrick Ryecart (Lysimachus) of *Pericles*, as well as David Giles, director of *King John*.

In addition to contact with the press, the BBC gets its own direct contact with the public through its weekly publication *Radio Times*, which provides information on upcoming BBC radio and television programming, somewhat analogous to America's *TV Guide*. Henry Fenwick, a free-lance writer who has for some years covered American television and film for *Radio Times*, did a special set of articles about the individual BBC Shakespeare plays based on his interviews with directors and cast members, often cover stories complete with color production photographs; these would appear on British newsstands the week of each broadcast. In America there was no such national vehicle for series's publicity, though the series's start did accomplish the near-miraculous feat of getting the cover of *TV Guide* one week, something public television had never before achieved.

In the United States press coverage was more difficult to arrange, explained Tim Hallinan of Stone/Hallinan Associates, the agency hired by the American underwriters to publicize the series in the

States. Few newspapers except the *New York Times*, Hallinan said, will write very often about public television; there is widespread resistance to running more than two or three stories a year,[50] yet there were twice that many productions televised annually. Stone/ Hallinan maintained a solid and ongoing publicity campaign but tried to give it extra momentum by starting with a splash.

For media publicity the series's broadcast in America was launched in high style, including a White House reception for visiting actors and BBC executives with First Lady Rosalynn Carter and lunch in the Folger Shakespeare Library on Capitol Hill (which the *Evening Standard* unkindly reported to its London readers as "a perfectly awful occasion" and "a desperate afternoon" of long-winded speeches before lunch, typified when "a radio reporter pushed a microphone into the face of Anthony Quayle who plays Falstaff, saying: 'I suppose you realise that to most Americans Falstaff is a brand of beer?' ").[51] That press conference was the unhappy initiation of the debacle over casting James Earl Jones as Othello, the revelation of which prompted two days of transatlantic telephoning culminating in British Equity's adamant refusal. Jones, the *Manchester Guardian* stated on its front page, "was ready to appear at the Washington press conference until he heard of the conflict."[52]

Nonetheless, British actors proved especially appealing to the American press. Richard Pasco (Brutus in *Julius Caesar* and Jaques in *As You Like It*), Celia Johnson and Patrick Ryecart (the Nurse and Romeo of *Romeo and Juliet*), Helen Mirren (Rosalind of *As You Like It*), and Anthony Quayle (cast as Falstaff) had made the trip and were frequently interviewed. Looking back on the series, WNET's Jac Venza said one of the best aspects for U.S. publicity was bringing some of the artists over to promote the productions, and he lamented it could not have been done more often because it is so important for the press.[53]

The publicity effort in the United States was hydra-headed compared to the BBC's, which centered comfortably on London. Not only is America's television industry split between the coasts, in New York and Los Angeles, but after covering those two cities there are still Chicago and Dallas, Atlanta and Boston, and many other urban areas. Getting coverage is a greater agency challenge in the United States because of this dispersion. Since critics could not as easily be gathered in America as in Britain, Stone/Hallinan distributed impressive publicity materials by mail to pique the press's interest, varying the format to overcome the sense of an assembly line or thirty-seven cloned releases. To help the cause, the underwriters also contributed some extra promotional efforts of their own. Exxon's agency produced ads for the productions in newspapers and sometimes in national magazines such as *The New Yorker* as well as some radio and television spots. Metropolitan Life sponsored some additional activities, too, setting up an Elizabethan fair in its New York headquarters when the series began and printing posters and viewer guides for its agents to distribute with every season.

Within the series, the inevitable publicity challenge in the United States was *The Merchant of Venice*, frequent subject of controversy in this century. Once WNET announced the broadcast date, the station received a certified letter and a telegram in protest from the Holocaust and Executive Committee of the Committee to Bring Nazi War Criminals to Justice in the U.S.A., a protest statement from the Anti-Defamation League of B'nai B'rith, and a letter to the editor of the *New York Times* from Morris Schappes, the editor of *Jewish Currents*. The Holocaust and Executive Committee stated that Shylock can arouse "the deepest hate in the pathological and predjudiced [sic] mind" and urged "that reason and a reputable insight into the psychopathology of man . . . will impel you to cancel [the play's] screenings" or demonstrations would ensue,[54] later adding that "our objection is not to art but to the hate monger, whoever the target. . . . This includes the singular and particular work of art which when televized [sic] is viewed by millions and alarmingly compounds the spread of hate."[55] The Anti-Defamation League, after deploring censorship, said a broadcast of *Merchant* would be "awash in bad taste" and would be "providing a forum for a Shylock who would have warmed the heart of Nazi propagandist Julius Streicher."[56] In his letter to the *New York*

Times Schappes, after pointing out that in 1960 Orson Welles cancelled his production of *Merchant* because of continuing anti-Semitic activity in the world, asked, "Are we in [a] safer epoch?"[57]

Both PBS and WNET responded to the objections in a joint statement sent to all PBS stations, acknowledging that groups sometimes protest certain programs, as the Saudi Arabians had the previous year when *Death of a Princess* was shown, and quoting PBS President Lawrence K. Grossman on this subject when he accepted the 1980 Media Award of the American Jewish Committee. "The healthy way to deal with such sensitivities is to air the concerns and criticism," they stated, "not to bury or ban them." They pointed to Miller's introduction to the show and his follow-up conversation on this issue with Warren Mitchell, the actor portraying Shylock, and added, "Incidentally, Mitchell and Miller, as well as the director, Jack Gold, are all Jewish." They said they would no more think of banning Shakespeare from broadcast than many school libraries did of removing *Huckleberry Finn* when it was called a racist novel: "That is not the American way."[58] WNET published a 45-item list of its "programs of interest to Jewish viewers" since 1975, and Exxon issued a statement that the interpretations in the productions were the BBC's, not the underwriters'.

The press mentioned statements from both sides;[59] also frequently quoted were comments about the interpretation by Miller and Mitchell from the Stone/Hallinan press materials (they had anticipated the controversy and prepared for it), "To Warren Mitchell, Shylock is not a murderous, money-grasping villain, but a sympathetic and much sinned-against man," Jack Gold's view that Shylock's Jewishness in dramatic terms "becomes a metaphor for the fact that he, more than any other character in Venice, is an alien," and Miller's belief that "it's not about Jews versus Christians in the racial sense; it's the world of legislation versus the world of mercy." No other production elicited such a response, and it must have been an ironic switch for the public relations people not to urge viewers to watch but to defend what "the millions" would see when they did watch.

The point of scheduling and advertising campaigns is to attract viewers, and during the planning of the series no one was quite sure just how big a draw it would be. There was the feeling, the hope that it could be a major television event, and its potential for importance excited those who thought television might be the key to the public's appreciation of Shakespeare. Looking back on the series, a wistful note steals into some people's voices for a moment as they consider why that did not happen. The audience figures suggest the Shakespeare series was a modest achievement for arts programming, with nowhere near the audience of Britain's *Coronation Street* or America's *Hill Street Blues* during the same years. This reaction, the tinge of regret and puzzlement, was especially strong in America, where good Nielsen ratings make a show worthy, and low ratings almost always damn a show regardless of its quality. Those at PBS asserted and reasserted that ratings do not and should not matter in public broadcasting, but the pervasive mindset of the industry had a way of creeping back into the discussion. In the BBC's Drama division much the same attitude prevailed, a sanguine interpretation of what must have been slightly disappointing numbers, if numbers matter.

In Britain and the United States, viewership varied both from one play to the next and from early in the series to late. The Shakespeare series usually drew a few million British viewers (one to three million) for a production, but sometimes as few as half a million. In the United States (though figures are not available for the entire series since PBS does not get fifty-two weeks of audience measurements) the highest viewership recorded for the series was *Hamlet*'s with about 5½ million viewers, and a number of the plays had 4½ to 5 million viewers. In any anthology series, even *Masterpiece Theatre*, the audience is selective and far from consistent, and statistics suggest there was a fair amount of coming and going during a Shakespeare broadcast. Overall the PBS figures suggest the Shakespeare viewership was comparable to most PBS opera broadcasts. John Fuller of PBS Market Research said he was rather pleased the Shakespeare plays did as well as they did, then mentioned (as everyone did in considering viewership) that these figures should be compared to how many people had seen the plays in the theatre. *Hamlet*'s 5½ million American viewers in one night is equivalent to 5,500 sold-out theatre performances of *Hamlet* in a 1,000-seat house, enough to make Joseph Papp or the RSC envious.

Citing figures for only Britain and America, however, excludes the fact that by 1983 the series was sold to and shown in thirty-seven other countries as well, including China, Iraq, Japan, Kenya, Peru, and Poland. By 1987 sixteen more countries had purchased the series, as various as Czechoslovakia, Egypt, Jamaica, Mexico, and Sri Lanka.[60] Such international exposure suggests the series may well have effects as yet little known. Director Elijah Moshinsky once mused briefly that although the series is not very well thought of in England, he was invited to a conference at the Sorbonne to speak about his *All's Well* and was sent a copy of a French paper delivered on the semiotics of that production.[61] At its annual convention, the Shakespeare Association of America sponsored a number of seminars on televised Shakespeare and the BBC series during the late 1980s. It would be ironic but not uncommon were the value of the BBC effort only belatedly recognized at home.

EDUCATIONAL OUTREACH

The worldwide sales of the productions were a corollary goal of the series; the primary focus for this "Shakespeare phenomenon" was the nations of the funding corporations, Britain and America. In line with the major objectives of the Shakespeare series, to attract viewers and to enhance education, a second major public relations effort concentrated on educational programming. Fundamental to these programs was the emphasis on studying Shakespeare in performance, not just as a text on a page. Although Shakespeare is almost universally taught in English classes, the planners, especially the Americans, realized that numbers of students have bad experiences with and bad memories of studying Shakespeare. Many of those who worked hardest and were most dedicated to supporting the productions and educational programs for the series, as they discussed the value of the programs as supplements for teaching, would add, almost as a confession, "Well, I never liked Shakespeare myself when I was in school." Some had never before willingly read an entire Shakespeare play, but all found productions to enjoy and moments to savor in the series. The possibility of the productions helping make the experience of Shakespeare's work a positive one spurred the development of educational supplements to the series.

In Britain the BBC sponsored a three-pronged educational program for the public based on books, television programs, and radio broadcasts. Because the texts focused on the current production and the radio broadcasts on performance history, the BBC effort extended the usual literary commentary to a practical concern with playing the material that was appropriate to the educational goal of the series. To facilitate any serious study of the productions, BBC Books published the texts as scripts, annotated with textual cuts used, production scene numbers, and details from the camera scripts; to each of these were joined a literary analysis by the series's literary advisor John Wilders of Oxford University, an invaluable essay on the production by Henry Fenwick based on interviews with director, designers, and actors, color and black-and-white production photographs, and a glossary. The texts give a reader a quick reference and a full account of each production. The early volumes appeared promptly, expedited no doubt by the work of the script editor and production assistant in preparing the text. But once Alan Shallcross (Messina's script editor) and David Snodin (Miller's script editor) left their posts to become producers in the Drama division, there was no script editor for the remainder of the series and thereby no one to expedite the preparation of copy for BBC Books. Perhaps this factor contributed to the late publication of the last four scripts, delayed until 1986, over a year after the series ended.

The background of the televised *Shakespeare in Perspective* educational programs offers an additional glimpse into the history of the series. Early in the discussions, the BBC's Continuing Education division offered to plan a series of educational programs to complement the productions. Seizing on the support, Messina incorporated televised educational programs into his ideas for the Shakespeare series. From various possible formats, Victor Poole, Executive Arts Producer for BBC's Continuing Education, chose a

"Shakespeare in Perspective" approach for the programs, with an interesting individual giving his or her perspective on the play, but because the Drama division wanted Continuing Education to make "trailers" for the productions composed of interviews with directors and actors on the problems of producing and playing Shakespeare, as Victor Poole recalls, "there was tension from the start, and instead of collaboration, each project went its own way,"[62] as did so many aspects of the Shakespeare series. The greatest problem this independence posed for Continuing Education was with scheduling. The original plan had called for the 25-minute *Perspectives* to precede the productions by an hour or so on the same night, but they were sometimes scheduled two or three days ahead of the productions and in a few instances even followed the plays.

Victor Poole's intention and the idea that actually shaped the educational series for its three directors—Barbara Derkow, David Wilson, and Sally Kirkwood—was "to enlighten a new audience for Shakespeare on television, attract people to the plays, and give them some background material." Consequently Poole sought as speakers "people from all walks of life—authors, politicians, performers, barristers, businessmen," all public figures familiar to British television audiences. The speakers included authors Anthony Burgess, Stephen Spender, and Germaine Greer, journalists Malcolm Muggeridge, Clive James, Anna Raeburn, and others, a Minister of State, a former chairman of the British Rail Board, a general—a real variety. "It was a requirement," Poole explained, "that they liked Shakespeare, that they encapsulated the stories of the plays, provided an historical framework, where feasible, and offered some original thoughts which might intrigue those already familiar with the text or stimulate thoughts in those ignorant of the Bard's output," but these were guidelines rather than a formula, and the speakers were encouraged to follow their own best inclinations, especially regarding their own opinions. Poole most wanted interesting ideas about the plays, a thesis to prompt viewers to think and respond instead of being passive recipients of the action.

Poole's other major consideration was audience educational level: "The level of the Perspectives had to be gauged for 6th form— O- and A-level examinations—because I saw a potential audience among students as well as general viewers," so the speaker could assume the audience had some familiarity with Shakespeare and would know what the plays were and generally when they were written. Students proved to be a constant audience in Britain, and demand for the free booklist of background reading issued by the Continuing Education department was "very high: usually 600–800 per play and mainly from schools and colleges," Poole added.

In theory the Continuing Education division would receive a list of the season's plays from Drama and begin arranging speakers, who would write their own scripts and be filmed in a location appropriate to the speaker or play, such as the Inns of Court for judicially focused *Measure*. In practice, any number of glitches and predictable snags appeared. In the course of the series, the scripts differed in quality, some exciting, a few trivial. According to Victor Poole, "The success of the Perspectives varied with the choice of presenter. Sometimes, as in the case of Wolf Mankowitz on *Merchant*, it resulted in a programme that was a powerful plea for the tolerance of minorities in our society and by placing the jew in the historical perspective made the play more powerful than ever." Once when the film crew arrived to shoot a *Perspective*, the eminent thinker who had agreed to provide the commentary merely stood before the camera and stated, "This is one of the silliest plays ever written and I have nothing to say about it." (The play was *Hamlet*.) In that case, there was little choice except to start over.

The size of the television audience for the *Perspectives* was gratifying for Continuing Education, Poole reported: "Our audience figure for the 'Perspectives' was around the 1,000,000 mark." In many cases, at least, it seems those who tuned in the productions were willing to learn more about them or to review the play's context as an enhancement to viewing and so watched the *Perspectives* as well. (A critic or two also tuned in, prompting at least one scathing review of these shows.)[63] The *Perspectives* also proved quite successful as part of a Shakespeare "package" when sold with the productions. This auxiliary appeal of the Continuing Education programs was undoubtedly part of their attraction during the early deliberations about the series: they might enhance the plays' marketability.

The other aspect of the BBC outreach programming in conjunction with the Shakespeare series was the radio series, "Prefaces to Shakespeare," which aired a famous British actor commenting about a specific play and his or her experience in major Shakespeare roles. The list of those participating is a Who's Who of British theatre: Dame Peggy Ashcroft, Sir Michael Redgrave, Janet Suzman, Anthony Quayle, Michael Hordern, Judi Dench, and many more—all offering lively anecdotes and a wealth of personal knowledge about performing Shakespeare. The BBC thought enough of these "curtain raisers," the *Perspectives* and the "Preface" programs, that BBC Books published transcripts of the broadcasts as essays in two paperbound volumes titled *Shakespeare in Perspective*, both edited by Roger Sales. These together with the scripts provide a well-rounded, publicly accessible account of BBC programming in support of the Shakespeare series, which focused on education in the broadest sense, adult and student, unlike educational efforts in the United States, which focused on programs for schools.

In America planning for the BBC Shakespeare series began in 1975, almost as soon as in Britain; even as Morgan Bank, Exxon, Time/Life, and WNET sought to complete the funding, they proceeded to plan outreach and educational programs. Unlike the BBC, the underwriters did not have educational divisions, television and radio production units, or book publishers built into their corporations. And unlike the BBC, which therefore plugged its efforts into the existing units and the existing approach, the American underwriters began asking questions, seeking answers. Exxon with its extensive experience in arts programming guided Morgan Bank in the early going; for instance, they introduced them to Tel-Ed, the educational branch of the Stone/Hallinan public relations firm they had contracted to provide publicity for the BBC Shakespeare series in America. (Metropolitan, which only became involved in 1978, missed most of this planning phase.) No one was quite sure what the effect of the BBC Shakespeare series would be in America, but the general feeling was that it could be significant. Messina's statements about the cultural and educational value of the series—never untrue, but somewhat laced with public relations amid the power-brokering inside the BBC—were probably taken more seriously and no doubt more earnestly in the United States. Here was a great opportunity; what could be done with it?

The American exuberance did not, however, create a state of complete harmony among the participants. If the BBC units vied among themselves, the broadcast and publicity firms also vied in the United States. Yet even this competitiveness backhandedly attests their commitment to the Shakespeare series and its potential for profit or education.

Initially the planning involved every avenue of access to the public: television, radio, books, high school classrooms, adult study groups, special lectures. Many of these materialized, many did not. The book proposal for a special American edition of Shakespeare's plays to accompany the BBC series died in prospectus when Time/Life said the project would have scheduling problems and be difficult to coordinate. WNET had lined up some of its finest people to produce and direct half-hour televised introductions to the plays—an idea that drew Joseph Papp's ire when he was asked to host them—but discovered the programs would entail twice the cost of the American underwriting of the plays themselves, so the idea withered. In fact, the greater expense of television production in America was an element often overlooked in the American challenges to the BBC series; the dissension grew along artistic lines, as if the issue were only cast, not cost. Nonetheless, frustration at the comparative economics probably fueled as many fires as did wounded integrity.

Radio programming in conjunction with the series fared better, especially with National Public Radio's (NPR) "Shakespeare Festival" in 1979, the BBC series's inaugural year in America. In addition to a special series of Shakespeare-based operas and Renaissance music programs, NPR produced a two-hour docudrama, "William Shakespeare: A Portrait in Sound" by William Luce, starring Julie Harris and David Warner, and broadcast a WNET lecture series from Lincoln Center in April 1979 with scholars Sam Schoenbaum, Maynard Mack, and Daniel Seltzer. And for every production, NPR station WQED in Pittsburgh planned a half-hour radio introduction to the play to be aired the week before the telecast. Such an outburst of radio programming was both hype and tribute; the tribute was genuine, but when the Shakespeare series did not immediately revolutionize the cultural climate of America, the major programming efforts for radio ceased. Even television planning was similarly affected. A two-hour Shakespeare variety show gala planned as a PBS fund-raiser in 1981 (with stars such as Richard Chamberlain, Charlton Heston, Chita Rivera, and Robin Williams) could not find an underwriter.

The other corollary outreach program planned before the series went into production was the Folger Shakespeare Library's "Shakespeare: The Globe and The World." Comprised of artifacts and books to illustrate Renaissance daily life and Shakespeare references, paintings on Shakespeare subjects and performances, and clips from Shakespeare-based films, this multimedia touring exhibition was a major event, traveling to museums in San Francisco, Kansas City, Pittsburgh, Dallas, Atlanta, New York, Los Angeles, and Washington, D.C., and supported by both a companion volume by Sam Schoenbaum and an audiovisual instructional kit for teachers and students. As John Andrews, then Director of Academic Programs at the Folger Shakespeare Library and publications editor and conceptual consultant for the project, reported, the exhibition spawned a host of ancillary activities: lecture series, film festivals, concerts, Renaissance feasts, Elizabethan dance and fencing demonstrations, dramatic presentations, and satellite publications and exhibits. It met with acclaim across the United States, but it was an exhibition that happened amid funding difficulties only by the sheer persistence of those believing in it, very like the Shakespeare series itself.[64]

These programs enhanced the broadcast of the BBC Shakespeare series in America; the primary emphasis of the pre-broadcast planning, however, went into education. The underwriters suggested a plan to use the series in schools and asked for proposals. Since Time/Life adamantly refused to grant off-air taping rights for educational purposes, allowing only rental or sales—a policy that led some to charge them with greediness—educational programs had to be planned to work with on-the-air viewing. There was an effort from the West Coast to support postsecondary uses of the series,[65]

and a broader, more informal educational effort led to the dissemi-
nation of family viewing guides, produced for seasons one through
three by WNET/Thirteen, for season four by McCaffrey-McCall
and enclosed in *Time* magazine, and for seasons five through seven
by Metropolitan Life.

By the end of the first season, however, it was apparent that the
focus of the education program in America would fall almost entirely on secondary education. The underwriters were most interested in this grass roots educational outreach, to the extent that
they spent at least as much on the educational program, which they
awarded to Tel-Ed, the educational subsidiary of Stone/Hallinan, as
they did on underwriting the series itself.

Tel-Ed insisted that educational programming for the Shakespeare series should focus on the junior and senior high school
level, where most American students first meet Shakespeare. Re-
education would not be as necessary if the initial introduction to
Shakespeare was strong and appealing. In planning the Tel-Ed program, executive officer Tim Hallinan said they had three basic
objectives: getting more plays taught (most curricula teach only a
few, such as *Romeo and Juliet*, *Julius Caesar*, and *Macbeth*), encouraging teachers to think of the BBC series as a resource, and
having Shakespeare taught more often.[66] During the work on the
educational materials, Hallinan and Tel-Ed encountered only two
formidable problems. The first was Time/Life's not allowing off-air
taping, a decision Hallinan found indefensible and certainly coun-
terproductive to education; the second was the length of the productions after the first two seasons. With shows three or more
hours long scheduled to start at 8:00 or 9:00 in many cities, some
schoolchildren simply could not stay up for the duration of the
production.

The Tel-Ed approach was to make educational materials on the
productions available to every high school in the United States.
Because the first season was laden with the plays usually taught in
American public, private, and parochial schools, Tel-Ed emphasized those plays and sent out more than 36,000 education pack-
ets to English department heads, receiving between 17,000 and
18,000 responses about the materials. During that first season Tel-

Ed also tried to anticipate and help with problems teachers might have with plays outside the usual curriculum. In the material, Hallinan said, they "put out hooks" about lesser known plays with very good BBC productions. As a result, 4,000 to 5,000 teachers, mostly in urban areas, tried *Richard II* in their courses with good response.

Based on this experience, they thereafter spent their money on the best productions, and since many of the best productions were of the lesser known plays, the base of plays being taught broadened. Through the televised series every play in the canon, Hallinan reported, has been taught in several thousand American classrooms; 11,000 to 12,000 teachers undertook *Antony and Cleopatra*, for instance, and over 17,000 taught *Merchant*. Largely as a result of this educational effort, he added, Shakespeare classes at many universities grew markedly; some professors who experienced this response in their classes considered it an outgrowth of the students' high school experience with the series, for almost every student had seen one of the productions. While that degree of viewing saturation does not hold true for the entire country, it attests the great positive effect such production-oriented education programs can have.

In assessing the educational program, Bruce Roberts of Morgan Bank called it the greatest success in underwriting the series. Hallinan remarked that of all his publicity and educational work, he was proudest of this set of materials and its educational effect. The American Theatre Association gave Tel-Ed and the underwriters its 1984 Founder's Award, and the National Council of Teachers of English also recognized their efforts with an award. Everyone was so high on the educational value of the series that by 1981 John Andrews of the Folger Library, chairman of the underwriters' advisory panel for education, and Bruce Roberts began long-term thinking about how to extend the educational potential of the series. Of the series's three American underwriters, ultimately only Morgan Bank continued the educational program, and they were pleased to have reserved renewal rights from the beginning. When John Andrews suggested they model their program on *Masterpiece Theatre* and divide the shows into one-hour segments dubbed "The

Shakespeare Hour," Morgan Bank readily adopted the idea, and late in 1984 the National Endowment for the Humanities awarded funds for a new series to begin spring of 1986.

The Shakespeare Hour was planned as a different approach to the Shakespeare productions, a "recycling" more specifically educational in focus. A three-year series, it would treat five plays per year in a fifteen-week season, with repeats the following fall. The plays each season would be linked thematically—love, power, and revenge respectively—using what Roberts characterized as the fifteen best, most widely taught plays and with taping rights for schools to facilitate their use of the shows. Walter Matthau agreed to host the series and became quite committed to it: "since 1952, when I did Iago on the 'Philco Playhouse,' no one had offered me a job connected with Shakespeare. And when this came up, I jumped at it like a hungry tiger seeing fresh meat again."[67] Along with his comments, the programs would include "minidocumentaries" to highlight the themes of the season and to round out the hours when a section of the play ran short.[68] New educational materials were prepared, and a book for the general audience was also published by Signet, *The Shakespeare Hour: A Companion to the PBS-TV Series*, edited by Edward Quinn, containing a thematic introduction, essays on each play in the season, and a select bibliography. The total cost projection for the series was $600,000 to $650,000 per year, and all parties agreed to reexamine *The Shakespeare Hour* at the end of the first season.

"We thought we had a winner," reflected John Andrews, "like with the series." The cancellation of *The Shakespeare Hour* immediately following its first season hit all participants hard—Hallinan, his advisors, Matthau, Andrews, Morgan Bank. Suddenly it was really all over, after ten years of planning and implementing. In a sense, the second end of the series in America came too fast for its planners, as if untimely ripped from them. Causes abounded—too many stations did not show the series in prime time, it was not publicized thoroughly enough, it was not given a proper test. PBS affiliates were tired of Shakespeare after seven years; the new format came too fast on the heels of that programming marathon, so the local programmers axed it. Nonetheless, Hallinan affirmed, "the underwriters wanted a lasting legacy; they got it." Then with an understandable mixture of pride and regret he added, "The high school English teachers are the only ones who realize what the series has meant." As a result of the series, he continued, high school teachers are more adventurous in planning curriculum material and more students going into college will be Shakespeare-literate. Andrews maintained, "The series's reputation will improve because the series gets better the more you see it. It is a wonderful resource."[69] Hallinan stated his view a bit more assertively: "The series will be seen as a monumental achievement fifteen years from now."[70]

CRITICAL RECEPTION

Assessing the Shakespeare series was the continual task of the critics as well. They not only worried whether the series was a boondoggle or a mere flourish when it was announced, but at the end they also made some retrospective comments of their own, such as Cecil Smith's in the *Los Angeles Times*: "The series has been the target of critical catcalls on both sides of the Atlantic, shabbily treated by many PBS stations, often ignored or damned as dull, dull, dull."[71] The generalizations about catcalls or yawns at dullness were not uncommon at the series's end, as if much of the series's reception had been a long, fairly consistent detraction. That is the mathematical magic of criticism, which can add a string of largely positive reviews and get a negative total; no critic wants to appear uncritical. Certainly the charge of dullness, rephrased to suit individual critical temperaments, had been bandied about, especially early in the series, yet even in the first year the reviews of individual productions as they appeared were predominantly appreciative. Of course, one rather expects critics to disagree, but it may be salutary to remember that they do disagree about the value of the Shakespeare series, its best and worst productions, its finest directors, perhaps the more so in a realm as open to various tastes and strictures as Shakespeare on television.

Some of the criticism stemmed from the nature of the endeavor itself, the production of a collected works. As one critic wrote of the series approach:

> One can admire the producer's motives and calling without necessarily endorsing the results—which have been erratic. Might the worst [productions] ∴ be more counterproductive than no Shakespeare at all? It can be argued that the sexless and passionless "Romeo and Juliet" . . .—to take one example from the marathon—could serve as a form of aversion therapy for teen-agers who saw it. . . . Why, promotional expediency aside, is there a need for a marathon? Would it be more worthwhile to do some of Shakespeare's plays with deliberate care rather than to mount three dozen at a sprint simply so the culturally acquisitive can say "I've seen it all"? . . .
>
> To date, the marathon has been so inconsistent. . . . There have been good productions, in-between productions and barely nominal productions. There has been no unifying principle . . . to galvanize the entire enterprise, to make the marathon seem like an exciting journey for audience and company alike rather than merely a stunt.[72]

Of course, this is Frank Rich writing about Joseph Papp's New York Public Theatre "Shakespeare Marathon" in the late 1980s. The comparisons are irresistible; Papp began with the same star-centered and anticonceptual biases that Messina had in the BBC Shakespeare series, and the results, whether on stage or screen, are the same: such a series is uneven.

It was apparently Clive James of the *London Observer* who dubbed the BBC series "the Bardothon." He also set the long-range critical tone about the early technique with his arch description of the set in *Romeo and Juliet*; though some critics commented that "the settings are beautifully presented" or "the sets and costumes are lavish and beautiful, so that almost every frame is a visual treat,"[73] James asserted: "Verona seemed to have been built on very level ground, like the floor of a television studio. The fact that this artificiality was half accepted and half denied told you that you were not in Verona at all, but in that semi-abstract, semi-concrete, wholly uninteresting city which is known to students as Messina,

after the producer of the same name,"[74] a setting often characterized later as "1950s Old Vic." The familiarity of approach struck
critics long accustomed to Messina's *Play of the Month* and BBC
televised drama, and so some pointed to the obvious: "The BBC
Television Shakespeare . . . will be, above all else, stylistically safe.
Tradition and consolidation, rather than adventure or experiment,
are to be the touchstones,"[75] and others raised questions and offered prescriptions for the BBC's monumental effort:

> And yet, with two plays down and 35 still to go, is it churl-
> ish already to raise doubts?
> So awed, so reverential, so safe have these first two produc-
> tions [*Romeo and Juliet* and *Richard II*] been, that the BBC
> appears in danger of embalming, not offering Shakespeare for
> the delight of a wider public.
> Thus it must be more adventurous. They must be less stagey
> and more willing to let the camera get up to some of its
> tricks. . . .
> The BBC have been munificent. They should also steel
> themselves to be bold and ever so slightly bloody.[76]

If not manifest early on, "bold" and "bloody" might well express
the attitude toward both text and production style in some of the
later Shakespeares.

During the first season, even the admired performances of Celia
Johnson and Michael Hordern, Derek Jacobi, Sir John Gielgud,
Kate Nelligan, and Timothy West, among others, could not stave
off the feeling that although "there was very little for purists to find
fault with" in a production, "that perhaps may be the most damn-
ing thing you could say about it. . . . There was nothing to stir the
blood either to hot flashes of anger or to the electric joy of a new
experience. What we got was some more of the BBC's ghastly middle taste."[77] In searching for causes of this perceived blandness,
moreover, critics occasionally looked beyond those immediately
responsible: "Perhaps the fault was that this was an American
co-production and Americans have a false, churchy respect for
Shakespeare on television."[78] (Americans, be it noted, had no

part in production decisions except for the brief presented by the underwriters.)

Yet in this sifting of the series, even early on some critics saw what became apparent to all by the end: "It is not *Romeo and Juliet, Macbeth,* or *Hamlet* to which I look in this series for the most interesting contributions, but to exactly those plays which some have objected are not worth televising: to *Henry VIII, Pericles, Titus Andronicus* and so on which I have never seen in the theatre."[79] Traditional approaches would have greater difficulty inundating the less popular plays, those with less tradition encrusting them. And as other production concepts were enunciated and could be assessed, some critics even saw a wisdom in the BBC's approach to the plays. Commenting on director Michael Bogdanov's 1983 half-hour analytical series *Shakespeare Lives* on Britain's Channel 4, Sean Day-Lewis concluded: "Yet in his compulsion to chop the plays about, and perhaps to translate them into our own comparatively impoverished modern English, so as to make them totally relevant and meaningful in this day and age, Mr. Bogdanov chiefly underlines the need for the philosophy behind the BBC Shakespeare."[80]

WNET executive Jac Venza said that given the BBC's interest in producing works with a long-range use, the production guidelines were a "very sensible decision," for their goals were unlike those of theatrical companies such as the RSC or San Diego Old Globe, which are interested in only one season and have narrower, more select audiences accustomed to Shakespeare so ever-fresh ways to present the material are essential to attract artists and directors as well as patrons.[81] All the critics and reviewers of the Shakespeare series, however, were part of that narrower, more select audience experienced with Shakespeare production, a fact that accounts for the nature of some of the criticism, which asks for something other than what the BBC intended to produce. Whether they succeeded or not, the BBC set out to engage the widest possible audience; consequently, novelty was not necessarily their first consideration.

In addition to such contextual perspectives, a number of critics offered technical analyses of the series, a closer look at how the plays were televised. The most optimistic version, surely a rendition of the BBC party line, came from New York as the series began its American broadcast: "These versions of Shakespeare will be vigorously adapted for television, with attention to the particular demands and drawbacks of the medium." Expecting technical facility, therefore, the critic not surprisingly finds it in that inaugural *Julius Caesar*: "The techniques used in filming 'Julius Caesar' are very evidently—and often very successfully—geared to the small screen," she said, for "instead of pausing for reaction shots or close-ups of individual players, the camera swoops in upon them, or remains fixed on the actor who's listening while the actor who's speaking strides in and out of the frame. This may look sloppy at times. . . . But it's also . . . introducing an element of visual suspense."[82]

The most evenhanded and useful consideration of BBC technique in starting the series is Sean Day-Lewis's assessment of the first season. His initial coup is to point out that there is no one style in the productions but a number of different approaches: "In my view the first season has contained three duds ('Romeo and Juliet,' 'As You Like It,' and 'Julius Caesar') and three successes ('Richard II,' 'Measure for Measure,' and 'Henry VIII'), but I found redeeming features even in the former trio. It has therefore not been such a bad start, given some directors new to the problems of translating Shakespeare to television, and the casting policy of collecting stars rather than a company." While he prefers the RSC's televisual style of defining space by lighting rather than sets and of focusing on talking heads, he also adds that this may be a style for a specialized audience and that the BBC productions have shown "there is no one way that is obviously right or wrong in televising all Shakespeare."[83] As examples, he looks at various productions' soliloquies, settings, and sense of audience, describing the successes as well as what can be learned from the less successful.

Such a constructive analysis was all too rare in journalistic criticism of the series, which was more nearly characterized by grand and sweeping generalization; for instance: "It must now be apparent as the BBC wind up their complete Shakespeare with *Titus Andronicus*—that the whole venture has been reckless and misguided. . . . Messina's first productions were clumsy and unspecific, badly shot in the main, and indifferently cast. Miller's productions were a clear improvement: their visual style was precise and distinctive and the casting, on the whole, intelligently done. . . . But the series has not been a success."[84] More than an early and a late view of the series, these illustrate two different styles of criticism, one that initiates discussion and one that terminates it.

Reviewers and critics were not the only assessors of the BBC's work; the Shakespeare series also underwent the scrutiny of the British television industry during its years of production and gained its share of acclaim. Awards for technical excellence appeared almost annually, starting with *Measure* the first season, among them a British Association of Film and Television Artists (BAFTA) award in 1981 to Geoff Feld as Best Cameraman for *Merchant* and in 1982 to Jim Atkinson for camera work on *All's Well, Othello, Timon,* and *Troilus and Cressida.* Don Homfray received a design award for his work in the series, especially for *Merry Wives,* and in 1984–85 the Royal Television Society gave *Much Ado*'s Jan Spoczynski its award for Designer of the Year and presented a special Judges' Award to the BBC for the series as a whole. Lighting designers were also recognized with awards: John Summers for his work, including *All's Well,* and Dennis Channon for the lighting in *Henry IV* and *Henry V.*

But by the end of the BBC Shakespeare series everyone—BBC production staff, underwriters, outreach and publicity personnel, and critics—admittedly, was tired; it had been an arduous though addictive project for those who saw it through. The natural exuberance of beginning paled by the finish, which in itself was an exercise in discipline more than enthusiasm, a factor that the choices of new producer and new directors in the stretch may have been meant to alleviate. And the BBC itself was less deferential in scheduling broadcast slots as the years wore on and hierarchies changed. Over a short space of time, as Alan Shallcross indicated, a series can maintain a unity of style because taste and fashion do not radically change; seven years, he suggested, may be too long for unity in television terms. Thought in the popular culture and in the theatre shifts; what seems immediate and catching at the moment may not maintain those effects a few years later. Miller frequently said he thought the shelf life of the series—that is, the length of time the productions would remain fresh, viable, undated—would be about ten years. The underwriters, on the other hand, hoped and planned for much longer usefulness in the United States.

In London during February 1985, one last end-of-series party celebrated the conclusion of the seven-year, 37-play effort. Gathered to dine were many of those who had had responsibility for productions in the series—directors, the three producers, underwriters' representatives, leading actors, and the permanent production staff. Through the evening they basked in the satisfaction of finishing their considerable task and joked about producing all the works of another prolific playwright such as Shaw, at which everyone groaned. They had done it, the first televised canon of Shakespeare's plays. It was not a night for asking why; it was a night for all the participants to come momentarily together in an unreal unity held together by the genuine gaiety, politeness, and forced conviviality common to such gatherings, and next day everyone turned to new tasks and the next drama production.

We, however, may ask why or perhaps for whom—a question that elicits an answer suitable for both. There is, of course, the skeptical critic's answer, offered even before the series started, to "the big question: Why? ... The BBC says it's all to do with mass education and with British prestige abroad. But the State-supported theatres already put on enough Shakespeare for our educational needs. There are also ... mutterings from English Lit. teachers and pupils to the effect that what's needed to stir curiosity about Shakespeare is a new and challenging interpretation of the text, not the traditionally lavish and literal reading. Prestige and foreign sales are probably the real answer."[85]

But there is another answer as well. When asked, some of those long involved with the series invariably responded, "We did them for ourselves," an answer that is not as solipsistic as it sounds. "Ourselves" is not just the Drama group of the BBC nor even the BBC itself. "Ourselves" is more nearly a term for British television viewers, especially the nonurban British audience, removed from a theatrical center, whose only opportunity to see great theatrical texts performed is by means of a mass medium. Alan Shallcross described this audience based on his personal experience, telling of growing up in northern England where he saw live theatre perhaps once a year in Liverpool; otherwise Shakespeare and all drama came from television. His first television *Othello*, he recalled, "bowled me over; it was like the road to Damascus." And, he continued, "we must remember there are young and old people out there who are also on that road."[86] Not primarily for fame or profit or self-aggrandizement, the series came about for those involved in its production for the same reasons most artistic performances come before the public—because they can, and because someone may see them and enjoy them, appreciate them, be moved or disturbed by them, and understand them afresh.

2   Transatlantic Shakespeare

When news of the BBC's proposed Shakespeare project became known in the United States, one of the frequent early criticisms stemmed from the fact that the productions would be British. In New York City, the Public Theatre's Joseph Papp not only protested U.S. companies sending artistic funding to England but also complained "that young Americans should not be faced with a British-accented Shakespeare as it will cut them off by labelling Shakespeare both foreign and highbrow."[1] Of course, even the fact that Shakespeare's plays are performed more frequently in America than in Britain, as the myriad Shakespeare festivals across the continent would attest, does not make Stratford-upon-Avon a suburb of St. Louis or Shakespeare a Yankee Doodle Dandy. Shakespeare comes from another time and for Americans also from another place; no accent alters that. And although the series was intended to make the plays available worldwide via the twentieth-century's most popular medium of communication, television, the Shakespeare series is nonetheless British in ways more pervasive and far-reaching than accent, ways that point up the differences between British and American television. Those differences account for much of what the series became in the United Kingdom and the United States.

In looking at the place of the Shakespeare series on British and American television, more than a footnote's worth of consideration should go to the general difference between the series's being broadcast over BBC 2 at home and over PBS in America. Though BBC 2 does have a somewhat higher-brow reputation than one of Britain's commercial channels, it is nonetheless one of the regular channels, one that in the schedule-checking and viewing habits of Britons has a place like NBC's, ABC's, or CBS's in the United States. Even though the two BBC channels are noncommercial,

each offers a full range of programming: sports, news, current affairs, features, music, light entertainment, and drama. They are
meant to be complementary, with BBC 2 described as "slightly
more 'up-market,'" and they compete for viewers with the commercial stations.

The reverse is the case in America: when PBS was founded, three
well-established commercial networks were already broadcasting,
and PBS's noncommercial status and programming guidelines did
not leave it an equal competitor. It was started because of gaps in
commercial programming and offered an important alternative to
the networks before the rise of cable television, especially in arts
programming, much of which the American commercial networks
would not touch. But federal funding for PBS supports a wide
range of arts programming, as Jac Venza, Executive Producer for
Performance Programs at WNET, the New York City PBS station
that produced the Shakespeare series for broadcast in the United
States, explains:

> [The arts] shine best in the hands of the best living artists, and
> that's where the media is the perfect way to distribute them
> globally and nationally . . . at one time and very efficiently.
> That's the reason the National Endowment is interested in a
> series like *Great Performances*, for in a sense it allows some of
> the most important arts organizations they support to [be
> widely seen]. You can't tour ballet theatre or the Metropolitan
> Opera very readily to more than a few cities, but you could, on
> television, make sure everyone is getting value for the taxpay-
> er's dollar. So that's why the idea of this national system in line
> with those arts support organizations makes great sense.[2]

Yet PBS's somewhat highbrow arts programming proved both a
blessing and a curse for the Shakespeare series. As a result of its
programming reputation, some American viewers do not even click
by the local PBS station on their television dials, whereas comparable households in England would have watched BBC 2. Had the
Shakespeare series been picked up by one of the commercial networks in the United States (if that fantasy does not collapse on the
spot of its own unlikelihood), its impact might have been more far-

reaching because of viewing habits and the assumptions viewers have about those stations' general-appeal programming. Even on PBS, Shakespeare was considered fairly erudite subject matter, and programming the series was a challenge. As Venza observed, unlike contemporary drama, "Shakespeare has a connotation that separates it from what people usually associate television with being: entertainment, diversion, rest, [a source of] information." American television programming needs "immediate accessibility" and usually lacks literary quality, he continued.[3] As classic drama the Shakespeare series was at home on PBS; PBS, however, has a special, if not quite central, place in American television.

The Shakespeare series, as the BBC touted, was a huge project: 37 plays, most 2½ hours long, some up to 4 hours. Put in practical television terms, the series presented a scheduler's nightmare, but far more so in America than in Britain. In Britain, television shows can run any length and start at any time—11:02, 7:48, 6:13—different on every channel, different every day. Thus the BBC Shakespeare productions, as is usual, ran to various lengths—2 hours and 18 minutes, 2 hours and 34 minutes—with no rigid consistency. The 2½-hour limit was a guideline, not an absolute. In Britain shows are rarely trimmed to fit specific program slots; instead, the slot is chiseled to fit the show. In the early seasons the BBC did edit Shakespeare's text to bring the shows close to the suggested length, but such editing was not an exact science guided by a stopwatch.

Exporting the Shakespeares to America posed difficulties, however, because of the rigid half-hour and hour time slots on American television. In the United States a television show cannot run 2 hours 18 minutes followed by the next show; it must run either 2 hours or 2½ hours. Moreover, regardless of length, the BBC divided its Shakespeare productions into halves—giving, as if at the theatre, a 5-minute interval of news and weather—whereas PBS had to break every hour. Therefore American television immediately faced the need for adjustments and had to start looking for fillers to complete the time slots of the productions. As their varied lengths indicate, the shows certainly were not made with a strict eye to the needs of American television.

During the first season of Shakespeare productions, only *Measure for Measure* and *As You Like It* easily fit American slots; the other productions necessitated fillers, some of up to 17 and 18 minutes. In the second season all the supplementary programming involved Renaissance music performed by the Waverly Consort, sometimes brief pieces but twice that season a 23-minute miniconcert. During Miller's producership another concept governed the American fillers, one proposed from the series's inception by the BBC Drama section. WNET taped Miller (a proven television instructor after his series *The Body in Question*) giving "wrap-around" comments—2-minute introductions to each show—and then afterward, as needed, interviews between Miller and a leading cast member, such as John Cleese (Petruchio) from *The Taming of the Shrew*, Warren Mitchell (Shylock) from *The Merchant of Venice*, Jane Lapotaire (Cleopatra) from *Antony and Cleopatra*, wherein they chatted about the play, the nature of the particular character, the historical context of the play, the production concept—in other words, the sort of "meet the director" or "meet the star" program that can fill a theatre as a special offering. Whatever the general response to these supplementary bits, many American academics objected to them, considering them condescending, almost as if they thought the fillers were Miller's idea, a means of self-promotion and lecturing to the colonials, and not special fillers arranged by WNET for the American broadcasts. Such miscues can occur when the origin and purpose of programming are left unexplained, as they were in this case by WNET.

By the end of Miller's producership, the WNET funding for even these fillers had been exhausted, and since no more money was available, the only alternative was to edit the tapes of the plays to fit the time slots. Throughout the series, WNET had silently edited for American broadcast, nibbling bits out of *Hamlet* (about which the series producer informed the BBC production office, which benignly left the issue to WNET's discretion) and others. WNET felt it best not to call attention to the editing, for that left them with fewer restraints. The American attitude as stated by WNET's Jac Venza was, "when they would go three minutes over the half-hour we felt that if they couldn't cut three minutes out of 3½ hours, we could."[4] Much of the editing early in the series had been slight, but later it became more significant as pressures from the local PBS stations increased. Faced with numbers of Shakespeare plays that took up hours of their valuable prime-time programming, some stations started to mutter and complain, especially as the shows began to run longer than 2½ hours once Miller instituted the more complete scripts. The programs could not be moved earlier ("You can't bump *The MacNeil-Lehrer Report*"), so they ran late.

The productions that felt the brunt of the American editing and the stations' concerns were those in Jane Howell's *Henry VI–Richard III* tetralogy. In England this sequence, shown on four successive Sunday nights in January 1983, proved to be the surprise hit of the series; fan mail poured into the production office. Howell's integrated concept with one basic set and a repertory company of actors was fascinating and addictive. But the Americans feared a different response and formulated a different plan, which was the nadir of the Shakespeare series's programming in America. Faced with four straight productions of 3, 3½, 3½, and almost 4 hours respectively—14 hours of what were for the most part little-known plays—PBS and WNET balked. Heeding stations' criticisms, WNET moved the *Henry VI* plays out of the usual Monday evening slot to Sunday afternoon, known in the trade as the "ghetto" of programming, following the lead of a number of local stations that were already rescheduling the series this way. In addition, they divided each *Henry VI* play into two parts, so the audience saw only half a play on a given day and the tetralogy stretched over seven weeks. *Richard III* with its famous villain-protagonist was allowed to return to the Monday night broadcast time. Lastly, they edited the *Henry VI* tapes, not just deleting 3½ minutes as with *Richard III* but well over an hour (about 77 minutes), roughly 13 percent of the *Henry VI* plays' taped length. And the editor felt virtuous doing it, for he considered he had improved the tapes. Whatever it may imply about the artistic integrity of the director's finished product, the American attitude toward editing reveals the unmistakable aesthetic differences between British and American television production.

WNET felt its editing had been very discreet, and the last of the series's coordinators at WNET bragged that only one play had forfeited an entire scene for transmission: *Troilus and Cressida* lost act III, scene 1, the Helen/music scene (which Miller had taped entire). If Americans buy the Time/Life videotape, they see the scene; if they watched the series on television, they did not. In approaching the *Henry VI–Richard III* editing, the first task was getting it into chunks, since only *Richard III* would be shown entire on one day, and even then it had to have hourly breaks. According to Roger Downey, the coordinator who edited these tapes, "Anything that wasn't words went,"[5] which meant that the battles, a carefully patterned part of Howell's overall production concept, were the first to go. He allowed "scenic voice-overs" for essential battle scenes; otherwise the motto was "tighten, tighten, tighten," which was sometimes a matter of minutes, more often a few seconds here, a few seconds there. Downey also made inroads on long establishing or tracking shots and on exits. Where he could, Downey said, he strove to maintain the tape's effect in his editing; for instance, if he had to cut a long camera move, he would let it start, then fade to black as a transition for the cut. In one scene during the *Henry VI* sequence he cut a rather large section from a tent scene, he explained, then had to run the tape backwards to get a head turning in the proper direction to cover the edit.

Richard III lost almost nothing in the editing, 3½ minutes; on the other hand, the play full of battles, *3 Henry VI*, was cut over 35 minutes, one-seventh of the tape, for its television transmission. Just before the final edit, WNET executives decided the tapes needed an introduction on the Wars of the Roses. James Earl Jones agreed to provide the voice for the introduction, which thanks to Jones's renown as the voice of Darth Vader was quickly nicknamed the "Star Wars of the Roses" introduction, and a few more seconds were nibbled from the plays.

Throughout the series, WNET experienced the typical problems of preparing foreign tapes for broadcast. The first concerned receipt of the tapes, which often arrived just six weeks before their airing date. Those at WNET frequently commented on the delays in receiving tapes and on the productions' delayed BBC editing—

the tedious problems of coproduction broadcasting. In a few cases such complaints had justification, for although most of the productions were edited within three weeks of taping, eight or so had postponed editing. These included a few of Miller's and all of Moshinsky's productions, for Moshinsky's schedule was always very full. In the case of *Love's Labour's Lost*, for instance, he taped in early July 1984, then immediately left to direct an opera in Australia; he returned to edit *Love's Labour's Lost* in November. And while communication between the BBC and WNET was generally good, changes in the BBC's production schedule could wreak havoc on the other side of the Atlantic, where PBS planning is done a year in advance.

On arrival at Time/Life all the tapes had to be converted from British to American television technology, for the two countries' televisions have different resolution, that is, different numbers of lines scanned on the screen: Britain with 625 lines scanned 50 times per second, the United States with 525 lines scanned 30 times per second (a difference that the British and Europeans claim improves the clarity and color, though American television personnel disagree). Especially during the first two seasons of the series a number of different conversion houses worked with the tapes, so that conversion was uneven at best, sometimes substandard. When broadcast was imminent the tapes would bypass Time/Life and go straight to WNET for conversion; that eased the schedule crunch but did not solve the problem of quality. Furthermore, for most of the series the BBC was still editing on 2-inch tape rather than 1-inch tape, though the 2-inch is less efficient. While preparing *King Lear*, for example, the challenge was mechanical; in editing from a 2-inch onto a 1-inch tape, WNET's machine devoured part of the 2-inch tape at the beginning of the first heath scene. The videotape engineer manually spliced the 2-inch tape; nonetheless, Downey confesses, in the American broadcast Lear still got to the heath very quickly.[6] The best thing that happened during the series, Downey observed, was the BBC's change to 1-inch videotape for the last few productions.

But in addition to these broadcast issues, there were others more specific to the BBC Shakespeare series and to an aesthetic judgment of what is good television. Since there is no agreement among Britons or Americans about what makes for good Shakespeare or effective television, evaluative comments abounded. Even within the BBC some called certain approaches "old-fashioned" or disagreed about how to shoot certain action—the usual professional undercurrents. Some Americans felt the productions had not had enough rehearsal time, though the actors in the series felt otherwise. Ian Hogg (Banquo in *Macbeth*) said there was ample rehearsal time for the televised productions; the difference between a television and a theatrical performance, he added, is not in rehearsal but in the run of a show during which performances often grow.[7] Lack of rehearsal time was not a significant problem in the productions. A few performances may not have been stellar, but that was a matter of talent; none was half-baked. Even stronger comments from America usually focused on one of three BBC production elements: camera work, pacing, and sound.

Early on, television-savvy American academics lamented the BBC's constant use of what they often mistakenly considered two-camera taping in the productions, but the greater item for comment among television professionals was Jonathan Miller's reliance on single-camera scenes. Not only did Roger Downey say they were impossible to edit, but WNET's Jac Venza explained, "The idea of never having a cut in the midst of a long literary speech sounds right, I mean, when Jonathan [Miller] describes it. The fact is it belies that there is an audience looking at very sophisticated cinematic editing and cutting, so that if anything this will look more strange. . . . [Miller] took the position that whole scenes should just be performed for the literary style, and there should be no interruption by intercutting, . . . five or six or eight minutes' worth of no alternation. He may be right that at first people listen and don't look as much, but I'm not sure it served the dramatic impact of the pieces as well as it might."[8] In addition to these concerns, there were comments about the prevalence of triangular blocking as a standard device in the series, that is, placing two speakers in the foreground of a shot with another figure visible between them to the rear.

More than on camera work, however, technical criticism of the series focused on its pacing. To some extent pacing is a subjective matter; what is fine or subtle for one viewer may be slow and laborious to another. But in general American television—epitomized during this time by *Three's Company* and *Miami Vice*—is very fast paced, full of quick cuts, which are partly dictated by the need to overcome commercial interruptions. Briskness makes good television, and anything less prompts impatience, or so the aesthetic maxim runs. Even *Sesame Street*, the mainstay of children's educational television in America, is programmed in modules of thirty seconds each. Accustomed to that rhythm and reinforced by the visual assault of rock videos, some viewers find anything less than scarcely contained chaos a slow pace. As Jac Venza pointed out, insisting on such a pace does a disservice to much arts programming, for Shakespeare, ballet, and opera take longer than thirty seconds to build or to "hook" an audience. BBC programming, on the contrary, because it is based on a noncommercial system, is not driven by commercial breaks. Devotees of *Masterpiece Theatre* appreciate the uninterrupted development and juxtaposition of scenes, the careful building of effect over time. Admittedly, the British see far more of American television than Americans see of British. Consequently, Britons notice the difference between American and British television pace; Americans, for lack of comparison, do not. Some people at the BBC along with some at WNET felt a few of the productions were very slow, but the American response in general results from overlaying an American standard on the BBC without acknowledging alternatives.

The technical element that provoked most concern, though, was the sound; WNET and PBS repeatedly complained to the BBC that the audio was bad, that the actors could not be heard. Critics, too, registered concern throughout the series, one saying *Measure* was "a production marred only by this series' continuing annoying variation in sound levels,"[9] another charging of *Timon of Athens* that Miller "could have at least made sure every actor was adequately miked; some of the speeches evaporate into air downstage."[10] For their part, the British often comment on the bland uniformity of American sound: "It all sounds alike," all levels evenly high. The difference is not a matter of technology but of aesthetics. The Americans believe every sound should be crystal clear, as if close. The British use another standard, unapologetically valuing perspective sound, which means if a character speaks far from the camera, he or she should sound far from the camera, even if that means faint.

Sound is not overlooked in the BBC studios; in fact, so zealous was the sound crew to capture every syllable of Shakespeare that the most prevalent visual flaw in the series was boom shadows. The sound supervisors were exceedingly picky about the sound, bursting out of the sound suite and virtually wearing a path to the director's chair to explain a problem or register a complaint. During the Shakespeare series, horses' hooves were swathed in booties and the lids of silver dishes padded to avoid intrusive or inappropriate sound. At the end of the first park scene in *Love's Labour's Lost*, for instance, the three lords were to run across the steps, catch Boyet, and each inquire a lady's name, but as they ran in heavy eighteenth-century–style shoes, it was very obvious, as the sound supervisor pointed out, that those steps painted to look like weathered stone were actually wooden. They echoed hollowly at every footfall. (One reviewer commented on just this phenomenon in *The Tempest* when a solidly shod Miranda ran across "the wooden beach.")[11] The actors tried tiptoeing, but that altered their gait too noticeably on the quick moves, so the only solution was for them to remove their shoes and sock-foot their way across shot, which conveniently excluded their feet. Furthermore, the concern for sound extended beyond the studio; in editing the sound levels were again carefully monitored and adjusted. The varied sound levels were no accident; the BBC wanted perspective sound.

Timon is a case in point, for in that production any number of characters either speak from afar or exit speaking at the opposite side of the studio; they not only sound far away but occasionally a word is even garbled or lost, as it naturally would be in such circumstances. *Othello*, too, has a striking example of this approach to sound. As Iago asks Cassio about Bianca they sit in a window seat in the main hall; Othello is hidden behind the open door to the next room. The scene is almost entirely shot from behind Othello, so the viewer sees what Othello sees, and, more importantly, hears what he hears—snatches of the deceptive dialogue, Iago's muttered questions, Cassio's muffled replies. A cut to a close-up on the pair of officers shows Iago chuckling and jollying Cassio along, then returns to the distant view. Though not every word is audible here, the viewer shares the subjective effect of the revelation. To the British this effect is not actors' bad projection or bad audio; it is perspective sound, a realistic sound effect that establishes the depth of the picture.

Nonetheless, not every director in the series favored perspective sound. Elijah Moshinsky, for one, insisted that he wanted American sound, no variance, and fought to avoid perspective sound in *Love's Labour's Lost*. The dilemma about audio also from time to time prompted videotape editors on the other side of the Atlantic to bump up the BBC sound level. In other words, in transmitting them, WNET to some extent Americanized the productions, editing for speedier pace and more uniform sound. Clearly these productions were not seen as works of art (the changes prompt views as strongly held as those about adding color to old black-and-white films), for the implication of this American response is that either the BBC does not know what it is doing or does it badly, though neither is in fact the case. They know what they are doing and mean it. The two countries are divided by their views of a common medium.

The rigor of these aesthetic differences points up how closely linked television is to popular culture. We all know the accepted patterns and methods; if those are diverged from we tend to see the divergence as a problem or flaw rather than a creative difference. Some of the American response to the Shakespeare series may have been affected, for instance, by the contemporary vogue for television miniseries, lavishly filmed affairs involving big-name stars and extensive location work. By comparison, the Shakespeare series may have seemed cramped or confined in the studio and certainly not lavish. The battles came in for special criticism in this regard; with the exception of Achilles' pushing Hector's battered head into the slime during *Troilus and Cressida*, several television professionals found the studio battles unworkable and as the only feasible approach sanctioned instead the work of Olivier and Akira Kurosawa—film work, not television.

In another sense, too, the aesthetic differences deserve reckoning, and that concerns the issue of medium itself. Were Americans given novels rather than television productions, they would immediately recognize their British context and call any quick criticism based entirely on American cultural values a misreading. Yet a comparable response to the televised Shakespeare series is not called a misviewing. What we get from the Shakespeare series, however, is partly determined by what we see and partly by how we see and what we look for.

Consequently, there is the British cultural context of the series to consider. Theory of the television medium asserts that "the television message is made meaningful only at the moment when the semiotic codes interlock with the cultural awareness *supplied by the viewer*, whose own context will play a part in shaping the cultural awareness."[12] The BBC Shakespeare series provides an excellent laboratory for testing and proving the ways this statement is true, starting with casting. Much of the casting in the BBC Shakespeare series brought good actors from the British stage and television to classical roles, playing on the connotations of the actor's famous roles or just as earnestly playing against those connotations, while often seeking to counter traditional concepts or longstanding characterizations. In *A Midsummer Night's Dream*, Elijah Moshinsky said, instead of following the British stage tradition of portraying Puck as a sweetly mischievous sprite, by casting Phil Daniels he consciously sought an effect closer to *A Clockwork Orange*. This approach to casting developed along with the series, changing as the series changed. Innovative casting was more frequently mentioned during the Miller years, for as a director he often discussed the concept with the press and as producer fostered it, and Moshinsky insisted on using casting as a means of interpreting the plays. Retrospectively, the Messina productions were criticized for their conventional, uninteresting casting, even though reviewers at the time praised a number of the performances. The first big press treatment of Miller's casting involved John Cleese as Petruchio, the actor's first classical role. John Gorrie had had a similar prompting in *The Tempest* the previous season for casting in his first classical role (Trinculo) Andrew Sachs, an actor well known as the waiter Manuel who was regularly battered by Basil Fawlty (John Cleese) in *Fawlty Towers*.

Yet Americans have almost no way of fully appreciating the contributions of casting to the series except where such figures as Sir John Gielgud, Claire Bloom, Roger Daltrey, John Cleese, and perhaps Derek Jacobi are concerned. These actors have ready recognition in the United States. But despite their being well known in Britain, many of the fine television actors who took part in the series go unnoticed in America because they have not been weekly visitors on Americans' sets as they have been at home. American viewers lose the frisson of recognition, the extra edge of watching an actor move from weekly series to classical drama. What would be the effect for Americans if they saw Alan Alda of *M.A.S.H.* in jerkin and codpiece spouting iambic pentameter?

Consider an example from the Shakespeare series. Though the name of Leonard Rossiter is not a household word in the United States, it is in Britain, where he was (before his untimely death between the taping and transmission of *King John* in 1984) revered for his comic characterizations. The memory of a single shifty look could send critics writing about him into joyous chuckles years later. Playing the executive Reginald Perrin in the long-running series *The Rise and Fall of Reginald Perrin* and the seedy, lecherous landlord Rigsby in *Rising Damp*, Rossiter and his facial expressions in these roles became so well known that one critic of *King John* observed: "The unaccustomed beard which he adopted in the central role could not conceal the occasional wild and oddly lunatic leer which was the essential rampant Rigsby."[13] Yet no American would see Rigsby in Rossiter's King John. No American viewer could feel what so many British reviewers, admittedly in a eulogistic mode, lamented as the untapped classical abilities of this fine actor. A similar case in the same cast is John Thaw, who played Hubert, previously seen in Britain (without a beard) chasing criminals as the star of *The Sweeney* series.

Non-Britons have no way of appreciating the effect such casting has on the native audience; even when told of the actor's fame and credits, the foreign audience finds these just empty titles, evoking no connotations or vital memories. British reviewers, however, regularly commented on the actors' television "identities," such as the fact that Kenneth Colley, as the Duke in *Measure*, had just been seen as "a flea-bitten, pathetic accordian man" in the highly successful *Pennies from Heaven* (which also starred Bob Hoskins, the BBC *Othello*'s Iago), or that Bernard Hill's convincing characterization of the unemployed Yosser Hughes in the BBC's *Boys from Blackstuff* made it difficult for some viewers to grant him aristocratic status as *Henry VI*'s Richard, Duke of York.[14]

But this is good casting, better than many viewers can know, and it happens repeatedly in the Shakespeare series, encouraged by Miller's inventive tapping of John Cleese as Petruchio and carrying through to the end. For example, Warren Mitchell, who played Shylock in the BBC Shakespeare series, is famous in Britain as the bigot Alf Garnett on *Till Death Us Do Part*, the show remade in America as *All in the Family*, so that casting Mitchell therefore provides the British equivalent of Carroll O'Connor (Archie Bunker) playing Shylock. Another lead in *Merchant*, Gemma Jones (Portia), was star of the popular British television series *The Duchess of Duke Street*. When Elijah Moshinsky called to offer television comedienne Maureen Lipman the part of the Princess in *Love's Labour's Lost*, she paused and then responded, "But . . . I'm Maureen Lipman!" implying, "I don't do classical drama." But she showed she can do classical drama, bringing a lively refinement to her performance and stunning the studio with her delivery of the emotional change at Marcade's act V entrance and mournful news: on every take her eyes filled with tears as the banter and laughter left her lips. Moshinsky was particularly proud of this casting. He pointed out that the role of the Princess starts in a comic scene and ends with a serious one; that is the surprise he wanted for the audience—to be startled by Lipman's effectiveness at the end.[15] The associations a performer has for the audience are not an inconsequential part of the BBC Shakespeare productions in Britain, though they are lost in other countries.

Lost to Americans in the same way are British allusions and

mannerisms, the "in" jokes. One example is the depiction of Peter Quince in *Dream*, which drew a good deal of praise. A few critics also wryly noted that Peter Quince talked and behaved exactly like the retiring Director-General of the BBC.[16]

In other areas of production, too, the British cultural context figures significantly. From the cockney Luce in *The Comedy of Errors* to *The Winter's Tale*'s west-country Perdita, the class and regional accents used throughout the series—that vocal shorthand that tells the British ear so much—to other listeners can seem an aural impediment, the words harder to discern. These British accents do not say to an American audience, certainly not to students on first viewing, what they quickly say to a British audience more discriminatingly born to the manner of class distinctions. Because accent often functions as an interpretive signal in British drama, a character's entire background and world view can be suggested in a few syllables if the audience knows the code. Of course, there were two different kinds of accent at work in the series—natural and assumed. National origin was subject to comment by British critics with Anthony Hopkins's Welsh lilt and Ian Charleson's Scots burr, and Britons accused Edward Petherbridge of sounding American as Gower in *Pericles*.

Americans usually protested any non-Oxbridge sounds: "[Miller] tends to cast his British television productions from ranks so Cockney they sound like leftovers from the first stage run of 'My Fair Lady,'"[17] or, "Some BBC presentations can be a tiresome sort of challenge to us poor 'hempen home-spun' Americans, sometimes unable to cut through the thicket of British accents."[18] The British critics did not challenge the *use* of accents so much as who used them; whereas the depiction of Joan la Pucelle, the French spitfire of *1 Henry VI*, took some flack for using a rural British accent, the other lords of that *Henriad* were once chastised for not speaking "u" enough: "Jane Howell does what she can to help by providing a wide range of physical types and, more questionably, by endowing them with a variety of regional accents. . . . But most local accents inevitably create something of a plebeian impression which may seem at odds with the dignity and status of the aristocratic and royal protagonists."[19] Evidently they can behave like savages as long as they speak like gentlemen from the same club.

If the accents of the characters drew varied transatlantic responses, so did their appearance in that more nebulous aesthetic category known as beauty. Pulchritude formed the basis for publicity and also for some criticism of the series. Particularly at the series's opening the British press ran features on the actresses, the "beauties" involved in the productions; perhaps it was a BBC promotional ploy. One of the earliest production-related pieces to appear is titled "A Date with Bard's Birds," which sports individual pictures of Janet Maw, Helen Mirren, Kate Nelligan, Rebecca Saire, and Angharad Rees in their Shakespeare roles, the hook for an otherwise factual account of the series's opening.[20] A more thoroughly beauty-focused article was London's *Times Sunday Magazine*'s spread, "Beauty and the Bard," which provided color pictures of Helen Mirren, Virginia McKenna, Rebecca Saire, Kate Nelligan, and Penelope Keith with Ciaran Madden (of that first *Much Ado About Nothing*). After a brief set of facts about the series, Milton Shulman continued with interview material about how the actresses looked in the parts, their opinions of their own beauty, and also whether they would perform nude (to spare you the research, Mirren and Nelligan already had, Keith would, Madden would not, and fifteen-year-old Saire apparently was not asked).[21] As the third season was launched the *London Daily Mail* reported with a photograph of Sarah Badel, Angela Down, Anna Calder-Marshall, and Janet Key, captioned "Four New Girls for the Bard."[22] Such a standard advertising gimmick—like draping a chic female across the hood of a car—provides the sugar-and-spice of publicity, a slant common with many London papers.

Amid this glow, comments also surfaced in reviews about those portraying the lovelies or the femmes fatales in Shakespeare's canon. Jane Lapotaire's Cleopatra elicited some quibbles about sex goddess expectations, for instance, and the remarks about Rebecca Saire's Juliet focused on her youth. In America, where the audience had fewer associations with the performers' other roles or reputations, viewers tended to judge looks more absolutely against the stereotypical American television standard of beauty. Whereas British television seems to offer a greater range of what is considered attractive, the harder, colder eye of American consumers often responded on a yes-or-no causal basis: if the characters were considered good-looking, they were accepted in the roles; if not, they were rejected. Especially for American students, a romantic lead had to be perceived as good-looking to appeal. Yet defining what is attractive gets into cultural determinations distinctive on each side of the Atlantic, based on both tradition and current popular culture.

This issue complements a related aspect of the series's presentation and audience's perception—that the BBC Shakespeare series was part of the contemporary fabric of British dramatic production and demonstrated its fashions and fads. Moshinsky's punk Puck, that Brixton tough of a sprite, was in 1981 part of a spate of punks on British stage and television, even Shakespeare punks that ranged from the beige *Dream* fairies at the National Theatre to the young and provocative punk witches of the RSC's 1982 Brechtian *Macbeth*. Even Tamora, Queen of the BBC Goths in *Titus Andronicus*, as carefully period-costumed as she was, also conveyed a wildly up-to-date ferocity with her nose ring, large bone-and-bead jewelry, and cascade of shocking red hair. Such characterization reads on several levels to a British viewer, but while Americans pick up some of the connotations, these are not as rich or full as they are to those viewers confronted by punks every day in the street or on the Tube. Punk is a political and social statement in British society, whereas it is derivative, more nearly a rock video fashion in America. Predictably, the context provided more nuances for the British viewers.

If the current production styles in London and Stratford-upon-Avon influenced the BBC Shakespeare series's style, that influence may have been two-way. Television and theatre all arrived at the punk mode simultaneously, but the contemporary aqueous stage craze may well have been encouraged by Moshinsky's forest pools in *Dream* and Miller's battlefield puddles in *Troilus and Cressida*, for subsequently the RSC used an on stage drizzle over Henry V's English army at Agincourt (1984) and very nearly a Tommy Tune

My One and Only splash dance in the 1985 *As You Like It* as well as the Capulets' swimming pool in the 1986 *Romeo and Juliet.*

Even within the medium of television, there is a richer context for viewers of televised Shakespeare in Britain than in America, for as the BBC Shakespeare series began in 1978 the RSC was just televising two of its productions on ITV, perhaps as a competitive challenge—the Ian McKellen–Judi Dench *Macbeth* and Trevor Nunn's musical *The Comedy of Errors*, both using very different production values and styles than the BBC, as reviewers remarked. Americans, were it not for the occasional televised Joseph Papp/Shakespeare in the Park production, would see even less than the very little American Shakespeare now on television. William Ball's lively *Shrew* from San Francisco's American Conservatory Theatre (shown on PBS) and a few Hallmark Hall of Fame broadcasts can be singled out because of their rarity as noncable televised Shakespeare.

Thus, the different cultural contexts in which the series was broadcast make it in many ways a different phenomenon in America than in Britain. Americans—whether they consider the BBC Shakespeare series on technical, aesthetic, interpretive, or educational grounds—must acknowledge their special and sometimes limited perspective on what the series is. It was not made specifically for American audiences. It was conceived and carried out in Britain, and when finished, the series bore the mark of its origin; it was made for a British audience and then successfully marketed worldwide. In planning, production, and aesthetics, the BBC Shakespeare series is very British indeed, a fact that both limits and enhances its effect on its international audience.

Two

Using the Medium

> *This is an art*
> *Which does mend nature—change it rather; but*
> *The art itself is nature.*
> —The Winter's Tale

> *In framing an artist, art hath thus decreed,*
> *To make some good, but others to exceed.*
> —Pericles

3   Medium, Message, Style

*T*he fact that Shakespeare wrote for the Elizabethan and Jacobean stage has not deterred subsequent ages from printing his plays, revising and improving them, illustrating them, setting them to music, using them as the basis for ballet and opera, broadcasting them over radio, and making films of them. Like Cleopatra, Shakespeare's works offer an infinite variety. The plays have most recently been put on television, yet this last technical translation or adaptation seems to have aroused more skepticism than the performance of Shakespeare's work in any other medium. The general suspicion is that the plays are somehow diminished because Shakespeare cannot be put in a box, much less on a tube. His premises are defiled or negated, it is implied, his effects and power lost.

Why then, one gingerly wonders, would it be possible to adapt Shakespeare in so many other ways but impossible to put his works on television? Why is this medium radically incompatible with the stage? Or is it perhaps our expectations of what Shakespeare in performance should be that limit our perception of the plays when televised? Certainly we think of Shakespeare as a writer of large effects and heightened rhetoric, the more so because for several centuries the plays have been performed mostly in large theatres where just to be heard or seen the actors' line delivery, gesture, and movement have had to be histrionic. The difference between seeing a Shakespeare production staged at the Royal Shakespeare Theatre and at The Other Place in Stratford-upon-Avon, at the Olivier and the Cottesloe at the National Theatre in London, at the Festival Theatre and the Third Stage in Ontario, or at any venue with over 1,000 seats contrasted with any 200-seat house quickly demonstrates the way circumstances and environment affect audience response. The large auditoria provide spectacle; the smaller allow presence and intimacy. It stands to reason that an audience will not respond the same way to an action three yards away as to one thirty yards away, and they do not, else why would the best, that is, the most expensive, seats be those front and center?

Not only audiences notice a difference, but actors as well. In talking with RSC director John Barton during one session of Barton's televised series *Playing Shakespeare*, actor Ian McKellen observed that "it's surprising how doing a play in a small theatre can release it in some ways," then proceeded to compare this to performing on television:

> Another important ingredient [in our contemporary approach to Shakespeare] is the spaces we work in. Have you been struck, watching your actors work at a conversational level in this studio with the camera very close, how speeches have taken on a life that you haven't heard before? You may recognise it because you sit in the rehearsal-room. . . . But it's so rare in the theatre—even in the small theatres where we sometimes work—to get that intimacy in which the audience can catch the breath being inhaled before it is exhaled on a line, and feel the excitement and certainty that what is happening is for real. The voice is wonderfully communicated but it isn't projected. The force behind it isn't exaggerated; there's nothing getting in the way. That's a level at which I like to work.[1]

If the effect of a play can vary remarkably even within the theatre, its effect will certainly vary when we shift the means by which we experience it, perhaps, as McKellen proclaimed, revealing new possibilities for the material.

Once we accept that televised Shakespeare will in some ways differ from staged Shakespeare, just as filmed Shakespeare differs from staged Shakespeare in scope, focus, pace, and effect, we are ready to consider the exigencies and possibilities of televising Shakespeare, and not until then. The subtle, insidious prejudice against television as a high-quality production vehicle, especially strong in America, obstructs the viewer's attentiveness to production and sometimes even to the television set itself. Watching is too often not a process of seeing or understanding or appreciating; it is vegetative and simply critical in the worst sense. In the mid-nineteenth century, Professor of Natural History Louis Agassiz of Harvard began to teach Samuel H. Scudder entomology by asking him to look at and describe a fish until Scudder, after hours of staring at a formaldehyde-soaked specimen, finally realized how much there was to see and how little he had seen at first. The same method might be beneficial with televised Shakespeare.

One of the common criticisms of putting Shakespeare on television is that the plays are primarily verbal, that is, aural, while television is a visual medium. There is some truth in that but only necessary and not sufficient truth. Film is a far more highly visual medium than is television (in Marshall McLuhan's terms, film is "hot"), yet viewers and critics often embrace filmic renditions because film is based on the grand scale, as is much theatrical performance. In contrast, television is smaller, more intimate. But as McLuhan explains, television requires a synesthetic response, an involvement and completion by the audience that is analogous, if not entirely equivalent, to the demands of Elizabethan performance on its nearly bare stage. The Elizabethan audience had to fill in the visual; so in its own technological way must a television audience: "The cool TV medium promotes depth structures in art and entertainment alike, and creates audience involvement in depth as well."[2] It matters, therefore, which aspects of the production medium we examine and compare; we need to look from more than one perspective.

Media specialists and scholars from McLuhan on reiterate that, unlike other media, television uses oral modes of presentation, not the dominant literate modes that have shaped much of Western culture since the Renaissance:[3] "Its mode is the reverse of literate or formal logic: its mode is that of rhetoric. For instance, the television message is validated by its context, by the opposition of elements (often visual/verbal), and not by the deductive requirements of the syllogism."[4] In television these modes interact, so that television, like some other forms of mass communication, does "not have the abstract and solitary quality of reading or writing, but on the contrary share[s] some of the nature and impact of the direct personal interaction which obtains in oral cultures."[5] One of the critical ironies we must consider, therefore, is that while television looks like a visual medium and is commonly considered as such, it actually works like an oral one. Even while the BBC Shakespeare production staff focused on the visual element, they often commented that of course on television the words would dominate. In this way the Shakespeare plays are not so different from a nightly news program; in both, one starts with the story, the text, and selects the visuals to complement or illustrate it. In both, meaning emerges from the combination as the viewer experiences them in context.

In the nature, and perhaps the quantity, of their words, Shakespeare's plays pose their first challenge to the television medium. Shakespeare's shortest plays are as long as many of the longest special television dramas, and his longer plays at three to four hours exceed the length of almost all regular and special programming except for sports events such as a five-set Wimbledon match. Whereas the standard guidelines for thirty- to sixty-minute teleplays, the kind most frequent on American television, emphasize action over all other components, character second (but only character of a type that can be quickly developed), a plot of essentials, and no long speeches, Shakespeare's plays are nearly the inverse: character over all other components, action second (often with much willing suspension of disbelief), a composite plot often counterpointed, and any number of long speeches and bravura passages. No wonder those trained to television at the BBC quote a former head of Plays who said he would cheerfully produce Shakespeare if he could just send the scripts back for a rewrite. Shakespeare sometimes builds huge, intricate scenes in the plays, while television depends on the shorter, more frequent breaks in action necessitated in America by commercials. Our response to Shakespeare's dramaturgy when used as teleplay depends on the dramatic rhythms we are accustomed to on television, though in theory his natural depth of development should complement the depth of participation the television image requires.

Given their length, Shakespeare's plays experienced two kinds of editorial attention as they were prepared for BBC production: cuts and changes. As the script editors pointed out in the BBC texts, many of the cuts were practical: if the camera clearly shows Marc Antony approaching there is no need for a mechanical line announcing, "But here comes Antony." If we see Brutus pull Casca by the cloak to get his attention, we do not need Casca to respond, "You pulled me by the cloak"; his "Would you speak with me?" is sufficient. And, likewise, since the camera usually discovers characters in place rather than waiting for their entrance, a line such as Bolingbroke's "Bring forth these men" would be cut, and the action would begin with his addressing them.[6] In each case the excisions are essentially stage directions redundant for the camera.

Also ripe for cutting were period allusions now considered obscurities, such as Pandarus's "It should be now, but that my fear is this, / Some galled goose of Winchester would hiss" or in the long list of Thersites's curses some of the less clear diseases, such as "limekilns i' the palm . . . the rivelled fee-simple of the tetter," for after mention of ten other vile diseases his point is already generously made. Many of the scripts are filleted, losing one line here, two lines there for pace and clarity, as is often done in theatrical productions. The only excision to elicit an apology from the BBC script editor is in *The Comedy of Errors*, where amid Dromio's bawdy geographic banter (III.2), the marginal note reads: "Lines 131–135 omitted, with apologies to our cousins. This ['Where America, the Indies?'] is the only mention of America in Shakespeare."[7] Such cuts are fully within the bounds of most theatrical performances, many of which silently cut lines, speeches, characters, or whole scenes depending on production exigencies. In fact, so common are cuts that performance of an uncut *Hamlet* is a widely publicized event—and a long evening in the theatre.

Nearly every Shakespeare production tinkers with lines. More significant to the BBC adaptation of Shakespeare's plays to television are the changes made in scenes, changes of three types: division of scenes into smaller units, combination of scenes, and omission of scenes. Twenty-eight of the plays in the BBC Shakespeare series experience scene divisions; sixteen combine scenes (four of which join more than two scenes); from eleven of the plays twenty scenes in total are omitted, five of which are from the scene-wealthy *Antony and Cleopatra*. While the standard scene divisions are far from sacrosanct, or even accurate according to James E. Hirsh in his *The Structure of Shakespearean Scenes*, these televised productions display a noticeable degree of change. The fact of change, however, means less than the nature and cause of the changes, for television depends on frequent scene shifts and habitually works with much smaller units than Shakespeare does.

Almost half the productions (eighteen plays by eight different directors) change two to four scenes in a play, eight productions change five or six scenes each, while seven of the productions make changes in a total of over sixty-five scenes, individual plays ranging from having seven scenes changed to the protean *Coriolanus*, in which changes occur in at least twelve scenes. Even these numbers do not fully reflect the degree of change,[8] however, for while the text of *Romeo and Juliet* shows twenty-five scenes, the BBC version has forty-two scenes; eight scenes are divided, some into three parts, one (V.3) into eight smaller pieces for the camera. Similar shifts occur in *Henry VIII* (18 textual scenes to 38 television scenes), *A Midsummer Night's Dream* (9 to 19), *3 Henry VI* (18 to 35), *Cymbeline* (27 to 39), *Coriolanus* (29 to 39), and *Love's Labour's Lost* (9 to 18), among others. The opposite change—combining scenes—also occurs, but to a much lesser extent, in *Timon of Athens* (17 to 11 scenes), for instance, and *Antony and Cleopatra* (42 to 31). Moshinsky is therefore the great divider, Miller the great combiner.

Yet the scenes are not divided simply for the sake of division or for the television medium itself. Many take advantage of the possibilities offered by taping to shift settings, a shift difficult, sometimes impossible, to accomplish quickly on stage. Television scenes move from exteriors to interiors (and vice versa) or from room to room, often implying small passages of time as well. A few of the shifts establish a sense of simultaneity, as when the scene in *Coriolanus* cuts from the battle at Corioli to Volumnia and Virgilia sewing in Rome and then back to Corioli, or when the meditating Proteus in *The Two Gentlemen of Verona* suddenly joins his father's conversation, which had just been shown before his soliloquy.

Yet the most strongly interpretive use of scene division indicates passage of time rather than change of place. Some of these divisions cover short time spans, as when Oliver summons Charles the wrestler in *As You Like It,* followed by a scene shift to Charles's entrance; or when back at home after the opening of *Romeo and Juliet* the Capulets discuss the fracas in the street; or when the old shepherd finds the babe left by Antigonus in *The Winter's Tale.* Other scene divisions suggest longer passages of time, as in the shift from morning to evening in III.3 of *All's Well That Ends Well* when Helena chooses Bertram by day and Lafew discusses the marriage with Parolles later that night, or in the shift from one day to the next when *Dream's* Helena hears at dusk of Hermia's plans to elope with Lysander and next day formulates her own tactics in soliloquy. These and the scene divisions that clarify the progress of a battle in the Wars of the Roses plays are the common uses for scene division showing time passage, but in *Henry VIII* we see scene division effectively used for an even longer passage of time with the fall of Wolsey in III.2, where Wolsey first recognizes his fall in the royal palace, then receives the lords in his own palace, obviously later, and finally moralizes his experience to Cromwell in an abbey some time after that. Whereas the gargantuan scene runs nonstop on stage so that Wolsey's responses are a series of stiff-upper-lip exercises in dignity and wounded pride, in the televised production the divided scene shows a growth process; Wolsey has endured his fall and learned something. The scene does shift place as well as time, but the former serves to supplement the latter, and both changes clarify character. Such a change combines television and text to the benefit of both.

The final kind of BBC script change in scene structure does not divide or combine; it moves, transposes, reshapes the order of scenes to reflect what the director considers a clearer logic of material or action. In *Twelfth Night,* for example, the production transposes II.1 and II.2 so that Malvolio leaves Olivia to return Cesario's ring and, completing that action immediately, finds Cesario in the next scene—one scene within the garden, the next just outside it. That move postpones Sebastian's first entrance until after Viola's soliloquy, "I left no ring with her; what means this lady?" Oxford's John Wilders, literary advisor to the series, was wary and perturbed by such tinkerings with order but conceded to some of the rationales, as in this case, where the irony of twinness is not lost, merely

inverted. In *Titus Andronicus* the opening challenge between Saturninus and Bassianus moves to the middle of the scene, so that the
production opens with Titus's entrance to Rome. In *The Merry
Wives of Windsor*, IV.3 precedes IV.1 so that the beating of Falstaff
dressed as the old woman of Brainford leads into the women including the men to plan their last trick. This change also involves
picking up nine of Falstaff's lines from IV.5 and inserting them in
IV.4 as a comment before the last plot is revealed.

Several times almost an entire scene is cut, with only a few of its
lines retrieved and tucked in elsewhere, as in *Timon*, where V.2 is
cut, but lines 15–17 are used to close V.1. In *1 Henry VI* the thirteen lines of V.2 left after cutting are played at the end of IV.7 so
that the French leaders comment on their good fortune at facing a
divided English force and learn of its reuniting in the same scene,
a move that creates a balance of issues bracketing both sides' discovery of Talbot's body. Such changes occur in at least eleven of
the plays, affecting our perception of action, character, and issue.
Love's Labour's Lost, on the other hand, inserts a passage from
another Shakespeare work, six lines from his sonnet in *The Passionate Pilgrim*, into an invented scene following II.1. Yet because
these lines from poem five of *The Passionate Pilgrim* are a variant
of Berowne's poem read in *Love's Labour's Lost* (IV.2), this change,
in essence, suggests Berowne's drafting the sonnet we later see mis-
delivered to Jacquenetta and hear read aloud by Nathaniel.

In three plays there are no changes at all in scenes, although both
The Comedy of Errors and *King John* lose between forty and fifty
lines each. In terms of the script, then, of all the canon only *The
Merchant of Venice* is presented without textual change of any sort.
While that may seem a formidable statistic, it should be acknowledged that no 37-play span in any major professional Shakespeare
company would have a much purer record. Plays are written to be
performed, performance is embodiment, embodiment is adaptation
and interpretation. Nor should change be looked upon as negative;
these scene changes are many times narrative or interpretive clarifi-
cations made possible by television technology. And since the emphasis here has been on changes, it should be noted that overall

we are considering hundreds of scenes, most of which appear un-
changed in substance or order, so we can conclude that much of
Shakespeare's work adapts very comfortably to television. In that
there is no surprise. One of the first bits of advice in guides to
teleplay writing is to look at great drama.

Once the words are in place as script, the next step is to integrate
the pictures, and a great deal more worry and planning went into
the visual than the textual aspect of the BBC Shakespeares. Even if
the scripts were not ideal contemporary teleplays, they were usually
compelling drama and thereby workable. But how to envision the
plays for television? Here the producers' and directors' theories of
the television medium become apparent because the result depends
upon the assumptions and the approach.

Put simply, there are basically three ways to televise a play—to
tape a staged performance in the theatre, to tape in the studio, or to
film on location—and these approaches run the gamut of possible
collaborations between the play as drama and the television medium. The first forthrightly admits that a play is a play, a theatrical
performance, and takes us along to the theatre via camera, often-
times including shots of the theatre audience with whom the home
viewers share the experience. The third considers a play a script for
camera but insists that the visual medium and the locale predomi-
nate, whether filmed for big screen or small. But what of drama in
the television studio, that no-man's-land of aesthetics, that undis-
covered country from whose bourne no critical theory returns, the
medium like Mistress Quickly, apparently neither flesh nor fowl so
a viewer knows not where to have it?

The core of the stylistic debate about Shakespeare on television
rests on whether televised drama should aspire to film or to theatre, in other words, to a realism of location or verisimilitude of
actual place—a strong representationalism—or to a suggestivity—
a stylization of place common in open staging, a visual imagery. In
camera terms, the difference is between montage and depth of field,
that is, between using cuts and different shots—the more cinematic
approach—and developing within shot—a perspective closer to the
theatrical.[9] As his initial inspiration for the series shows, Messina's

views were deeply rooted in the filmic approach, in an effort to approximate reality.

The technical approach of the Messina years was to get, if not a real place to shoot on location, at least a large representational set—twice, with *Measure for Measure* and *The Tempest*, a 360-degree set so action could move fluidly from locale to locale, so actors could walk through the streets of Vienna (by circumnavigating the studio eight times)[10] or pass without break from beach to cliff face to orchard (an orchard comprised of actual apple trees).[11] John Gorrie, who directed *Tempest* and *Twelfth Night*, felt strongly about establishing a sense of geography in the settings, whether interior or exterior. In viewing the productions, we might not be able to get from Capulet's hall to Juliet's bedroom on our first attempt or find Abhorson's room in the prison, the Duke's camp in the forest of Arden, or anything in Henry IV's London as we are presented it, but with Olivia's house in *Twelfth Night* we quickly pick up the relationship of room to room by means of halls and of rooms to garden by means of doors and windows.

What this realism becomes during the first productions is often obvious studio work, a clean, fresh, flat area and some freshly painted, sharply angled buildings—a space meant for the machinery of television rather than a worn, weathered, or dusty space that has seen time, inclemency, and human inhabitants. The *Romeo and Juliet* set is a case in point: the piazza is noticeably a stage set on a studio floor rather than an actual place; so is the arbor with its painted drop, the balcony, the Capulets' hall and tomb.[12] All are a step removed from reality, as is some of the acting, especially with the young Juliet, whose fresh face alone cannot convey the powerful emotions the part demands. Likewise, the tournament grounds, the dock, and the battlements of Flint Castle are all obviously studio exteriors in *Richard II*. Such half-realism repeatedly belies the very verisimilitude that was its goal. *Twelfth Night* is better at rendition of particular place, but only late in the series with *Merry Wives* and *Cymbeline* is there a credible studio verisimilitude of exteriors, of places that work like filming on location rather than on a somewhat realistic stage or studio set.

Filming at Glamis Castle, Scotland, made nature a major and at times overpowering character in Shakespeare's pastoral As You Like It *during Messina's first season. Rosalind (Helen Mirren) and Celia (Angharad Rees, rear).* © BBC

John Wilders, scholarly advisor to the series, defends the half-realism as being "studio sets designed to appear fabricated," an approach that he considers "much more satisfactory [than taping on location] because the deliberate artificiality of the scenery works in harmony with the conventions of the plays." Then he adds, as if acknowledging the problem, "Unfortunately it may create the impression that we have tried to build realistic sets but have failed for want of skill or money."[13] As setting, such "deliberate artificiality"

Romeo and Juliet *was taped in obviously studio-bound environs; its design was more admittedly a stage set than an effort at verisimilitude. Tybalt (Alan Rickman, left) and Mercutio (Anthony Andrews).* © BBC

may not be deliberate enough as it tries to satisfy both the television medium and the conventions of Renaissance drama.

In the early productions under Messina, the production decisions were shaped by a concern for the audience's assumptions about the television medium: the nature of the audience, what television is to

them, how they view Shakespeare. As Henry Fenwick reports of
Alvin Rakoff's view in directing *Romeo and Juliet*:

Both Rakoff and Messina were sure that the play should be
staged as naturalistically as possible. "You have to see a proper
ballroom, a balcony, the garden, the piazza," Messina insists.
"In order to grab the audience's attention you've got to do it as
realistically as possible," Rakoff stresses. "You're asking the
audience . . . to do a hell of a thing: the most real medium in
the world is television; they're watching the news at nine

Later in the series, efforts at recreating the outdoors in the studio prompted such approximations of reality as the lovely Tudor village set for The Merry Wives of Windsor, *designed by Don Homfray. Anne Page (Miranda Foster) and Fenton (Simon Chandler).* © BBC

o'clock and they're seeing real blood and real violence and suddenly we're saying, 'Come to our pretend violence.' I've done stylised productions before, and it takes the audience a hell of a long time to get with you. You could do *Romeo and Juliet* against white or black drapes but I think you'd alienate a hell of a lot of the potential viewers. I would love to have tried to do *Romeo* outside in a Verona town somewhere. . . . In a medium which is half-way between theatre and film I was trying to go for the visuals, trying also to go for the words.[14]

The demand for the realistic or the representational was the most formidable challenge many directors felt in the initial years of the series, for the overriding production view was that television was a realistic medium, and therefore Shakespeare had to be realistic.

With two productions being filmed on location and consequently providing ultrarealism during the first season, the other directors and designers were drawn or forced toward that approach. Tony Abbott, designer of *Richard II*, explained, "You can stylise Shakespeare right down to black drapes and lighting . . . or you can make it realistic. These Shakespeare productions are going to be reaching a very wide range of audience, some of whom won't know the plays at all. They certainly won't be all a sophisticated theatre audience. We've also got to mix studio productions with outside broadcasts [filmed on location]. . . . Any form of extreme stylisation was just not on."[15] What these views reiterate is the belief that while there are a number of styles and production methods possible for the Shakespeares, the general audience can only deal effectively with realism because they also watch news and documentaries. One might also inquire whether the audience is offered other production styles often enough to build acceptance and understanding. The audience, in addition to students, was supposed to be the news and sports group, the live-action crowd curious about these famous plays; their need for a straightforward style was widely assumed.

Herbert Wise, director of *Julius Caesar*, commented about setting the play in Elizabethan England rather than ancient Rome: "I don't think that's right for the audience we will be getting. . . . It's not a jaded theatre audience seeing the play for the umpteenth time: for them that would be an interesting approach and might throw new lights on the play. But for an audience many of whom won't have seen the play before, I believe it would only be confusing."[16] Wise consequently erases all visual evidence of the Elizabethan despite his view that "*Julius Caesar* is not really a Roman play. It's an Elizabethan play and it's a view of Rome from an Elizabethan's standpoint."[17] A Renaissance theatre audience, even groundlings, would understand the convention of a toga draped over contemporary dress, but with a modern audience watching television such an approach was deemed chancy.

Notice that these remarks championing television realism for the productions consciously link stylization with theatre and an appeal to a "sophisticated" or "jaded" theatre audience well versed in Shakespeare (a description that covers most of the critics, professors, and teachers viewing the series). The historical context of these comments made as the Shakespeare series began is instructive, for during the late 1970s, when the BBC was planning the series and working on the early productions, the RSC was also televising some of its productions in Britain using a remarkably different style, exactly the sort of "drapes and lighting" stylization here decried. The contrast provides grounds for a clear debate about technique and style in televising Shakespeare.

But to acknowledge the disproportion of this comparison, the BBC set out to televise the entire canon, whereas during this time the RSC (which, after all, is not formally in the television business) produced only three Shakespeare plays for television. The first, Trevor Nunn's *Antony and Cleopatra* (1972), aired in Britain in 1974 and in the United States in 1975 on ABC (with frequent commercial interruptions). The other two, Nunn's 1976 *The Comedy of Errors* and his *Macbeth* from The Other Place the same year, were transmitted on British television in 1978 and 1979 respectively, in other words, just as the BBC series was beginning, so that for British viewers and critics comparisons were inevitable. American viewers were offered the RSC *Macbeth* on PBS in 1980. These two groups' simultaneous efforts demonstrate the interest in televising drama at the time and also probably indicate a latent rivalry. The RSC felt they were the Shakespeare-producing experts, and their latter two televised productions may have been partly prompted by a desire to show off their abilities—a "this is what *we* can do" response aided by their preempting most of the BBC series with the timing of their broadcasts. Nonetheless, the BBC and RSC productions illuminate the issues surrounding studio-based drama.

Of course, both the RSC and BBC have successfully tried the straight tape-it-on-stage approach. The RSC's *The Comedy of Errors*, for instance, is a taped stage play, or rather a taped stage musical, for the show, updated and set in a modern Greek island tourist trap, included nine full-scale song and dance numbers in addition to the familiar Shakespeare dialogue. Using the convention of off-we-go-to-the-theatre, it opens with a shot of the theatre across the Avon, then the crowd mingling in the lobby, people taking their seats, and later, after applause and reaction shots are cut into the action intermittently, it even includes a shot of an audience member wiping her eyes at the family's reunion, the director teetering near the pathetic fallacy. For the most part the taping just had to keep pace with a quickly paced and very funny show, the camera itself adding close-ups, some interesting angles, and a few self-conscious maneuvers. What this production does have that the BBC's comedies do not is a built-in laugh track, that staple of television comedy, because of the live audience being taped at the production. The experience of the stage play in the theatre was by all accounts magic; with the camera, for all its virtuosity, the production was a bit slower—great fun still, yet some of its magic gone.

But the other two RSC televised Shakespeares, the tragedies, come to the studio from the stage, and the televised versions are quite striking, even though television was not their original goal. The RSC performances are full and rich down to the last spear carrier, a quality attributable not just to the depth of the company but to the fact that these are mature performances reaching tape after a complete repertory run in Stratford and London; five to six weeks of rehearsal and eighteen months on the boards will season any good production. The *Macbeth*, for instance, had enjoyed 108 performances and eighteen months in repertory before its videotaping; *Antony and Cleopatra* had 103 performances in the seventeen months it was in the repertory with *Julius Caesar*, *Coriolanus*, and *Titus* during the 1972–73 season of "The Romans." Such a long run is a luxury the BBC never had, for four weeks after their first rehearsal, the BBC Shakespeares went into the studio, and for television work even that amount of preparation time is considered luxurious. Yet time and experience in a role can make a great difference in performing Shakespeare.

Unlike the filmic school such as Messina's that sees only the actual as credible, the RSC style explodes any belief in the need for absolute realism of locale on television. Their technique takes the contemporary theatrical interest in the empty space and open staging and translates it to studio videotaping. The productions are special cases, admittedly, since they adapt for the camera already extant productions. But true to its roots, the RSC technique for televising Shakespeare stems from a current theatrical mode rather than a filmic one. These RSC productions of *Macbeth* and *Antony and Cleopatra* had spare, suggestive sets on stage, and if anything, they got sparer on television; there are virtually no sets for either production, no attempt at recreating a full-scale physical reality. The television style of *Antony and Cleopatra* achieves its elemental effect from a series of conscious production choices between stage and studio, a visual translation and simplification that show what reexamining production values for television can achieve. Given Richard Johnson, Janet Suzman, and an impeccable cast, television director Jon Scoffield and designer Michael Bailey decided to let the camera and the visual medium highlight them. They abandoned the stage set of mechanized stairs and large white panels as well as the panoply of set dressings (a silk canopy added for Egypt, a sail and spar for Pompey's ship, an SPQR banner in Rome). The set in the studio is a plain, lit cycloramic curtain or occasionally a bit of thin drapery; only lighting, a pile of pillows, a table, or smoke dresses the set. Scoffield and Bailey bring to television the willing suspension of disbelief, the willing use of the imagination so essential for theatrical open staging, creating strong visual images by means of actors, costumes, shadows, or a single golden throne against a backdrop of solid color instead of intricate detail. Against this background, both director and set designer exploited the iconographic, even the hieroglyphic, value of the visual images.

On videotape, Egypt is colorful, loud, and kinetic. Even the soundtrack registers not just wind, thunder, and water lapping, but dog, horse, gull, and fly noises, and from Caesar's camp amid the cadenced marching of soldiers can be heard the far-off cheers and laughter of Antony's Alexandrian revels. Early on, the backdrops for Egypt are white or pale yellow and once a sunset red; nearer the play's conclusion they are more frequently stark black. And against these backgrounds the design and camera achieve some striking visual images. For example, the scene that brings Cleopatra news of Antony's marriage to Octavia (II.5) opens with an extreme long shot—as if Egypt were far away, seen from the Rome of the preceding scene—a careful grouping of very distant figures, while over the scene stands a very tall, stark, lovely sunshade, like a huge waterlily pad floating on a long, angled stem. On stage they had used a large, tasseled beach umbrella; on television the visual aspect is more formal and impressive. The scene's last shot returns to that distant perspective before the cut back to Rome. The director, in essence, supports and parallels the textual shifts with the camera's perspective shots.

Equally striking effects occur in Rome, which is usually portrayed as a white expanse peopled with senators. For instance, III.6, the scene in which Octavia returns to Rome, opens with a high shot straight down on first the shadows and then the forms of Caesar and a host of senators marching from bottom to top of frame across a row of alternating bands of bright light and shadow, as if a row of columns stood just off frame. The shot cuts to track behind this moving group, which is discussing the news from Egypt, while the director intercuts brightly colored shots of Antony in state in Alexandria, Cleopatra as Isis, and her children, so the viewer sees what Caesar is describing. A similar shift from black and white to color is achieved during the opening dialogue of the play; the shot of the soldiers is desaturated of color, so the cut from these gray figures to Antony and Cleopatra reveling startles with its sudden gold and orange, another successful combination of camera and text.

Such shots, sparingly used, are very potent. More than the striking long shots and high shots, however, more than the dialogue shot through Cleopatra's thin gauze boudoir drapes, more than the soft halo frame sometimes used on shots, more than the shimmer that suggests distance and heat, the power of this production's camera work lies in its close-ups, as in the cut to a shot of only Antony's eyes as he sees Thidias kiss Cleopatra's hand, the move in on Enobarbus's tortured face in Caesar's tent, or the close-up of Cleopatra's face luminous under her heavy black bangs that blend into the backdrop of shadow, monument, night, and death. These tightly framed camera shots make the viewer very aware of these characters who are very aware of themselves. Scoffield and Bailey essentially created the RSC television style in adapting this staged play for another medium; they took a strong show and improved it with their acute visual sensitivity, using a minimalist doctrine for setting to deemphasize the "where" while emphasizing the "how," a special versatility afforded by the camera, and showing that with televised drama less can indeed be more.

In taping the RSC *Macbeth*, television director Philip Casson could not have improved the performance or design, which already had stark, powerful qualities in the theatre, so he captured them alive with the camera. In the theatre *Macbeth* took place against black drapes on a bare platform with a large black circle painted on its dark boards, the action presented within that charmed space. A group of crates were the only additional pieces, serving as chairs or throne or piled to be whatever. That is essentially the way it is televised, very theatrically. Casting is equally spare; many secondary characters double parts—Donalbain as Seyton, Ross as the Porter, Fleance as the goose-faced Messenger, the second Witch as the Nurse, the youngest Witch, played as a medium drooling in her trance, as Lady Macduff. In the studio, changes from the theatre are minute; the painted circle is gone, Malcolm no longer wears jodhpurs in the early scenes, and a television viewer loses some of the simultaneity of witches' keening and Duncan's prayers that opened the play as well as losing a sense of the actor-observers who in the theatre had sometimes watched the action from their boxes (for instance, the Witches stayed to watch most of the Macbeth–Lady Macbeth dialogue).[18]

In general, however, the stark black-and-white design of the production is translated without variation to television. Only Duncan and Lady Macduff appear in solid white; Malcolm has an off-white cable knit sweater, while the rest of the cast wear black suits, white shirts, and soft black Edwardian ties in the case of the lords or black leather and fancy black military garb in the case of Macbeth. Lady Macbeth, too, wears a plain, solid black dress and a black turban. The backgrounds again are plain and bare, either total blackness or a dark blue-gray; there is even less set in the studio than on stage. Lighting is usually angled from the side so that in many shots parts of the faces are shadowed. A sudden flash of light serves as the convention for an opening door in the Porter's scene. The way to Duncan's room is behind a dark, backlit wall, so Macbeth's figure is silhouetted as he turns and approaches it. Light

alone creates the space in this production. Because of these transferred theatrical choices, this televised production is far starker
than the RSC's *Antony and Cleopatra*, which used color and opulent costuming to good effect. Appropriately, in this almost emblematic *Macbeth* the only splash of color other than flesh tone is
blood red.

The visual construction is again careful and acute. The televised *Macbeth* opens with a high shot straight down on a circle of
boxes; shafts of light saturate the scene. Into this circle the actors
step simultaneously, ritualistically, so that their shadows meet like
spokes of a wheel at the center of the circle. They sit in unison, then
the camera pans the serious, expressionless group and the scripted
rituals begin, the witches' necromantic rites and Duncan's prayers,
complete with organ accompaniment. The camera moves in for
extreme close-ups during Macbeth's soliloquies, and the production is also rich in direct address, most noticeably by the Porter, a
vaudeville comic, who plays sportively with the camera. Another
camera effect, a freeze-frame, occurs after Banquo's murder; as his
dead body is lifted, the image of his bloody face, upside down in
the frame, is held for several seconds. The same technique recurs at
the end of the play, making a strong visual statement, as Ross picks
up the crown and Macduff holds up the two daggers Macbeth had
just unsuccessfully fought him with, bloody once more, so crown
and daggers are juxtaposed in a final close-up.

The production as a whole has power without histrionics; the
performances are intense, both tortured and implosive, as in Lady
Macbeth's long, strangled, unvoiced scream during the sleepwalk-
ing scene—Judi Dench's head twists and her mouth opens, but
the only sound is a jagged intake of breath. Such agony is the
strength of the performances, kept close to the viewer by effective, tight camera work and by the visual emphasis on these figures fading into or standing out against the darkness. The overall
quality of this production's achievement is expressed by *London
Daily Mail* critic Herbert Kretzmer: "Television is honoured by this
Macbeth."[19]

Thus tragedy can be stripped down to essentials for television,
radically by the RSC, which transfers a theatrical bareness almost

directly to the camera, although these are not just taped stage plays. Their combination of camera distance and proximity, angle and effect, makes the camera an essential character in and a genuine asset to the productions. Yet it should be noted that the plays *are* both tragedies, and that the BBC is also more radical in setting the tragedies than in most of their Shakespeare productions. The BBC *Hamlet* has a successful open and stylized set, the *Macbeth* uses a similar approach, and except for the heath scenes, the *King Lear* is performed on boards before drapes, the essence of Elizabethan open staging. These productions are not always as visually extreme and striking as the RSC productions, partly because, even stylized, a set is a set, and also because they do not seek the studied visual elegance of the RSC *Antony and Cleopatra*. The closest approximation to this RSC style within the BBC series is probably in Jane Howell's Wars of the Roses productions.

Because the RSC productions appear to be state of the art, very modern, stylish, and up-to-date technical renditions of Shakespeare that play off of the latest theatrical conventions, they contrasted as fully as anything could to the early BBC productions, which appeared at the same time. Recognizing this contrast and its basis in fundamentally different attitudes toward drama on television, we can not only learn about televising Shakespeare but discern the source of some of the initial critical reaction to the BBC Shakespeare series, why some of the early BBC productions seemed "old-fashioned" by comparison.

An interest in stylization came to the BBC Shakespeare series only at the end of the second season, and it grew out of the directors' response to the plays. Giles rightly felt that *Henry V* is a much less realistic piece than *1 Henry IV*, as the Chorus passages admit, and sought to create that feeling in the production's design with long establishing shots to give context and with shifts of place to be indicated by turns of large, polygonal columns, like ancient Greek *periaktoi*, painted on the various sides to suggest necessary locations, such as England and France. But because whole columns were rarely included in shots, their effect was minimal. Even more thoroughly stylized was *Hamlet*. Director Rodney Bennett recognized that the play uses "a theatrical reality." He explained, "The way to do it is start with nothing and gradually feed in only what's actually required."[20] Accordingly, Don Homfray's set, the least realistic of the first twelve, provides ambiguous space, openings without architectural definition, a combination of large open halls, trompe-l'oeil panels in smaller rooms (thematically linked to the ambiguity of appearance and reality in the play), and empty space. Of all these BBC studio productions, Hamlet is the first to affirm a theatre-based style rather than aspiring halfheartedly to the nature of film. Yet for the series to attempt various approaches to the plays and to studio production was only a boon for the audience.

The audience did not watch a television screen capturing a glimpse of reality through its pane during the Miller years, however, for Miller had an entirely different view of television and of its audience. No standard practice of videotaping stood in the way of his willing experiment with the medium. If the Messina productions were predominantly set in the historical periods referred to, Miller's were insistently Renaissance in dress and attitude. If television was supposed to be based on realism, Miller took the productions straight into the visual arts of the period. If most earlier productions had been visually filmic, Miller emphasized the theatrical. If the previous interpretations were basically solid and straightforward, Miller encouraged stronger, sharper renditions, cutting across the grain, vivid and not always mainstream. This was not just difference for the sake of difference; his critical and aesthetic sensibility is simply that distinctive. You do not hire Jonathan Miller as producer and director unless you are ready for fresh ideas and a new theoretical slant.

Miller did acknowledge the inherent realism of the television medium (though "realism" is not a term he readily uses) but drew his own conclusions as to what that meant for production. In his view the representational concern impinged on different aspects of the plays; he refigured the equation of art and reality. On one hand, he argued, the medium made the text easier to deliver. Miller embraced the intimacy of television because actors could speak rather than orate; a more natural, less grandiloquent communication was possible, a far greater range. Not just the nature of the medium but the nature of the text affected the delivery, and in fact it influenced

By the second season of the series, directors and designers began to explore more stylized settings in addition to variations on the filmic option of "reality." In the various scenes of Henry V, designer Don Homfray turned the two background towers to serve as castle ramparts or, as here, interior walls in the French court scene; this square, blue, fleur-de-lys-studded sea of fabric was the production's most stylized space. © BBC

In Hamlet *designer Don Homfray used the design concept of open space—a bare studio floor, a small ramp, and a cycloramic curtain—for the tragedy's exterior scenes.* © *BBC*

the entire production process. Miller explains: "I think that as soon as you put Shakespeare on that box where . . . people are accustomed to seeing naturalistic events represented, you are more or less obliged to present the thing as naturally as you can. There are, of course, limits upon that because of the sort of language that is being spoken. First of all, it comes from the past, and secondly, it doesn't come from the naturalistic past. It comes from the artistic past, and it's got a style and an idiom of its own which can't be violated."[21] In other words, not only is the language poetic in terms of imagery, but much of it is actually verse. The conversation at most offstage social gatherings, Renaissance or modern, would not be rhymed or metrically regular, yet in Shakespeare's aesthetic world Romeo and Juliet speak a sonnet at a Capulet party. The mode of expression is an art form.

Whereas that poses one set of tensions and challenges for performance, the visual aspect poses another: "I think it's very unwise to try and represent on the television screen something which Shakespeare did not have in his mind's eye when he wrote those lines. You have to find some counterpart of the unfurnished stage. . . . [In *Antony and Cleopatra*, for instance,] he's talking about a Rome and an Egypt as they would have appeared to the sixteenth-century imagination. . . . What details you do introduce must remind the audience of the sixteenth-century imagination."[22] With works such as Shakespeare's, then, Miller believes you must capture not a realism of the eye, a guided tour or postcard reality, but a realism of the mind, a realism of the sensibility and world view, perhaps best rendered by staying within the realm of the arts at that time.

Because realism for Miller is not an absolute referentiality but the particular way certain people see or represent something, one major production attitude in the plays Miller directed and in others he produced is an art-based style, a conscious aestheticism. Jonathan Miller and Elijah Moshinsky consider the television screen like a canvas; they recreated works of pictorial art for the camera, especially Dutch interiors out of Vermeer but also using Veronese, Watteau, and others. They recognized the medium as a surface and worked accordingly, experimenting to gain depth and experimenting with materials. This approach could be considered a variation on the television-must-be-real doctrine, but with a painterly rather than a photographic model, a realism once removed. Or it could be an abstraction, an art-affirming means of countering the realism by allying director and designer with others who have artfully rendered the illusion of a scene on a surface, a more self-conscious and more highly referential use of the medium's natural realism.

For Miller, "it's the director's job, quite apart from working with actors and getting subtle and energetic performances out of them, to act as the chairman of a history faculty and of an art-history faculty."[23] Thus, Miller's is a far more serious and scholarly approach to producing a work of Renaissance art. The essential reality is not ours but theirs: "Here was a writer who was immersed in the themes and notions of his time. The only way you can unlock that imagination is to immerse yourself in the themes in which he was immersed. And the only way you can do that is by looking at the pictures which reflect the visual world of which he was a part and to acquaint yourself with the political and social issues with which he was preoccupied—trying, in some way, to identify yourself with the world which was his."[24]

Such a view respects Shakespeare's artistry and historical place and also the audience's awareness and perceptivity. If earlier productions were posited on a naive audience (naive in performance terms, inexperienced with the material) who expected television to be visually realistic, Miller's productions were posited on a somewhat more knowledgeable, adaptable, and intellectually curious group. Miller is one of television's great teachers, and most of his works are instructional as well as entertaining (consider *The Body in Question*). In the Shakespeare series, he used Shakespeare's words and the production elements of television to create and comment on the work of art. Miller saw the plays as entities that must be staged, and he encouraged the audience to consider them in the same way. Knowing that in some regards his style of visually integrating history, art history, and drama would seem unconventional, he explained: "I think two things should always happen when you go to the theatre or when you watch a play on television, particularly a play from the past, a classic. One, you should enjoy the drama, but also should be made to think always about the staging of the drama. Your attention should in some respects be drawn to the problem of the play as an art form as well as to the problems that the art form is being used to express."[25] For Miller, Shakespeare production is both denotative and connotative, both narrative and reflexive. It *is* art, is *composed* of art, and is to some extent *about* art.

These two basic orientations—one to television as realistic no matter the subject, the other to Shakespeare as Renaissance dramatist no matter the medium—function like magnetic poles of production values in the BBC Shakespeare series. But variation rather than rigid pattern best describes the mode of the series, and to understand more fully the issues of Shakespeare production on television we need to be more precise and look at the work of individual directors on specific plays in the series to see how they sought to use camera and setting along with the other production elements to express themes, images, character, and conflicts on a small screen.

4   Jonathan Miller

PRODUCER AND DIRECTOR

onathan Miller, Elijah Moshinsky, and Jane Howell share a theatrical bent, perceptive minds, striking scenic senses, and a willingness to develop action before the camera rather than insistently cutting. Miller brought Moshinsky and Howell into the Shakespeare series, and these three directed nearly half the canon, seventeen of the thirty-seven plays. Fostering his directors' different strengths, Miller encouraged experimentation, and the directors developed along the lines of their own interests: Howell to abstraction, image, and ensemble; Moshinsky to art-for-art's-sake or at least art-for-production's-sake, a performance aesthetic grounded in a period look and style. As a director himself, Miller was interested in all these approaches and explored or combined them throughout his own productions.

Because he both produced and directed, and because his productions were done within a comparatively short period of time in the series, Miller worked on Shakespeare by total immersion, dealing with the whole canon, never just a single play. In fact, thinking of other Shakespeare plays while doing a specific one is for Miller a natural result of his work on the series; he believes that "Shakespeare becomes intelligible when you undertake his work in close order . . . and to use a fashionable phrase in literary criticism, the work of an artist can be used to disambiguate the sentences that he uses in any one of his plays."[1] But seeing the plays in relationship to each other was for Miller also a process of not looking at a play's encrustations, at whether it is called a tragedy or a comedy, but at the serious and comic elements in each work. Miller believes the basis of Shakespeare's drama is the ordinary, the commonplace, a view that complements Miller's own attitude toward performance in general: "I think that this is what makes Shakespeare so readily producible, and that although he seems to deal with very exalted

Jonathan Miller working on The Taming of the Shrew *with Gregory (Leslie Sarony, left rear), Petruchio (John Cleese, at table), Curtis (Angus Lennie), Grumio (David Kincaid), and Katherine (Sarah Badel).* © BBC

events, like high moments of state and the fall, the tragedy of kings and queens and of the aristocracy, there are in fact all of the representative people, and I think that he's principally a fairly domestic playwright, even when he deals with noble themes. . . . What Shakespeare is constantly drawing our attention to . . . is the commonness of mankind."[2]

Shakespeare's characters behave "much like people who live in ordinary circumstances," and that, according to Miller, is their strength. He asks the same strength of his actors in performance—to behave like people who live in ordinary circumstances. That is why he mentions social psychologist Erving Goffman's work so often, because we *all* make and recognize public remedial gestures, and why he sets actors specific tasks—to avoid generic "acting."

Miller is not interested in actors who strike poses or who "twin-kle," that is, who play too broadly or mug for the audience; he is interested in ensemble. Actors should be like secret agents behind enemy lines, Miller once told the acting company of the Alabama Shakespeare Festival; if they are noticed or call attention to themselves, they are shot.[3]

Because acting should look real but not be real, Miller also has little respect for method acting, which he feels loses the proper focus, involving the actor in personal irrelevancies rather than in the character. For all his emphasis on authenticity of action—or on the appearance of authenticity—Miller insists on the artifice of theatre or television. Like Hamlet's mirror up to nature, Miller would have theatre capture the details of reality but be aware that it is itself a reflective surface, not life, for otherwise people would stand on street corners watching each other instead of buying theatre tickets. His attitude toward sets is analogous to this view of acting based on the artificiality of the medium: "One need not use materials which are exactly the same as materials you're trying to represent; there's some sort of knight's move that you can make, that you want to indicate without necessarily reproducing them exactly. So that, for example, you can in fact build a palace out of rough plywood; as long as it's got the architectural features it needn't be an imitation of architectural surfaces."[4] Representation is the art of illusion.

In relation to acting, Miller's greatest contribution to the series was undoubtedly his attitude toward casting. Where Messina, in the *Play of the Month* tradition, would cast the biggest name available, at times someone who had done the part recently in the theatre, Miller recognized that casting was interpretation and so went for the unexpected, the interesting possibility, as was immediately apparent when he convinced John Cleese to play Petruchio and throughout his producership in the casting of Warren Mitchell (Britain's Archie Bunker) to play Shylock or Bob Hoskins as Iago. Moshinsky certainly shared some of this attitude, for he used it with calculation in his productions. All Miller's decisions for these productions, in fact, are based on what seems interesting to him rather than what seems safe, traditional, or definitive (a term he disavowed). Consequently, the productions under Miller's tenure in general have sharper edges and clearer lines, often times more intensity than those that preceded them. They make assertions, and they make demands on the audience. They reflect the working of Miller's mind, and few of us could stand up to a contest of intellectual acumen or diversity with Miller. Even with that exceptional mental kilowattage, however, Miller does not talk down to his audience through his productions; he speaks to cast, production staff and, implicitly, to audience with the benevolent assumption that ideas are a vital part of life and that everyone will naturally think while watching.

Miller told Henry Fenwick, for instance, that his insistence on the Renaissance focus in his productions' attitude and atmosphere was "not because I believe that's the way to do Shakespeare but because I happen to believe at this moment it's a rather interesting way to do Shakespeare."[5] This statement shows how alien Miller's views were to the "not for an Age but for all time" production rhetoric at the series's inception. Moreover, the very changeability of interpretation is exactly what Miller values in dramatic performance, for the very changes wrought upon it, Miller believes, contribute to the immortality of a work of art.[6]

Thus Miller's production choices emanated from his knowledge of Elizabethan history and culture, and they involved placing the plays within a context of their compositional era in terms of ideas and character, not just costumes and architectural setting. From the start, therefore, he incorporated more definite concepts and looks into his plays, as was obvious as his antiheroic, anti–high-tragic vein manifested itself in the first production under his sway, *Antony and Cleopatra*, which he ultimately chose to direct himself. Usually portrayed as the quintessential grand passion, *Antony and Cleopatra* under Miller's hand became a tale of two prominent, self-indulgent figures who were past their prime. As Miller described them, Antony was over the hill, like a football player who waited several seasons too long to retire, and Cleopatra "a treacherous slut"; their relationship was an exercise in the downhill slide, each scrambling to maintain a foothold—not a lovely sight. Miller also rooted the production more deeply in the sensibility of the

Renaissance than had previously been done in the series, permeating the design with the Renaissance view of the ancient world, for he observed that the Renaissance saw the classical world in terms of itself, with a contemporary rather than an archaeological awareness; they treated classical subjects but always dressed them anachronistically in Renaissance garments. This concept grounded his visual approach to the play. In *Antony and Cleopatra* Miller used Veronese's rendition of classical subjects as inspiration for sets (the drapes, the minimal literal scenery), for costumes (an anachronistic mixture of Renaissance and ancient world, as in the painting of the Darius family at the feet of Alexander in the National Gallery in London), and for staging, the organization of space.[7] Art provides not just a look in Miller's production; it provides a mode of being, a redolence of the air breathed in that world, an intellectual climate in addition to a physical space.

The Taming of the Shrew also shows the range of Miller's period references: the relationships are guided by two historical accounts, Lawrence Stone's *The Family, Sex and Marriage in England: 1500–1800* and Michael Walzer's *The Revolution of the Saints*. So while Baptista may be humorous in his economic interests, he is neither villainous nor vile but predictably Renaissance, and Petruchio's clear-headed, confident assault on Kate's temper and temperament is based on sound religious and social views of the time. The sets are equally footnotable—the Paduan street is an enlarged vista inspired by Serlio's comic street scene and the Teatro Olympico perspective; the interior of Baptista's house is straight out of Vermeer. And though Miller will publicly say such sets are in the spirit of the artist rather than exact, he will also flip open a huge Vermeer collection and indicate *Young Lady and Gentleman at the Virginal* (also known as *The Music Lesson*), which he reproduced exactly—furniture, fittings, and stances—in the course of the wooing scene in *Shrew* as an intellectually sportive allusion. Miller consistently combines such recognizably referential settings with less particular ones, such as the boards and curtains of Petruchio's barracks-like abode and the generic arches of the feasting chamber.

Miller chose to be unobstructed and unlimited by the BBC brief for the series, even if he found some of its strictures misguided:

The central figures of Veronese's The Family of Darius before Alexander—*where the kneeling Persian family is clad in Italian garments of the 1570s and the Macedonian general in a rendition of classical Roman garb—demonstrate the artist's anachronistic Renaissance view of the past that Miller drew on for* Antony and Cleopatra. *The National Gallery, London*

"The brief was 'no monkey-tricks'—and I think monkey-tricks is at least 50 percent of what interesting directing is about. . . . Had anyone been told in advance what Peter Brook was going to do with *The Dream* there would have been a great outcry of 'that's monkey-tricks!' The fact is that monkey-tricks are only monkey-

tricks when they don't work. A monkey-trick that comes off is a stroke of genius. If you start out with a quite comprehensive self-denying ordinance of 'no monkey-tricks' then you really are very much shackled."[8] So he found ways to respect the brief and enjoy some "monkey-tricks," too. If eras were prescribed, for himself he prescribed them even more.

With the brief's effort to prevent wild renditions of the plays by specifying setting, Miller quickly recognized how much latitude he actually had. His dedication to total Renaissance atmosphere in his first productions was partly an effort to move beyond open staging and variations on Peter Brook's famous approaches, which Miller felt had run their course. Part of his interest was to stretch the

For The Taming of the Shrew *Miller asked designer Colin Lowrey to build the Paduan street from virtually untreated plywood using the architectural principles of Serlio's famous sixteenth-century design for a comic scene, in which the audience looks down a street in forced perspective past various building facades and archways toward a distant edifice. Tranio (Anthony Pedley, left) and Lucentio (Simon Chandler).* © BBC

audience's perception of the television medium by working with the surface of its picture like a painter, sometimes adopting or adapting painterly solutions to spatial arrangements, color palate, or lighting. But Miller did not maintain just a single approach to Shakespeare on television. He reproduced the spirit of Vermeer in *Shrew* and a palace in Urbino for *Othello*; he also pared the setting down to boards and drapes in another part of *Shrew* and more thoroughly in *King Lear* and abstracted settings of Troy, Timon's home, and the Paduan street, suggesting architectural line without intricate architectural detail or realistic surface.

If Miller found liberty in style and setting, he found more in character and situation, for in directing the plays, he said, "I did

Miller's experiment with staging action on a board platform as at Shakespeare's Globe and with rear lighting to achieve depth of shot culminated in King Lear. Cornwall (Julian Curry, left), Oswald (John Grillo), Gloucester (Norman Rodway), Edmund (Michael Kitchen, partially hidden), and Kent (John Shrapnel, right). © BBC

what I wanted to do. . . . The sponsors . . . insisted that [the series] was a traditional thing, that it didn't disturb people by bizarre setting. And I said OK, fine, but I'll disturb them with bizarre interpretations. . . . You always remake these plays. But I was perfectly happy to remake them under the guise of a traditional setting."[9] Uninterested in repeating the standard approaches even if he could, Miller looked at the plays afresh, concerned with their Renaissance ambience and unconcerned with stage tradition. Thus we get an unheroic Antony and Cleopatra, an unsluttish Cressida, a nonfarcical Shrew, a brown, not a black, Othello, a less regal than familial Lear. Miller's firm belief that Shakespeare is essentially a domestic playwright as well as his skepticism about high tragedy also shapes his approach. Despite detractors who charge him with overintellectualizing, his interpretations are valid, not "bizarre" except insofar as they may be nonstandard, nor does he see them as whimsical. He attends to the text and develops his ideas with conviction; he explains them with force and characteristic pungency.

Like his view of Shakespeare partaking of the serious and the comic in every work, so Miller's production concepts have a solid intellectual basis and a genuine playfulness; his own dramatic roots in comedy and satire are always apparent. As a member of his production staff pointed out, Miller alludes to painters almost as a joke, as a jeu d'esprit, whereas Moshinsky does it seriously. Understood aright, there is much truth in that comparison. It may be that Miller sees the style through the action, whereas Moshinsky sees the action through the style, so that his productions naturally have a somewhat more integrated effect. It all depends on which concepts have priority.

Miller began his resuscitative efforts on the Shakespeare series with *Antony and Cleopatra*, experimenting not only with a painterly look but also with a wooden platform as set and interpretive casting. Veronese's use of drapes and suggestion of landscape are evident in this production especially in Cleopatra's pavilion, on Pompey's ship, and in Antony's and Caesar's tents. Pompey's ship also gave rise to another effect, one more related to the ways the cameras shoot than to what they shoot. On the ship the platform worked as a studio rendition of Shakespeare's stage onto which the camera itself never ventured; instead it shot by crabbing around the edges or craning over the top. The result—the sound of the actors moving on wood, the defined acting space—fascinated Miller; he returned to this effect for Petruchio's house in *Shrew* and for whole scenes in the bare and Shakespearean space of his *Lear*.

And Miller's casting of tough rather than stereotypically noble Colin Blakely immediately said something about Antony; he becomes the warrior who has fought for years, accentuating the contrast with young Octavius coming into his prime as Antony leaves his. Jane Lapotaire brought to Cleopatra a fire without the standard sex goddess qualities, which Miller sought to avoid. Lapotaire is not asexual, for she does a convincing bump-and-grind on the bed both here and later in the series as Lady Macbeth, but she is not Helen Mirren, to cite the actress Moshinsky taps whenever he wants a character to exude sexual allure. Miller wanted the power Lapotaire could bring to Cleopatra, and he got it; while taping the last scene in the monument her performance had the entire control room in tears. (The snakes nearly brought her to tears. She does not like them, and during camera rehearsal, story has it, a recalcitrant serpent started toward her breast, then dove down her back. She warily kept both hands on it during taping.) According to Miller, character interpretation is an issue posed by the genre of drama and its use of language, for drama, in its way, is all talk that is given meaning only in performance: "There is no way in which merely by reading the play over and over to yourself you can ever become acquainted with what's being said in that play. The phrase I always go back to is a phrase of Peter Strausen, Professor of Philosophy at Oxford: he said it was a mistake to believe that sentences mean things, although in a very general linguistic sense they mean things; but the full meaning of a sentence cannot be got till you've understood that *sentences* don't mean things so much as *people* mean things by the sentences they utter."[10] Therefore if Colin Blakely and Jane Lapotaire utter Antony's and Cleopatra's lines, a very particular meaning emerges, a meaning unlike that of other actors' utterances in the same roles.

Shrew brought not just the casting of Cleese and the Vermeer interior (complete with the lovely moment before the dialogue in one scene when we see the servant sweeping and talking to the caged bird, itself a suggestive image in this household, which is exactly the sort of moment Moshinsky's quick start principle would edit out if it somehow transpired); it also brought a pure Goffman comic creation in Hortensio, whose self-absorbed and emphatic finger gestures while he speaks bring a variety of puzzled responses from Cleese's Petruchio, who once simply steps out from under the finger mindlessly jabbing him and watches in fascination as it heedlessly continues to poke the air. Miller weaves an eloquence of gestures into his productions, born of the language but fleshing out the character visually. Petruchio's servants are a delightfully motley crew, and we see Miller working with similar naturalistic detail in the posh cocktail party atmosphere that opens

Timon of Athens as well as in the characterization of Nestor in *Troilus and Cressida*.

Miller's camera rhythm and the movement within shot also become more fluid and active as he proceeds. Some BBC insiders were critical of Miller's camera work, saying "he couldn't shoot anything" but nonetheless admiring the "tautness" of his work. Whereas some shots in *Antony and Cleopatra* seemed static due to statuelike auditors (as in I.2) and the actors a bit too carefully positioned for depth of shot, in *Shrew* there is more life, especially street life, with jugglers behind and apple vendor in front of the characters and a general bustle throughout. Because Miller has a higher tolerance than many for dialogue within a single shot and a dislike for television's continual "ping-ponging" between speakers, he often maintains shots when other directors would cut, a predilection more evident in *Timon* when the misanthrope is on the rocks than anywhere else in his work. When working with movement in a developing shot, Miller usually demonstrates his power.

Miller also gets fine visual effects in every production. The wipe that provides the initial shift from Egypt to Rome in *Antony and Cleopatra*, for instance, does not hurl us from one to the other as a cut would. It marks a transition like Antony's experience, for briefly both images are present simultaneously; though Rome pervades as the new picture moves in from the left, to the right of frame Egypt lingers like a memory then is gone for a time. Later after Enobarbus exudes praise of Cleopatra's spectacular presence, Miller uses a sound bridge to effect the comparison with Octavia; as Proculeius commends the Roman lady's modesty (in three lines after Enobarbus's forty-four about Cleopatra), the shot cuts to a close-up of Octavia—almost as if he conjured her—so we see not just the contrast but instantly the hopelessness of the match. Later, the gull cries, the sound of waves lapping, and the light reflected as if off the water add to the effect of being on Pompey's ship.

Miller can also be deft with the images that open and close scenes, though he often does not decide (or reveal) until in the studio what those images will be. In the middle of *Antony and Cleopatra*, for instance, he ends the scene of Octavia's return to Rome by placing her frame left, then cuts to a shot of Cleopatra from a slightly higher angle but in exactly the same position, frame left. As that scene ends, Cleopatra thrusts Canidius out of the way to look at the map with Antony, and Miller cuts to Caesar bending over his map in the same position as Antony had been. These visual notes chime as does the disposition of the battle orders portrayed in each scene. More controversial visually may be Miller's decision to cut III.10 and instead substitute the text about the battle at sea from North's translation of Plutarch's *Lives*, the passage overlaid on a painting of the battle—thus making multiple aesthetic allusions to art, to Shakespeare's source, and to the event Shakespeare uses. North's words move silently across the screen, and the camera stays focused on the painting; all the various arts' accounts are put before us as if underscoring the historic nature of the battle before thrusting us back into the characters' reactions, thus distancing us by adding history's judgment to the participants'.

By integrating the plays with their own world, the Renaissance, Miller revealed angles often shadowed by the Shakespeare-our-contemporary view that implies Antony lives in Hampstead or Georgetown and Baptista down the block. By working on the cultural assumptions of their day (he once said that he feared Americans thought period was simply a matter of frocks), Miller consistently established the ideas that went with the clothes, a total atmosphere or world. Yet in *Antony and Cleopatra* an important part of his decision was the clothes because Renaissance dress for classical characters, though the standard in Shakespeare's day, seems peculiar in our more archaeologically knowledgeable time. And though Renaissance dress is common for *Shrew*, it comes across as the more extreme interpretation when Petruchio acts as a Puritan of Shakespeare's era might have responded, a choice that does not go against the play but somewhat against stage tradition. Miller admitted from the outset that doing Shakespeare is interpreting Shakespeare, and by accepting the precepts of the series more fully than most, in his first productions he explored family and court life of the late sixteenth and early seventeenth centuries. Though some saw his attitude as "quirky Shakespeare," it was if anything more nearly another educational series from Dr. Miller—the Drama in Question—this time assuming that as audience we know enough to appreciate the overtones and to educate ourselves. If he proselytized on any topic, it was not Shakespeare but television; he encouraged directors to explore the medium, recognizing that the medium ineluctably affects the message.

If Miller was willing to talk and teach, he was as willing to learn from others and to share discoveries. His interest in nonrealistic sets, with suggestion rather than re-creation, was shared by Jack Gold in *The Merchant of Venice* and Jane Howell in *The Winter's Tale* and seen in Miller's own scenic abstraction in parts of *Shrew*, *Timon*, *Troilus and Cressida*, and *Lear*. Moshinsky shared Miller's passion for visual art and in *All's Well That Ends Well* rendered as richly detailed a Dutch-inspired environment for action as Miller had in Baptista's house in *Shrew*. Thus began a dialogue between Miller's and Moshinsky's productions—not necessarily an influence, for they already had common inclinations and strong individual opinions, but one sparking responses in the other. *Shrew* certainly convinced Moshinsky of the efficacy of using period space as Vermeer had, as we see in his *All's Well* at Rousillon and at the Widow's in Florence. Moshinsky's emphasis on lighting, however, gave more texture to shots, an effect Miller seized on and practiced in *Othello*. If Georges de la Tour can inspire the candlelight in various gatherings in Florence, he can also be the basis for candle-lit dinners in Cyprus.

Miller's use of lighting is richest in *Othello*; so are his use of interiors and his visual correlation of exterior and interior. In fact, though *Othello* would appear to be an exception to Miller's visual production attitudes in the series, actually it is a felicitous union of harmonious elements: Shakespeare's most domestic tragedy, an interior of interconnecting rooms, rich lighting effects, strong casting in the leads. *Othello*, of all Shakespeare's tragedies, seems ideal for television: it is a play of relationships, intense and personal, against a canvas of military events that never transpire; there are no battles, only a few brief outbursts of personal violence. Spectacle and public oration are not an issue—we are not in the Forum on the Ides of March, at court in Elsinore, or in battle at Actium. The camera brings us close to the characters' agony and deceptions, and

Miller uses both the camera and that intimacy to great effect, as the actors realized.[11]

Of course, *Othello* was the most controversial play in the BBC series long before Miller ever accepted the producership due to Messina's effort to engage James Earl Jones to play the title role. When a huge brouhaha arose with Equity and the press so that the production was indefinitely postponed, the problem simmered. Whatever ultimately transpired with the casting was bound to renew the controversy, but Miller shifted the grounds of concern because he did not try to get James Earl Jones to play the part. He even argued that race is finally irrelevant to the play (thereby raising hackles among press and scholars), besides which he added that Othello was a Moor, which means an Arab in the Mediterranean world of the Renaissance, and cited several period paintings, one of which inspired Othello's costume. So he cast Anthony Hopkins, an actor of enough stature to quash some of the comments, who played the character as a Moor, very clear and soft-spoken, exceptionally calm, sure, and confident on the surface, until Iago starts his private campaign.

Iago is not only the longest part in the play but also the play's focal point because he is the one who shapes and moves the events. Othello's first great action, eloping with Desdemona, precedes the play, and aside from slapping her, his role is reactive; his only other action is strangling his wife, the action toward which the play inexorably builds. But Iago is always a-doing, busy with scheme and innuendo and bluff, keeping everyone in the dark so he can strike undetected, literally with both Cassio and Roderigo and figuratively with Othello and Desdemona. Miller sought a working-class character, a gangster type, and found him in Bob Hoskins, who has been cast as a tough or a heavy in contemporary drama and gained renown as a gangster in the BBC's *Pennies from Heaven*. A combination of mischief and malice, this Iago has roots deep in folklore; as Hoskins reported, "My main note . . . was to do him like Rumpelstiltskin."[12]

We see that range of impish, trouble-making, destructive qualities immediately with Iago's mime of goatish copulation and the mischief of spraying Roderigo with water, then carrying a handful back to toss up onto Brabantio at the window, who on feeling the drops gazes in brief puzzlement up at the moonlit sky. Thus we see Iago's interest in the sordid and bestial (to him marriage is only the beast with two backs), his ability to lead Roderigo, his glee on arousing anyone's passion with his livid description. Then there are the Miller touches—Roderigo's shushing Iago, the water game, Brabantio momentarily distracted from disaster by the unlikelihood of rain. The image is apt, for Iago works as does the storm to bring separation and wreck to those in his way, though it does not appear so to them. Another such moment occurs in setting up Cassio, where Iago foments great conviviality, wine, and song, so that while Montano and the gentlemen tease by continuing the drinking song low-voiced, Iago baits Cassio and mocks him behind his back on his drunken exit. When no one is nearby to excite, Iago toys with the candle flame, always playing with fire.

Miller's camera work in *Othello* is also effective, both the regular group or 2-shots and his more characteristic single-camera sequences. Everyone in shot is active, often broken into smaller side groups with their own apparent conversations; there is no more stagey posing until a speaker finishes. And just as the line of rooms gives great depth to camera shots, so do the placement and movement of actors. Many of them walk the length of the hall while the camera waits and watches. In intimate scenes Miller uses the space more generously, putting the third party in shot farther back, as Iago or Emilia is often placed when attending but not party to a conversation. The reverse is also the case when we hear Iago talk with Cassio about Bianca from Othello's point of view behind the door, looking past him to the men in the window seat. The camera consistently supports and complements the action.

One of Miller's favorite uses of the camera is the single-camera sequence, which involves perhaps the most demanding taping circumstances for actors and technical staff alike. While he sometimes does short scenes on one camera, he might also decide to tape a blockbuster scene that way, as he did the scene of Troilus and Cressida's meeting or the temptation scene in *Othello*, a tour de force. It is a kinetic scene—actors and camera moving all over the room, shifting positions in relation to each other, the characters entering or leaving or returning—and to have the entire action build with only one cut is remarkable.

In this sequence all the changes usually wrought by switching camera shots occur *within* the picture by actors' blocking and camera movement. Once Othello enters, the shot develops, working in tandem with the actors, which calls for great precision, concentration, and consistency from them and from the cameraman as well, in this case veteran BBC cameraman Jim Atkinson with whom Miller regularly worked. In the course of the action Othello moves from table to table, as does Iago. He sits and watches Desdemona's entrance, and later Iago sits to malign her while Othello leans over the table (a difference indicating who is in charge, in the seat of power). It is a scene with deft images, as when the camera shoots through the handkerchief as Iago blows on it and celebrates how "trifles light as air / Are to the jealous confirmations strong / As proofs of holy writ." It is also a scene with near violence, as when Othello slams Iago into the wall, saying, "Villain, be sure thou prove my love a whore," and when Iago vows to second Othello's revenge not by kneeling beside him but by grabbing him around the neck like a wrestler working for a hold, so that he is nearly choking him in that infernal embrace. (And contrast the effect of this embrace from behind and that between Aufidius and Coriolanus at Antium in Moshinsky's *Coriolanus*.) The blocking throughout the scene, in fact, clearly interprets the relationships. As Miller said, on one camera "it seems much tenser, this long scene as a process of seduction of someone, and you have to have your camera *attend* someone very slowly and wander around him in much the same way Iago wanders around Othello; you wander around him with one camera and pay attention to him."[13]

Because Miller considers the play a "closet tragedy," he purposefully keeps it in interiors. Within those rooms, that "airy spacious confinement" that, as Miller notes, ends up seeming "an awful prison,"[14] he also builds a pattern around the opening and closing of the painted doors in juxtaposed shots at scene shifts; characters often leave the hall in close-up, shutting the doors behind them, and the next scene opens with the doors at the opposite end of the hall. In IV.1 action moves the length of the hall and into the ante-room, then for the first time into the bedroom for "strangle her in her bed, even the bed that she hath contaminated." The business with the doors is a choice, not an accident, paralleling the number of ideas and emotions Othello is now opening and closing himself to at Iago's instigation.

At the play's end, moonlight falls through the arches of the colonnade outside and through the windows of the hall inside, creating patches of light and dark, linking the scenes as does Iago's laughter that ends them both. Throughout Roderigo and Cassio's chase amid the arches, Iago is present only as a low chuckle and as a shadow running beyond the shot until he pops in to slash Cassio in the leg after Cassio fells Roderigo. The confusion, the quick shots of the chase—some by a cameraman with a handheld camera who ducked into a hollow column between shots—the shouts and echoing groans add to the effect of the scene. After Iago leaves, gleeful at the chaos, Othello is shown entering the silent hall and walking through bands of shadow and moonlight toward the bedroom. Miller uses the space well to tell the story, framing Emilia's discovery of Desdemona, for instance, from across the bed so we see the women reflected in the mirror and also Othello standing in the anteroom watching. Finally, we are left not with a shot of the tragic loading of this bed, the inevitable stage view, but of the moonlit hall as the maliciously laughing Iago and then wounded Cassio are led out, a camera shot that puts death behind us and emptiness before us.

Edited for straight dramatic drive, and thereby losing the street proclamation, the clown, and the musicians, the production is unrelenting and with its spacious interiors and moonlit colonnades has great beauty. Amid the more realistic space, the plentitude of black-and-white costumes has a richness and life, an appropriateness, whereas in *Timon* and *Lear* such a design choice used against drapes accentuates the theatrical origins of the work, the actors like cutouts animated against a backdrop.

Timon, the production that unexpectedly preceded *Othello* for Miller, clearly shows some of Miller's predilections and abilities because he had less time to work on that show. Usually his ideas would brew or distill for a year or more before the play went into production. During the summer of 1980, for instance, he was already describing attitudes or settings for the next year's *Othello*, *Troilus and Cressida*, and *A Midsummer Night's Dream* (which at that time he thought he might also direct, with fairies after Inigo Jones and Hieronymus Bosch), some of which changed over time, such as his initial inclination to put the women of Troy in huge medieval hats. But because he took over the production of *Timon* late, he had to work briskly. Timon's seaside shingle of gravel and gnarled trunks is littered with debris of past cities—walls or the edges of roofs at odd angles, the huge head of a horse from a statue half buried. Miller had been developing such an idea for *Troilus and Cressida*, the Greek camp built on the ruins of past Troys with broken columns and fallen statues seen amid the clutter, and appropriated the design for *Timon*. Timon's house is another, though grander, plywood edifice such as Miller experimented with for the street and also the banquet room in *Shrew*.

These banquet settings were alike in other ways as well, as in their incorporation of music. *Timon* calls for a masque, and Miller replicates the formality of masque music, costume, and dance as nearly as he can. We see a courtly entertainment. In *Shrew* no music is scripted in the wedding banquet, but in the spirit of Shakespearean comedy, Miller ends his account of Puritan attitudes both personal and marital with a hymn, Psalm 128, "How blest is he that serves the Lord," sung a cappella in four-part harmony and thereby testifying through words and action the renewed harmony of the family in the play. Rather than separate the gathering at the end with "Come, Kate, we'll to bed," that line is cut and all remain together.

Thus, some effects were very carefully planned; others, as usual, were more a matter of discovery. In trying to capture the feeling and to cover the angles he might want or need, Miller occasionally taped far more than he actually used. In *Shrew* he did repeated takes of the banquet scene, taping for every conceivable angle at the table, and still ran into one sight-line problem in editing as Baptista rises at Kate's unexpected entrance at the end of the wager. In *Timon* the first banquet was sumptuous and remarkably authentic; Miller had five Renaissance fish recipes prepared and a variety of meats. They taped the feast for nearly thirty minutes, almost all extemporaneous action; three minutes of that banquet made it to the master tape. Miller will sometimes use such taping to foster possibilities, whereas television-trained directors will not, for as Miller acknowledges, the BBC considers such an approach disorganized and bad planning, though he believes it is valuable artistically.

Miller brought vignettes in *Timon* to life, such as the three scenes in which Timon's servants ask his friends for loans. Each is given its own character, three small satires on social hypocrisy and prudence. The little moves tell all with Miller. Flaminius opens and closes the empty box as he paces Lucullus's hallway. From the end of the hall Lucullus enters in long shot (the camera throughout the scene never moves from the near end of the hall) and comes down the column-shadowed hall to Flaminius, moving confidentially into close-up with knowing looks and nods as he proffers his denial amid hollow lies, then moving back down the hallway. Flaminius, hurling the money and empty box after him, follows to shout his opinion after the now absent Lucullus and returns down the hallway to leave. The spaciousness suggested by the depth of shot, the effect of perspective sound (used consistently as actors repeatedly walk away from camera and exit in the distance, still talking but only half heard), and the detailed rendition of verbal evasion define the scene sharply.

A cut takes us to Lucius, seated at a table weighing his gold and counting his riches in a small room. He, too, is eager to receive but quick to fabricate excuses for not giving; at the end of the scene he knocks some stacked coins onto the floor with an expansive arm gesture, sending the disgusted Servilius around to collect them even as Lucius pleads lack of funds. After Timon's servant leaves, Lucius gives one last look over the table to make sure all the coins were collected—a lovely Milleresque detail—before resuming his accounts.

For the last vignette Sempronius sits foreground of shot munching on a leg of fowl from a table laden with food as Timon's servant Lucilius stands behind him. The blocking points up Sempronius's self-indulgence and self-concern. Thus amid reception, gold, and food—the items we have seen Timon bountiful in—Timon is denied. The detail of the different situations and the coloring of the speeches bespeak Miller's touch.

In working with Jonathan Pryce as Timon, Miller sought Pryce's ability to erupt, fabled since his award-winning performance in *Comedians*. Pryce's intensity manifested itself in the studio. In camera rehearsal for Timon's rage after the second banquet, Pryce reportedly told Miller he had no idea what he would actually do in taping. So Jim Atkinson took the camera and said he would follow him (this became a single-camera scene of necessity as well as choice). Watching the camera movement and framing of that scene shows not only an actor at work but just how good a cameraman Atkinson is, for only once, when Pryce interrupts a downward move, does the camera give even a hint of a hiccup in its presentation.

If *Timon* called for quick planning on Miller's part, *Lear* prompted the opposite. In 1969 Miller directed *Lear* at the Nottingham Playhouse using Michael Hordern and Frank Middlemass as Lear and the Fool. In 1975 Miller gathered Hordern and Middlemass and directed *Lear* for the BBC's *Play of the Month*, a two-hour version of the play that everyone found very powerful and that was the BBC's last Shakespeare production before the Shakespeare series started. A National Film Theatre (London) program book, in discussing this production shown during a Miller television retrospective, called it the "first (and better) of Miller's two television *Lear*s," adding that "its boldly-coloured backdrops serve to concentrate rather than distract our attention."[15] When he became producer of the series, Miller tried to get the BBC to use that 1975 *Lear* as part of the series, but they insisted a new one had to be produced. Still fascinated and drawn to the play in 1982, Miller essentially remounted his 1975 production and its interpretation, using more of the text but the same leading actors for Lear and the Fool, the same costume and design concepts, even some of the same blocking and characterization, such as indicating Edgar's madness not just with rags and gabbling but with a crown of thorns, basing it on the common Renaissance derangement of those who thought they were an apocalyptic figure such as Jesus.[16] (This interpretation shows Miller's personal concern with precision in acting: one is not just "mad," a generic aberration; one has a particular form of madness, a definite dementia.)

In directing Shakespeare's great tragedies, *Antony and Cleopatra*, *Othello*, and *King Lear*, Miller unified the design principles more than with his productions of *Shrew*, *Timon*, and *Troilus and Cressida*. They are not, however, the same design principles in each tragedy. Miller had a number of ideas about televising Shakespeare that he wanted to explore during the series, some based on Renaissance art, some based on Renaissance staging. In the course of his productions, he worked with both—*Othello* culminating the exploration of art by moving into Miller's most representational setting, *Lear* culminating the exploration of Renaissance staging by moving into Miller's least representational setting. But *Lear*'s setting is not a departure from the rest; it is closely linked to elements of almost all the other Miller productions in the BBC Shakespeare series.

The merits of the wooden platform as a stage or site for televising Shakespeare intrigued Miller from the start. Though Pompey's ship and Petruchio's house let him see how such a technique would work, these were limited scenes within larger productions. Only in *Lear* did he apply his plank-and-drape approach to an entire production. All castle interior and courtyard scenes were shot on or near the large wooden platform, the exteriors against a plain cycloramic curtain with dark tarpaulins spread over the studio floor, so that while interiors are distinguished from exteriors in *Lear*, neither is an actual re-creation of castle or heath but a suggestion much closer to the staging at the Globe. As Miller said, "You could do a large number of the tragedies like this. I think what we've shown is that you only need foils in order to give break-ups of space and shafts of light, and there really isn't much more necessary."[17] The BBC's *Hamlet* and *Macbeth*, *Lear*, and Miller's other two productions in the set of great tragedies, along with the RSC's televised *Macbeth* and *Antony and Cleopatra*, corroborate this view.

Miller's suggestiveness in *Lear* is also related to the studio spaces he used in *Timon* and *Troilus and Cressida*, especially some of their spacious and indefinite interiors. By contrast, however, the exteriors in these two productions, the shingle and the Greek camp, were far more detailed and defined than *Lear*'s heath. In fact, definition was absolutely denied objects on the heath, for even the pillars built for the interiors and the barrels and flats being used were wrapped in canvas.[18]

On such a set, as with the unit sets in Howell's productions, lighting becomes very important. Yet on a nonrepresentational set, there may be no traditional light sources. In *Othello* sunlight pours through the windows in the hall in Cyprus, and at night moonlight creates bands of silver light and shadow. Similarly angled shafts of light illuminate *Lear*; we simply assume more about sun and moon. And even more than in *Othello*, the light in *Lear* is very cool and white, the night scenes a bit icier than the day—no warm golden or rosy tones here—all in keeping with the basic design choices.

The interior scenes at Lear's and Gloucester's residences have a shaft of light at the rear shining from behind a drape so that figures pass through darker areas after entering, and at times many of the faces and figures are partially shadowed. This effect also causes much of the action to appear backlit, so hair and ruffs gain an aura, especially in the scene at Goneril's home, also strongly rear-lighted. And in the spirit of nonrepresentational staging, the direction of the light need not keep a realistic position.

The softer, whiter light is partly due to the lighting instruments and partly due to the technical treatment of the light, for lighting designer John Treays desaturated the color by 30 percent in *Lear*, far more than is usual for productions; "Certainly with tragedy the less colour the better," he observed.[19] Tragedy is often stark, and in the BBC *Lear* it is definitely so. Color was not the goal, as the costumes in "manichean black and white"[20] indicated.

Three Miller productions—*Timon*, *Othello*, and *Lear*—use black-and-white costuming, obviously a design element Miller appreciates. In *Lear* the costuming benefited from the setting, not only in terms of budget available[21] but in terms of focus as well, for the characters stand out starkly against the neutral drapes, and the eye can revel in every bit of costume detail without getting lost and

can catch the actors' every glance, gesture, and nuance of movement. Of course, to say the costumes are black and white general-
izes what is actually a richer range of tones—from grays to a blue
undertone;[22] a variety of texture and sheen—rough, velvety, crisp,
shiny; and different trims—silver, gold, black on white, fur. Even
actors' hair color and wigs complement the design palate: everyone
has either dark hair or white; there are no redheads or blondes at
this court. In this dark world, any flesh tone or white stands out,
and the white repeats as a make-up element in the clown-white
make-up on the Fool's face, which washes off in the storm, in the
white mask Edgar wears to challenge Edmund after the battle, and
in the white make-up on dead Cordelia's face (very apparent in the
last color photo in the BBC *Lear* script: "My poor fool is hanged").
Thus three supportive, suffering, good characters who help others
in need are visually linked. Moreover, the red feathers in the Fool's
hat, the red cross on Edgar's tunic for the challenge, and the red
welt on Cordelia's hanged neck leap out of these visual environs.

Being in a smaller studio with *Lear* (since *Richard III* was being
taped in the larger studio 1 at the same time) did not limit Miller's
continuing concern with depth of shot; he used every inch he had,
often placing entrances at the rear with action in the foreground of
interior shots and using the camera lens to blur those who enter
from afar on the heath. The composition of his camera shots further develops the depth; for example, Edmund loiters near the map
in the background as Goneril and Regan confer in the foreground
after the kingdom is divided, and for the blinding of Gloucester, an
elderly retainer is placed in the rear of shot, and as the violence
occurs in the foreground he beats his head in horror. And as in
earlier productions, in *Lear* Miller again has action shift within
frame, foreground to background to fore, rather than continually
cutting between cameras to maintain close-ups.

Thus for Miller *Lear* becomes the study of character and interactions it must be, moving inevitably toward its tragic close. Sinister
and insinuating tones are carefully modulated; the older sisters,
played by Gillian Barge and Penelope Wilton, are exceptionally deft
at manipulating and disposing of Michael Hordern's dottering,
outraged Lear. Hordern finds a different range of tones for the mad

Lear, a quieter insight amid the anger and a hearty, forthright, and spiteful flower-bedecked king out of his wits, who will even jab at Gloucester's empty sockets. The peace that comes to this shattered man and his shattered land is the peace of great grief and for those remaining, who hold the newly dead bodies, a feeble sense of shoring up ruins amid the wreckage.

Six months after Miller made the BBC *Lear* in 1982, Granada Television produced its own far more costly televised *Lear* starring 75-year-old Laurence Olivier. Using almost three weeks of studio taping and a $2,000,000 budget[23] (called "the most expensive production in British television history"[24]), it had roughly three times the BBC studio time and five-and-a-half times its budget. This star-studded vehicle, with a cast including Colin Blakely, Diana Rigg, Dorothy Tutin, Leo McKern, and John Hurt, which in the introduction to the U.S. broadcast Peter Ustinov touted as "probably the best Shakespearean cast ever assembled," displayed far different choices from Miller's for virtually every aspect of the play.

Olivier and director Michael Elliott set the play in Anglo-Saxon England with a Stonehenge studio setting and a patch of realistic grassy heath, with predominantly dark backgrounds and including a spate of animals—horses, dogs, a chicken, a mouse, a dead rabbit. Elliott's camera work in this *Lear* emphasizes the close-up, showing off his high-power cast and eminent central figure. Long high shots often establish or close scenes, and the occasional tracking shot covers the heath or the final duel, but the bulk of the visual element involves cuts to faces or medium close-ups, whereas Miller in the BBC production uses more medium shots and developing shots to gain a collective sense of the action. As Lear, Olivier goes for the pathos amid the cranky power, gently coaching Cordelia in the proper answers early on, sitting in almost serenely reflective madness beside blinded Gloucester while quietly registering the folly of human activity and kissing Gloucester's forehead gently, speaking in hushed whispers to the returned and later to the dead Cordelia—a performance far less public than private and personal, the white-haired man who after great railing against it finally admits to being old and foolish. The production offers a useful contrast of realism to Miller's stylization as well as a different interpretive balance of characters and action. The television techniques differ, too; Hardy Cook, in comparing the productions, argues that "Miller's televisual strategies enable viewers to watch Shakespeare on television in a manner that is similar to the theatrical experience" whereas "Michael Elliott's [do] not."[25]

Miller's work throughout the BBC Shakespeare series was thoughtful, interesting, crisp, clean, purposeful, and controversial. His presence was invigorating to directors, designers, and technical personnel as well as to the series itself. His own views on the productions were often a strange and characteristic blend of seriousness and cynical irony (his performance roots are in satire), as with *Troilus and Cressida*, which he spoke of and arranged in both ways. To Henry Fenwick he said: "It's ironic, it's farcical, it's satirical: I think it's an entertaining, rather frothily ironic play. It's got a bitter-sweet quality, rather like black chocolate. It has a wonderfully light ironic touch and I think it should be played ironically, not with heavy-handed agonising on the dreadful futility of it all."[26] This view is certainly apparent in Miller's production—consider the characterization of Thersites—and also in his producership. But during rehearsal Miller also often commented that the play is a tragedy, a denial of innocence, purity, clarity of motive. This view is equally true of the production, and both views are oxymoronically true of Miller's own art at the time, for he could exude a sportiveness, a frothy irony in public comments and in rehearsal yet also approach his work with intentness and great seriousness. Both prove to be essential qualities in his work.

Miller's interpretations of the plays were often more criticized than admired, in fact were savaged by many academics, especially American academics, as not just static but wrongheaded and in some cases a disservice to the plays. Miller is no stranger to such criticism; his daring views of classical works are sometimes acclaimed as genius and at other times excoriated. He never plays it safe and so gains no safe, modest response. As the BBC *Lear* production attests, Miller can be insistent in his revolutionary interpretation over the years. Miller's puritanical concept for *Shrew* first surfaced in a 1972 stage production at Chichester with Anthony Hopkins as the Puritan squire, though John Cleese added "certain disruptive tendencies" that freshened the character for Miller.[27] Miller became even more interested in Katherine's psychology through this process and focused on her mental aberrations in a subsequent staging by the RSC with Fiona Shaw in the role (1987).

Antony and Cleopatra, Othello, Troilus and Cressida, and *Timon*, on the other hand, were fresh looks at these plays for Miller, and in *Antony and Cleopatra* and *Othello* we see the familiar attack on tradition and get the expected cries of outrage. Nonetheless, Miller asserts that "it is essential that the director feels provoked by the text rather than responsible for it." He recognizes that his revolutionary urge "to overthrow a tired interpretation" arises in response to the theatrical tendency to repeat a "canonical performance": "I think there is a conspiracy in the theatre to perpetuate certain prototypes in the belief that they contain the secret truth of the characters in question. This collusion between actors and directors is broken only by successful innovation which interrupts the prevailing mode."[28] How to succeed at such innovation is the question.

Miller's style in the Shakespeare series is firmly based on his perception of drama and the medium of television. He worked for detail, but for detail in the action, in the characterization, in the interaction of speakers and listeners in a given situation, not for detail in or elaboration of setting. He perceives the other approach but denies it: "One is tempted to do it on the grand scale, but it's a different medium from cinema—space reads so badly on television. People always ask where events in Shakespeare are happening, but in fact they occur only between the people involved. You need no pretense at realism, just an austere, clear picture—against a foil of nothing, just one or two extremely detailed objects."[29] Thus Miller's style emphasizes not representation of space but representation of action.

What he strove for or says he strove for is quite clear, both during his producership with the BBC Shakespeare series and afterward in his own discussions in *Subsequent Performances*: ideally he wanted a stylization as elegant or austere as in the RSC television tragedies. In principle the success of such stylization as an approach to televising Shakespeare cannot be doubted, but in Miller's productions only Cleopatra's monument and the set for Troy maintain austerity and benefit from it. Though Miller's visual style could at times seem expressionless, the principles involved are admirable and, as always with Miller, interesting to contemplate, even if the results vary. Yet amid these explorations, though he discusses it less, Miller also worked representationally in parts of plays and achieved warmth and elegance with Baptista's rooms and Othello's Cypriot quarters.

In looking back at the series, with characteristic honesty Miller assessed his own experimentation and gave the other side its due: "Representationalism enforces itself upon the television producer however reluctant he may be to make use of it. In the television productions of Shakespeare for which I was responsible I am embarrassed to admit that the most successful were those in which the scenery was more real and more pictorial than the nineteenth-century stage versions I have reacted violently against when directing in the theatre."[30] And if we want to explore the validity of Miller's comment, the best place to examine the effect of pictorial scenery is in the work of Elijah Moshinsky.

5 Moshinsky's Television Artistry

In working on the Shakespeare series, Elijah Moshinsky not only shared many of Miller's interests and ideas, but he also saw additional possibilities in scenic effects and treatment of text, extending them to make them his own, not derivative of Miller; the men share an intellectual strong-mindedness and independence just as they share aesthetic concerns. One has, of course, only to watch the wooing scene of *The Taming of the Shrew* and Helena's first soliloquy in *All's Well That Ends Well* to recognize the similarities—the Vermeer look of activity in an inner chamber seen through the door, the softly diffused window light, the mirror over the spinet used for reflection shots, even the same spinet, cloned from a Vermeer painting. Yet the elements that give these scenes an aesthetic elegance Moshinsky takes even farther, and *All's Well* has the technical exuberance of one exploring a new medium. Any number of effects that become characteristic of Moshinsky's Shakespeare productions appear in that first show.

Moshinsky had never worked with television prior to the Shakespeare series, so the series became his training ground. With his many credits in opera and theatre, he obviously had the directorial skills and necessary production experience, and to help him adapt those skills to television Miller gave him an open invitation to the rehearsals and tapings for the four shows that preceded *All's Well* in 1980. Moshinsky also had two production managers assigned to him during *All's Well* so that in the studio one could manage the studio floor and the other could stay with the director in the control room to answer questions or discuss alternatives, though Moshinsky had very few questions; he worked confidently and firmly. From that production, he says, he learned to use more shots, for he

Elijah Moshinsky on the set of A Midsummer Night's Dream. © *BBC*

admits that during *All's Well* he "was too scared to do much," although he believes that reticence turned out to be "an unintentional virtue" of the production.[1]

From the beginning, however, Moshinsky was aware of how differently action comes across on television than on stage, a difference that most affected his casting because "television is Shakespeare with subtext" and not simply the theatrical challenge of vocal volume to fill the space. By way of example he praised Irene˙ Worth's very subtle, rich performance as Volumnia in his BBC *Coriolanus* and lamented how much of that was lost when she subsequently performed the role with the National Company in the Olivier Theatre. "If the actor is to perform Shakespeare on television successfully," Moshinsky once wrote, "he cannot afford to generalise. The television camera is merciless. It instantly exposes false and bombastic performances. If an actor is striving for theatrical effectiveness rather than for the truth of the role, the camera reveals the falseness."[2] He often chose actors who could "work small," Moshinsky said, and added that in some cases he would have cast very differently had he been working on a stage production.[3]

His textual editing does not entirely follow the same principles; he edits only for strength. When asked about textual editing, for instance, Miller responds that he cuts to achieve dramatic flow, as when he cut the musicians in *Othello*; it was not to maintain a tragic line or atmosphere in the play, he said, but to maintain the dramatic line. Moshinsky, working with the same script editor, David Snodin, edits the same way, and with increasing drive—or ruthlessness—as he proceeds. In *All's Well* he cuts much of the clown's banter and some of the elaboration during the capture and questioning of Parolles as well as Lafew's asides during Helena's choice of a husband. He does not like distractions or unnecessary interruptions; he likes a clear focus on the issue and characters at hand.

He will also rearrange lines, and in subsequent plays entire scenes, to give a clearer dramatic flow for television. The two scenes cut altogether from *All's Well* are the Florentine Duke's; they seemed extraneous to the director and also were potentially exterior shots in a production Moshinsky wanted to keep interior. The closest we get to the outside in *All's Well* is the women watching the passing troops out of a window in Florence. Parolles, supposedly in the street, gives his single line in a high angle close-up that cuts off any view of surroundings. In subsequent productions Moshinsky's editing is more strongly interpretive, as in *Coriolanus*, though he continues to work for interiors and utterly eschews battle scenes: the attack on Corioli is subsumed by one admittedly lengthy single combat amid the burning town, the battle between Romans and Britons in *Cymbeline* by a burning building without a blow struck on camera. In fact, Moshinsky changes more scenes in more shows than any other director in the series.

Within the productions Moshinsky keeps a consistent scenic richness and referentiality. Whereas Howell stylizes and Miller will frequently abstract, Moshinsky keeps every scene in a distinct space, even if by being against a painted backdrop that space is more aesthetic than realistic; after all, even his realistic interiors are aesthetic in inspiration and sometimes in effect. Moshinsky perfects the Vermeer perspective on inner rooms through doorways, but the doorways are more than an aesthetic effect. In fact, doorways become crucial in blocking and camera work in Moshinsky's productions: consider Bertram's and Helena's backlit entrances to the King's darkened bedchamber in *All's Well* and the shot of Lafew and the chastened Parolles exiting through the door at Rousillon juxtaposed to a shot of Helena and the other women entering the palace hallway in Paris. And consider how much Moshinsky keeps the camera on the doorway in the play's last scene; the King sweeps in through two doors (one off camera), the shot cuts to the doorway to catch Bertram's entrance and again for Helena's last unlooked-for entrance at the end of the play after Diana and those with her have stood in the doorway for much of her exchange with the King.

In *Cymbeline* and *Coriolanus* doorways are equally significant. In the former we wait with Cloten at Imogen's door and with Pisanio we enter it, and we also see several exchanges occur in doorways, such as the end of Iachimo's temptation of Imogen and the Queen's soliloquy about placing the English crown. In *Coriolanus* we not only watch Coriolanus enter the Senate Chamber and stop in the doorway to comment on the tribunes within, but we track before Volumnia and Virgilia as they pass through doors to confront those tribunes. Given interiors and multiple rooms, doorways seem inevitable; more than that, however, they are given visual significance in these productions.

Perhaps Moshinsky's most distinctive production element and the one through which he makes his greatest contribution to the series is his lighting, for he and lighting designer John Summers, who worked as facilitative genius on all five Moshinsky shows, developed a number of strong effects. Moshinsky introduced the Shakespeare series to the aesthetic of the shadow, usually the bane of all studio work, which traditionally uses general lighting with special portrait lighting for the actors so they will look attractive in close-ups. Yet *All's Well* is by design a heavily shadowed production because of the lighting—window light, candlelight, firelight. One detail of the Vermeer interiors that Moshinsky capitalized on was the windows and their soft white light. This gentle spill of light gave slight contrasts and a definitive angle to the light source; the chest topped with flowers and fruit in the main room at Rousillon was always brightened into an Old Master's still life by the nearby light. Parolles sat in the window by the spinet (a move Miller repeats in *Othello*, where the windows are a frequent stopping point), and not content with that, during Helena's soliloquy Moshinsky had the camera shoot a close-up of her head directly in front of the bright window, giving a silhouette. Later Parolles and Bertram are so shadowed they are very nearly silhouetted in the candle-lit hallway of the palace, and *Cymbeline* closes with a carefully arranged silhouette of Posthumus and Imogen that visually matches their earlier leave-taking.

Moshinsky favors strong dark/light contrast, as in these silhouettes, but more especially in the development of chiaroscuro effects in the productions. Wanting to shoot scenes with dark backgrounds and candlelight, Moshinsky showed Summers the work of Georges de la Tour, and Summers began seeking a way to light from a single small source such as a candle. Finally, by using a projector bulb carefully masked by other objects on the table, Summers got the bright localized light he and the director sought, though this effect called for tolerance from the nearly blinded actors and precision from the camera crew not to catch bulb or electrical line in shot.[4] The effect is stunning in the scene where the Widow agrees to Helena's wager and when the lords and Bertram bait the drum trap for Parolles. And we have only to look at the banquet scenes or the willow scene in *Othello* to see how sincerely Miller admired the effect by borrowing it.

The greater lighting challenge was actually the firelight, however, because the lighting instruments had to be so close to the frame of the shot in order to provide light from the same angle as the fire. During *All's Well* cameras regularly caught flares (the edge of a light in shot) in the candelabra-lit hallway scenes in Paris and during the scene between Bertram and Diana in Florence, and since the latter was a single-camera sequence with no cuts, a flare meant starting anew from the top. Candelabra and firelight recur in Moshinsky's productions; *Cymbeline* opens with a fire and burns untold candles in Britain and Italy, bedroom and great hall, until it gets to the burning building after the battle. Such flames give not only light but color, so any number of scenes are lit in flickering golden light as in *All's Well*, rosy-fingered dawn as in *A Midsummer Night's Dream*, reddish-gold or pinkish-red light as in *Cymbeline* (including the last silhouette against vivid deep pink through the windows), a red and golden hue as in Coriolanus's banishment scene—color chosen for the pictures, not reality. As Moshinsky told Summers early on, "Don't worry too much about the reality of it."[5] He continued his concern with lighting through *Love's Labour's Lost*, where several scenes have pinkish-red backgrounds, and where the women's private scenes and the pageant use footlights, one of the many eighteenth-century aspects of that production. Moshinsky uses lighting to sculpt and texture the atmosphere of the productions, enriching their visual element.

Moshinsky is almost as concerned with the camera and with framing shots as he is with lighting, and because he has such a strong visual sense he became increasingly prescriptive as he gained experience. In *All's Well* his camera supervisor was Jim Atkinson, one of the best in the business, the man without whom Jane Howell said she never could have done the histories. Atkinson is an artist with the camera; he sees good angles, frames exceedingly well, and maneuvers confidently. He also, as one production staff member said, works like a frustrated director, discussing improvements in shots and making suggestions. Howell and Miller were open to his approach and depended on his knowledge and ability, whatever

*Moshinsky's aesthetic interest in using the lighting effects in Renaissance
art is exemplified by the Georges de la Tour illumination achieved on the
candlelit faces in* All's Well That Ends Well *by lighting designer John
Summers. Widow (Rosemary Leach, left), Helena (Angela Down), and
Diana (Pippa Guard, right). © BBC*

their final decision about the shot; Moshinsky grew contentious
during *Dream* and never worked with Atkinson again, a difference
of temperament. In first camera rehearsals Moshinsky is exacting,
veritably scientific in the precision with which he defines the camera shots and their framing. In *Coriolanus* and *Love's Labour's
Lost* there is even an increased element of pose in the action, as if
he really were painting pictures on television.

In all his productions Moshinsky consistently uses long shots to
establish context for action and character, often as the opening
shot of a scene, after which the camera moves in to frame tighter
shots. In *All's Well*, for example, Moshinsky says, "I wanted to
start with a long shot of Helena and not move immediately to
close-up—I didn't want too much identification with her, I wanted
a picture of a woman caught in an obsession, with the camera static

The carefully angled sunlight in the Senate chamber of Coriolanus *is also indebted to Renaissance art. Cominius (Patrick Godfrey, left), Coriolanus (Alan Howard), and a senator (unidentified supporting artist, right).*
© BBC

In the more nineteenth-century romantic forest set of A Midsummer Night's Dream *Moshinsky put a shallow pool to gain reflections and comically sodden moments. Helena (Cherith Mellors, left), Demetrius (Nicky Henson), Lysander (Robert Lindsay), and Hermia (Pippa Guard, right). © BBC*

when she speaks, clear, judging her words. I wanted to start with long shots because I felt they were needed to place people in their context and for the sake of atmosphere. I wanted the atmosphere to help carry the story."[6] This comment describes his technique not just in *All's Well* but in every one of his productions—the long shots of Helena at the spinet and of the healed King dancing with her, the long shots of Puck or Titania's fairies in the pond or of Hermia awaking to find herself alone in the forest (an effect supported by the echo), the long shot of Imogen in the hall just before Iachimo's introduction or of Cymbeline and Lucius seated at opposite ends of a long table, the long shot of Caius Marcius entering the Senate or the shot down the table in the Senate Chamber, the long shot of the Princess's entrance to the garden at Navarre. In addition to getting depth of shot from his setting, Moshinsky will also move the camera back considerably to get distance from the focal figures, demonstrating that, carefully selected and prudently used, there is a place for the long shot in the close-up medium of television.

Definite surroundings are very important to Moshinsky's televised Shakespeares in both setting and camera work. But Moshinsky uses the camera as more than a documentary image-recorder; he uses it artfully to give impressions, and he blocks the action to set up specific kinds of shots. In addition to long shots, Moshinsky likes high angle or crane shots. One sequence in *All's Well* shows the King dancing with Helena down the corridor toward the camera, then cuts to a glass shot of their entrance into the great hall (the walls and ceiling of the room were painted on a pane of glass through which the camera shot, thus making the set appear far larger and grander than it actually was; a careful viewer will see one of the courtiers disappear into the left wall, which was painted on the glass, when he strays beyond the area of the set in shot), and finally moves to a crane shot through an oval opening high above the floor to see the King twirling Helena below. Other high shots in *All's Well* include Parolles's "Lose our drum" comment in the street, the capture of Parolles where the camera shoots past the First Lord prone in the loft onto Parolles lying below (a workable solution to this eavesdropping scene, one of the hardest kind to translate from theatre to television), and the high angle shot past Lavache hanging a garland of greens on the mantelpiece to Parolles standing obsequiously below (that last "looking down on Parolles" makes visual a dominant attitude in the play that is fully manifest by act V).

In *Dream*, any over-shoulder shot from Oberon on horseback is a high angle shot so that we often look down on Titania. We also get a high angle on abandoned Hermia fallen in the pond (III.2), and Moshinsky creates a link to the next scene by cutting immediately to an opposite angle high shot of Oberon dunking Puck, "This is thy negligence." Puck's own dunking of Flute is more violent and seen from a much higher angle. Moreover, when Bottom finally awakens, the camera, like a curious bird, looks down at him as he lies on the grass. *Cymbeline*'s high shots are few but striking:

we look straight down on soon-to-be-headless Cloten roaring for Posthumus in the forest—an eagle's-eye view, closely linked to the film clip of a soaring bird Moshinsky uses as image and as comment on the unacknowledged princes; the shot cuts to shoulder level as Guiderius enters and speaks. The other crane shot, predictably, is the one past Jupiter in the dream sequence, looking down on Posthumus and his family's ghosts.

Coriolanus, too, uses high angles sparingly since most of the angles, especially in close-ups, are low shots looking slightly up at Coriolanus whereas other characters are shot level. We watch the Roman battle formations from the crane and also the movement of the war machine; later we look down past Sicinius standing on a column's base to judge Coriolanus and observe Cominius defending him. In *Love's Labour's Lost* we continue this perspective shot in the King's library, where both Holofernes (certainly exalted in his own estimation) and later Berowne (likewise superior) are seen atop the spiral library ladder, with a shot past them onto those below, an angle especially important in the lords' eavesdropping scene. During taping, the crane camera, of course, is used far more often than this sam⁻¹e indicates, but in such shots as these Moshinsky accentuates the height and angle, usually with interpretive intent, since his camera effects, while noticeable, are rarely casual or indulgent. Like all other elements, they serve his productions visually.

A number of the high shots, especially those past Oberon and Sicinius and Berowne, point up Moshinsky's emphasis on point-of-view camera work—a standard television element, usually done by shooting over an actor's shoulder—that he thoughtfully incorporates in these plays. In *All's Well*, in fact, he takes the effect to its limit and substitutes the camera for the person, so it becomes Helena's eye searching out Bertram among the lords called to attend the rejuvenated King, and again at the conclusion the camera as Helena pans a line of startled and amazed faces, the last of which is Bertram's—moments of Helena's greatest vulnerability, the second also her long-sought victory. The same kind of shot, less self-consciously arranged, can also be seen in *Cymbeline*, when, as the King peers at the page who seems so familiar to him, Moshinsky cuts to a long shot of the King seen from behind Imogen so we share his puzzled scrutiny, or in *Dream*, when we watch some of *Pyramus and Thisbe* from behind the newlywed audience. These occasional shots are very useful to a viewer, enhancing as they do a sense of character and perspective.

As well as selecting the camera angles purposefully, Moshinsky also blocks the action to provide specific views for the camera. More than any other director in the series, for instance, Moshinsky shoots characters in profile for soliloquies and duet conversations. The silhouette shots are a special instance of this technique, but repeatedly we watch half a face: in *All's Well* as Helena confesses her love for Bertram, much of the Bertram and Diana exchange, the Helena and Bertram dialogue, and the kiss at the play's end; in *Cymbeline* the group shot of Iachimo's and Posthumus's chess game, much of the dialogue between Imogen and Iachimo, Pisanio telling Imogen of his orders, and Iachimo's confession to the King; or in *Coriolanus*—the images of which are as profiled as a Roman coin—when the seated Coriolanus is convinced to confront the people and speak them fair as the camera shoots past Coriolanus sideways at the head of the table to catch Volumnia on the other side (a scene that uses shift of focus from Coriolanus to Volumnia quite effectively), Coriolanus as Aufidius kneels and welcomes him, or Aufidius listening and taunting through the last scene. Only by realizing how often the camera has an oblique angle on the actors in most television work does the comparative rarity of such extended shots at right angles to the conversation become apparent. Typically a shot favoring one actor is alternated with one from a complementary angle taken on the other speaker. (Both approaches can be seen in the Angelo/Isabella interviews in *Measure for Measure*.) Moshinsky's nonfavoring profiles balance the shots of dialogue and give crisp definition when only one actor is in view. And, knowing Moshinsky's careful eye, one is also reminded how often subjects are painted in profile in Vermeer and other art of the Renaissance.

Moshinsky leaves no technical element of production unexplored; he uses sound as carefully as he uses lighting and camera. Not a great believer in direct address to camera, a device he does not use before *Love's Labour's Lost*, he instead incorporates voice-overs for soliloquies and for thoughts amid dialogue. Imogen's musings are voice-over prior to Iachimo's entrance in *Cymbeline*. Helena's first soliloquy in *All's Well*, detached from previous action as a separate scene, also begins as voice-over, shifts to thoughts spoken aloud and to music, then returns to voice-over to comment on Parolles as he enters. Later, as she turns to select a husband, Helena's lines to the goddess Diana are done voice-over, prayerlike. Thus even as Moshinsky says he uses long camera shots objectively on Helena so we will have emotional distance, he simultaneously incorporates two subjective techniques, the voice-over and point-of-view or subjective camera shot only for Helena, bringing us closer to her.

In *Dream*, a far more open play, Moshinsky takes advantage of dubbing to have Puck actually speak with Demetrius's and Lysander's voices as he supposedly imitates them, and then as he harries the women to sleep, each one speaks her last line asleep, that is, as voice-over, a neat trick to round out the scene's sound effects. Moshinsky also uses a reverse sound bridge in that sequence, for whereas in most sound bridges the new sound precedes the new visual, in this case Lysander's voice continues after the cut to Puck with Demetrius, thus working to support what Demetrius thinks he is hearing. Moreover, the sound track of *Dream* is full of nocturnal forest noises—owls, insects, who knows what lurking in the dark. Even unseen, those sounds lend credibility to that studio-bound wood and make the sound-track flies in *Coriolanus*'s Roman heat almost puny by comparison.

Cymbeline has two fine sound bridges, the first in the opening sequence, which moves from a close-up of the fire to the King's meditating, disturbed face amid the sound of attendants talking nearby, as if the King half overhears them, before the visual cut to Cornelius's and the gentlewoman's low-voiced exposition. The other sound bridge is an even more subtle visual and aural meld. The scene mourning Fidele's death ends with a close-up of the flower placed in "his" hand, and the picture fades to black, as many of Moshinsky's scene endings do. We then hear Imogen awakening in the dark before we get the visual of her drugged nightmare changing to waking horror—a crafty and effective use of the dark frame. By contrast, in *Coriolanus* Moshinsky again calls on the voice-over for the warrior but, interestingly, only when he is in a military context. The man so outspoken he does himself in at home proves circumspect before the enemy: at the gates of Corioli he chastises his troops not aloud but to himself as he overlooks them from horseback and again utters no word as he confronts his mother and wife come to beg pity for Rome. Before Aufidius, too, much of his initial response is voice-over, which well portrays the tension between his thoughts and his words by clearly distinguishing them.

On the other side of a consideration of sound, the technical rather than the artistic, is the nature of the sound man, in this case Derek Miller-Timmins, who like John Summers was a regular on Moshinsky's production team, working all five shows. He is very particular about what the microphones pick up in the studio and about the consequences of theatrical illusion for sound. For instance, in *Coriolanus* camera rehearsals every step the horse took drove him mad until he insisted the hooves be muffled, a move that also dictated the framing of camera shots. A similar concern appeared in *Love's Labour's Lost*, where of the four lords only Berowne was allowed to wear his heavy-heeled shoes at the end of one park scene, and the sound track registers every step woodenly.

Though not formally trained to the medium of television, Moshinsky readily appreciated the potential and limitations of cameras and studio. He bows to few traditional rules, has a keen sense of what he wants, and works with those who can help him achieve it. Like Miller, he approached his productions with a painterly aesthetic, but he was more intent, more thorough with the settings and style than Miller, who enjoys mix-and-match. Like Miller, Moshinsky relies on his intellectual background, bases rehearsal on talk, and will freely invent business in the studio. For her part, Howell works more to concept, and because the pieces are planned to fit, she adds less in the studio. In their productions Miller, Moshinsky, and Howell are in some ways more visible as directors than many of the others in the series, which is partly a result of sheer quantity, but also of style and control; we detect their presence. Yet of all the directors Moshinsky may be the most visible. Like designer clothing, he displays his signature and signs on the fabric of his work.

True to Miller's spirit, in a series accused of being traditional or trying to be definitive Moshinsky insists these productions are interpretations. In interpreting the plays, he welcomed clashes of interests and attitudes that he found in the text, and he built them into the productions through casting. One of his production managers observed that casting is paramount in this series because most of any production comes out of the personalities of the actors. Recognizing that fact, many directors used it to enhance the action or gained an additional edge with unexpected casting. Moshinsky would intentionally combine old-school with more naturalistic styles of acting, exaggerate generation gaps, and cast with an eye to weaknesses as well as strengths to convey character. He also emphasized the sexual aspects of the plays, partly as a consequence of the plays he directed, most of which encourage such an interest—*All's Well*, *Dream*, *Cymbeline*, *Coriolanus*. Sexuality is a key to character and relationship in Moshinsky's work.

Thanks to Donald Sinden's rendition of the King, *All's Well* became even more sexual than Moshinsky intended. Of course, sexual tensions abound between Helena and Bertram and between Bertram and Diana, since Helena was not sexy for Bertram, but Diana was. Moshinsky also nudged Helena's healing of the King toward the sexual, as a return to potency, and Sinden made the most of it. What was a restrained and entirely justified suggestion in rehearsal, it is said, unaccountably—or undirectorially—grew in taping to the theatrical and lascivious nods of the King's warning about "those girls of Italy" and the X-rated inflection that interjects itself in his "beware of being captives / Before you [knowing nod, growl] *serve*." Given such a warm-up, the scene with Helena, apparently set in the lusty month of May, could only be heated; for all the coolness Moshinsky intended Angela Down to bring to Helena, Sinden managed to make the scene an arousal of the King climaxed by his long, hard kiss. This is not the kiss Helena sought, but the supercilious Bertram denies her that kiss in the production. The hothouse atmosphere competed with the animal magnetism between Bertram and Diana in another very steamy exchange; helped along by cameras catching flares in several takes, the sexual and technical tension in that scene was palpable, and once when Diana leaned over and nibbled the end of Bertram's finger, every man in the control room shifted uncomfortably along with the young count.

Paralleling the sensuality and the enforced interiority of the setting is a pattern of public and private exchanges closely related to light and dark in the production. The farewell to Bertram, the corridor in Paris, the choice of a husband, the arrival in Florence, and the denouement are all daylight scenes, while Helena's confession of love to the Countess, the King's bedroom, the aftermath of marriage in Paris, the hoodwinking and exposure of Parolles, Helena's plan for the bed-trick, and Bertram's meeting with Diana are all either night scenes lit by candles or firelight or in intentionally darkened surroundings such as the sickroom. Only at the end do all the nocturnal truths see the light of day, and Bertram, learning that "dans la nuit tous les chats sont gris," both affirms the match (as he does not do when forced to marry Helena in Paris) and kisses her in what Moshinsky sees as a happy ending.[7] (Yet in an interview used in the American press materials, Moshinsky calls the ending of the play bleak because the young gain no wisdom and says he consequently made the production beautiful as compensation.)

Accompanying this dark/light strand of the production, Moshinsky uses what will become one of his favorite visual effects—the mirror shot. During her initial soliloquy we first see Helena's face reflected in the mirror over the spinet; our first meeting of Parolles is, significantly, also by means of that mirror. Helena chases Bertram in what was known in production as "the Mirror Room," and later that night Lafew finds Parolles preening before a mirror panel and then tries to warn Bertram about him as the Count dresses before two smaller mirrors held by servants (this last arrangement is duplicated almost exactly in *Cymbeline* as Cloten is dressed in Posthumus's clothes). The mirrors call attention to appearance in the play, a major theme, and Moshinsky will frequently use mirrors when appearance on one level or another is important: we get any number of reflections in the pond of *Dream* and in *Cymbeline* see mirrored reflections not just of Cloten but also of the King in the opening scene and of the Doctor and Pisanio when called to the scheming Queen about the cordial. These shots are artful (in every sense) and meticulously arranged visual effects.

By way of linking scenes in *All's Well* Moshinsky moves from scene to scene with quick cuts, but several times he opens a scene with a close-up of a detail, then pulls quickly back to establish context (an opening device Miller enjoys using for its enigmatic qualities). Thus in Paris we once open with a close-up of the King's hand as the lords kiss it in taking leave for Italy, and in the next scene with a close-up of Bertram's hand clutching a flask containing yellowish liquid. We move to Florence with a close-up of the casket of gold and Helena dropping coins through her fingers, a fine narrative touch as the camera pulls back to reveal the Widow's face as she eyes that gold; only after she gives her consent to the bed-trick does the camera move left to show Diana intently listening at the table with Mariana in the background, and their presence as auditors alters our sense of the scene. One of the deftest scene shifts in *All's Well* is not a cut but a fade: as Helena ends her first soliloquy by thinking of the King's disease, the visual of the King lying abed slowly rises under the shot of Helena, and the two shots are briefly held in simultaneous vision before we complete the transition to Paris.

Another effect Moshinsky had planned was letting the action itself close the scene in the palace corridor on Helena's return to Paris from Florence. It is late afternoon and sun streams through the corridor windows, motes dancing in the air (before the studio ventilation dispersed the piped-in smoke; the lovely effect never lasted until taping started); attendants stand ready with shutters, and as the Astringer agrees to help Helena they put them over the windows, plunging the corridor into darkness—an automatic cut. The movement was lovely and took only a moment, but in editing, it seems, Moshinsky worked for the quickest possible cuts, effects notwithstanding, and so instead of waiting he cut just as the attendants start to move. Moshinsky's major editing excision, however, is of the show's last transition. In the studio he taped the epilogue with a very theatrical effect; like Olivier at the end of *Henry V*, the King-as-actor appeared in heavy make-up before a stage curtain, his posturing taken in extreme long shot with a cut to a medium shot before the end. Yet the director chose not to include that last speech in the edited production but to let the King's meditative, brooding comment across the fireplace conclude the action.

If *All's Well* was not a fairy tale in Moshinsky's hands, neither was the more literal fairy tale of *A Midsummer Night's Dream* a traditional moonshine and gossamer romp. Again Moshinsky renders the darkness or the night in psychological and psychosexual terms. Though everyone may not find Bertram's Helena cold or unappealing, Demetrius's Helena is almost a parody of stereotypical librarianlike unattractiveness; costumed to appear angular and flat-chested next to Hermia's soft curves, she also wears granny glasses. On the other hand, there is as Titania Helen Mirren, on whom the camera lovingly lingers in mid-pool or mid-bower (while there may be no clock in the forest, there is a rather nice double bed). Moshinsky revels in such characterization, continually effecting unions out of disparates in this production. At the play's beginning, the gulf between Theseus and his prospective bride and between father and daughter, ruler and subject, older generation and younger is manifest: the first shot of Hippolyta's tense pacing develops into a long shot of her facing armored Theseus across the room, then continues to a 2-shot as he moves toward her. The next scene is equally formal, restrained, and stiff; the long shot of those arrayed in the library surrounded by books and ensnared by the Law pits Theseus against Hermia at opposite ends of the table. As the action progresses Egeus moves behind the suitors, but for the most part stands appropriately between Demetrius and Theseus.

The restrained physical movement in these two scenes contrasts with the more mobile forest scenes, where every lover is part of the chase: moving, touching, kneeling, falling. The kinesis of the forest world can be seen in the cut to the fairies, for we find Titania and her train in stately procession through wood and pool, and since these fairies tend to take the shortest route between two points, they spend a lot of time wading and creating lovely reflections for the camera. Their progress is consistently slow, however;

the most active, fastest-moving fairy in the forest is naturally Puck, who interrupts Titania's fairies with their dew-buckets, hurls Flute about the pond dunking him, and grabs the fairy guarding the bower. All Puck's motions are quick; he pops into and out of frame with sharp movements as if materializing instantaneously, and his curious, mischievous face, continually sniffing as he senses human presence, hovers in the midst of the lovers' confusions, half of which he causes. The attendants to the fairy royalty are also readily distinguishable; Titania is accompanied by slightly ragged Renaissance-clad children with small wings, Oberon by a few henchmen, one a dwarf, clad in dark formal court garb (and Oberon's followers never touch the water but carefully walk around it). The fairy royalty themselves are somewhat more dishabille, Titania in a long gauzy white gown and Oberon unjacketed and open-shirted. Puck is much of a muchness with his master, dark and entirely bare-chested, with a punk look and spirit of menace in his mischief that is exacerbated by his pointed teeth. Moshinsky did not want a sweet, impish Puck; he wanted a character from *A Clockwork Orange*.[8]

Puck's sprightliness in entering camera shots—as when he returns with the love-in-idleness blossom, not walking or running but nearly hurtling into shot, or when he drops into frame on his last visit to Titania's bower, both entrances angled—establishes the suddenness, the unexpectedness of events in the wood on a midsummer's night. Moshinsky carries this device over to the lovers; as Hermia faints with wandering in the wood, he cuts to a close-up of her collapsing to the ground across frame, and later the abandoned Hermia is hurled down by Demetrius in a comparable cut to close-up. Puck's quick moves seem infectious.

Quick talk also figures in the forest scenes. Just as Moshinsky blocks the lovers to turn and shift, changing configurations and angles with the camera, he has them tumble the dialogue, overlapping speeches, all talking at once in a very naturalistic effect, carefully orchestrated so the necessary lines can be heard. Aural confusion communicates the lovers' tangle to the audience.

The forest's freedom from restraint, for better and worse, seems all the greater to an audience once the lovers return to Athens and themselves become audience; they almost disappear into the formal occasion, the more so since many of their remarks about the entertainment are cut. They are matched and married; we need know no more. The conclusion takes its tone more from the intent seriousness of the mechanicals' performance than from any nuptial festivity; we are plunged back into a formality akin to the opening's, though more congenial. Theseus and Hippolyta, more relaxed and warmer together since their discussion of the story of the night, take the focus, and that part of the pageant not shot in close-up is shot from behind their chairs, from their perspective. It is a strangely sober ending until Puck and his broom clear the table and the fairies swarm onto it; the blessing, too, is unsentimental, almost businesslike, and whereas the previous dawn brought the hunt to awaken and amaze weary lovers, this dawn does not disturb the couples of either realm. Irrepressible Puck enjoys the incongruity of mastering the empty hall as he gives the epilogue. It has been their dream, not ours; the vigor and exuberance of the production is in the forest with the lyrical fairy queen, energetic Puck, and flower-crossed lovers, not with Bottom or the hempen homespuns—an uncommon balance of the play's possibilities.

Up until *Cymbeline* Moshinsky had made fairly typical script emendations, trimming dialogue for pace and focus, dividing Shakespeare's scenes into smaller television scenes and once moving one, shuffling the order of scenes, cutting small scenes, and moving lines. In *Cymbeline*, he changes the text far more, using the same approach more extensively: some scene openings and closings are omitted, leaving only essential action; wherever possible, characters act rather than talk (as when Imogen rips open Posthumus's letter and reads instead of waxing eloquent about the seal) and do not comment expositorily (as when Imogen's entrance disguised as Fidele is cut; on television, we discover her as Belarius does). In addition, there is much division and reordering of action from IV.2 through V.1, and the battle is cut altogether; we get men going to battle or captured afterward but do not see Posthumus defeat and spare Iachimo or hear Iachimo's comments thereon. While the political aspect of *Cymbeline* can be diminished but not expunged, its military expression is omitted and the action refocused on the disturbed personal relationships. Most of the shifts result from the difference in medium, of course, for whereas Shakespeare often accomplishes everything he can while one set of characters is on stage (as here in IV.2), television editing allows for seemingly effortless cuts between groups and locales, a difference Moshinsky exploits.

Cymbeline is part of the same sunset/candlelight/firelight/mirrored world as *All's Well*, and it, too, is full of tables—the game of symbolic chess over which the wager is made, Iachimo's return, the Queen's discussion of drugs, the payment of tribute, the disposition of prisoners all occur across tables. Because characters are seated, not moving, camera work with Moshinsky depends more on cuts as compared with Howell's camera work in the histories; because her actors were usually on their feet she often moved them rather than always using cuts to develop the visual element or change angles. Despite the tables, Imogen and Iachimo prove active enough; Posthumus, however, is remarkably static or at least restrained. He agonizes through soliloquies in close-up, very still (though once, it must be admitted, the stillness is due to his wrists being manacled to a chair); just once, on agreeing Iachimo has won the wager, he smashes a chair. The fray amid the battle would have given him a chance to show active valor.

But it is Imogen's show, and Helen Mirren, who as Titania was embowered with an orgasmic ass, now finds herself the sleeping victim of Iachimo's rapelike voyeurism in a far more claustrophobic environment than the forest, given the bed's hangings and tapestries. Iachimo's trunk scene is shot almost entirely in close-up and medium close-up, using television's intimacy sometimes uncomfortably. In most of the shots Iachimo is over or behind the sleeping Imogen, his shirtless torso stark against the white sheets. Presented with salacious slowness, it is a lurid scene, a nightmare, and one of Moshinsky's camera shots links it to Imogen's other nightmare scene in the play. Just before Iachimo leaves by backing out of frame there is a shot from over Imogen's head toward Iachimo examining her body; the little we see of her is upside down in shot. Later when Imogen awakes beside the headless Cloten, the initial shot once more has her upside down in frame, that is, we look down from her head to her feet, and she is tossing as she was when Iachimo returned to the trunk. The inverted images visually bind the perverse experiences, both nightmarish, both sleep related, both lit by one candle. The second scene is also a varied set of close-ups, an inescapable horror. The camera, which starts by looking down on the figures, crabs left and lowers until it looks up at Imogen, then a cut offers an angle up the headless body until a last cut gives a high angle down on Imogen grotesquely smearing her face with the corpse's blood (blood which is gone, however, when she and the body are discovered in the snow by Lucius).

In *Cymbeline* one also begins to sense Moshinsky's version of repertory casting amid the familiar faces—not only Helen Mirren from *Dream*, but Michael Hordern from *All's Well*; Robert Lindsay, who was in both *All's Well* and *Dream*; Paul Jesson, Geoffrey Burridge, and John Kane, who appear again in *Love's Labour's Lost* along with Mike Gwilym, who also appears in *Coriolanus*; and several others in smaller roles. As with Howell and Miller, this recasting is not lack of imagination on the director's part but an appreciation of and interest in actors' skills. Smaller visual echoes occur with the dwarf, Oberon's attendant in *Dream*, who appears at the rear of the long shot throughout Iachimo's wager with Posthumus, and also with the huge floor globe from Theseus's library, here whitened in the King's council chamber, a globe that also shows up like a grace note in Holofernes's first scene in *Love's Labour's Lost*.

Steaminess finds new means of expression in Moshinsky's next BBC production. The Rome of his *Coriolanus* is a city of alleys and very clean, bright narrow streets; its most spacious environment is the Senate Chamber. The sense of enclosure in the streets supports Coriolanus's attitude toward the commoners; if a few gather the space seems full (an effect that also helps mitigate the number of supporting artists needed to swell out the crowd; we know this bunch well by the end of the show, nineteen very familiar faces that sway amid the debate over Coriolanus's consulship). There is somewhat more air space in Corioli and Antium, though they still fight and creep in corners.

There is also weather in this world, with heat and flies pointed up in one scene. Moshinsky's productions do acknowledge nature's changes as opposed to the eternally balmy state of most studio work. Though *All's Well* had a spell of flawless weather and the Navarre of *Love's Labour's Lost* is blessed with sunshine, *Dream* is soggy and part of *Cymbeline* snowbound. There is a physiological acknowledgment of change here, too; people sweat in some of Moshinsky's productions and provide shots of glistening flesh— Iachimo's torso climbing out of the trunk, Imogen's face on waking by Cloten's body, Caius Marcius and Aufidius in their homoerotic clash (the Roman general fights regular Coriolian soldiers with shirt on but strips down to meet Aufidius, and then apparently puts that carefully preserved blood-soaked shirt back on, for he wears it in the scene in which he is given the garland of the war, the only disheveled figure in a room full of clean and neatly uniformed soldiers). Throughout the production the temperature and the tension rise whenever the two warriors meet.

For all this naturalistic touch, *Coriolanus* is also a world of pose, like its architecture, and especially with the title character Moshinsky builds scenes to end with poses or postures held for camera. The entire military campaign is abstracted, an operatic tableau amid choral chants and synchronized movement, but after his solo venture through the backlit gates of Corioli Caius Marcius reappears, leans on the wall in an assertively self-conscious posture, and smirks as he slowly raises his sword at scene's end. In his involved grapple with Aufidius that starts with spears, moves to swords, and ends up hand-to-throat, the combatants relax their grip at the end for Caius Marcius to sneer, and once again the shot is held briefly.

These moments are part of a collaboration between actor and camera, for seeing cold, ramrod-stiff, haughty Coriolanus posing lets us detect those moments when he is less than totally controlled, not just the obvious uneasiness of his begging for voices—which has the production's one comic moment as he edges to the corner of the ledge and peers around the column, fearing to find more voices—but also the extreme close-up of his eyes, uneasy, almost frozen, as he is presented triumphant to the public in Rome. He is stiff, but with a defensive stiffness, uncomfortable making the public gestures, self-conscious amid the clamor and acclaim. At the end of the scene, he greets mother and wife in the street as everyone cheers, then the camera watches him look aside, silent and separate from the noisy group around him. A similar moment occurs after he is given the garland of the war and proclaimed "Coriolanus." He does not hold up the garland like the captain of a winning football team holds up the loving cup to show the team and crowd; he does not lead cheers. Unable to respond in these circumstances, he does not even smile. Instead, after standing silent he says tersely, "I'll go wash," and slowly looks aside, as isolated as if he were on Saturn. In addition to the visual effect of these shots, the delivery of the lines in them is noticeably different, for Alan Howard is not trilling the sound as he does when Coriolanus is before the Senate. The delivery here is flat, vulnerably human rather than exalted, not projected at someone but quiet, flopped down like a small dead fish.

That tone occurs again as Coriolanus is visited by his mother, wife, and child, begging mercy for Rome. It is a family scene with two auditors, Valeria, the official patrician Roman presence, and Aufidius, before whom Coriolanus always poses. He has held himself rigid and unresponsive before Cominius, as we are told, and before Menenius, as we have seen. Aufidius's presence here is crucial for Coriolanus and for the audience. The two men are desirously wary of each other, whether hurling spears in combat or words in confrontation. When Coriolanus presents himself to Aufidius in Antium, Aufidius stands cross-armed, observant, and impassive behind him as Coriolanus speaks. Then as Aufidius kneels and greets him, Coriolanus sits almost motionless before him, listening with hauteur, showing nothing. The same poker game atmosphere exists as the women enter to Coriolanus later, and we watch the few conscious gestures, the kiss and avowal of fidelity to his wife, the kneeling in tribute to honor his mother, the nuzzle of his son. Coriolanus's words remain chilly and formal—and few—until he finally heeds his mother. The camera angle drops to catch their private handclasp. Then his line delivery changes; we again hear the still, small voice without resonance, "Oh, mother, mother, What have you done?" As he was offered up for consul earlier, here he is offered up to death.

Moshinsky refines that sense of sacrifice in his production. On the videotape as Coriolanus turns to wife and mother the capitulation scene ends with Aufidius's aside. In the camera script, however, Coriolanus's last speech in that scene is still present, with the camera direction to "go in as Coriolanus lifts young Marcius." But in the studio or in editing that speech was cut and with it any softening of the sense of personal doom that pervades Volumnia's victory.

The change is tonally significant but not as wide-ranging as the changes in the last scene. In the camera script the death of Coriolanus may be at the hand of Aufidius but results from a group determination just as in his banishment from Rome. Though the conspirators are cut, their lines are still in, given to "People and Lords." Aufidius is playing to the crowd, incensing them to sanction his imminent deed. When he says, "Insolent villain!" the script next reads: "All: 'Kill, kill, kill, kill, kill, him!' (Coriolanus is killed. Aufidius stands on his body)," to be taken in close 2-shot without showing the sword. But except for that last brief camera direction, that is *not* the way the scene plays in the finished production.

The scene is a duet; everyone else might as well be mannequins, even though a senator speaks ineffectually. The two generals never take their eyes off each other; they stand in 2-shot toe to toe, and Aufidius slashes at Coriolanus verbally. No commoners or lords cry out for vengeance; the rest is silence but for these two. Coriolanus mentions "my lawful sword" and Aufidius calls him "insolent villain." Aufidius goes for the sword as Coriolanus does, and they grapple for it, but not in mortal conflict. The scuffle is brief; then together they raise the sword and place it as for a Roman suicide against Coriolanus's midsection. They pause, then Coriolanus gives a clear, quiet order, "Kill," there is another pause, and at last a strong downward thrust on the sword. Coriolanus grimaces, the shot cuts to close-up, there is a second thrust, a stern, self-directed "kill" from Coriolanus with a smirk. His third "kill" is barked; on the fourth Aufidius joins him in crying "kill." Coriolanus cries it again, then with Aufidius a last time as he slides, mouth open in a half grin, half laugh, out of frame. Aufidius continues to cry, "Kill," building up to one last scream with sword held over his head in both hands as for a thrust. In all, Coriolanus cries "kill" six times and Aufidius seven.

But this is a very different exchange from the one scripted, not only in assignment of lines but in effect. The action is in a public place, before other people, but as enacted it is an exceedingly private and personal action. Aufidius taunts Coriolanus, dripping scorn as if calling Coriolanus a sissy with "for certain drops of salt" and hitting each syllable of "mother" with a sharp, accusing edge. But here Coriolanus wills his doom—banishment and death —as much as he is betrayed into it. The greatest violence of the play is this long-suspended consummation to their meeting in battle; there the sword was smashed out of the hand, here jointly held. In the BBC script the studio photographer offers us the shot Moshinsky had in the camera script but ultimately denied us: "Pull back—see Aufidius stand on Coriolanus' neck." Moshinsky has very definite ideas about staging, however, and changed the action in the studio because "there was no good shot there" and "a dead body is not interesting"; he found his new approach "more chilling," shocking rather than banal as it would be were the body shown. The nub of the story, he explains, is Aufidius's victory, and these shots tell that story.[9]

Of all Moshinsky's productions with their art-related effects, *Love's Labour's Lost* seems most like a painting momentarily come to life. Whereas his other shows were set in a period or atmosphere based on certain artists' work, this production is more; as he said in the studio, "If you say it's set in the eighteenth century, that is your conclusion. It is set in Watteau." The poses in the production are not a matter of individual character; they permeate the style and look of the play except for the comic relief of Costard, Jacquenetta, Dull, and Moth. The production's cultivated ruins in the park, the soft gauzy background of vivid pastels, the carefully placed and postured secondary figures all derive from Watteau, and the aptness of this artist for the society and atmosphere of this play has previously been noticed by other directors, including the twenty-year-old Peter Brook in his first production for the Shakespeare Memorial Theatre in Stratford-upon-Avon in 1946. The description of Watteau in any art history text reveals why:

The academy . . . invented for Watteau the new category of *fetes galantes* (elegant fetes or entertainments). The term refers less to this one canvas [*Pilgrimage to Cythera*] than to the artist's work in general, which mainly shows scenes of elegant society, or comedy actors, in parklike settings. He characteristically interweaves theatre and real life so that no clear distinction can be made between the two. The *Pilgrimage to Cythera* includes yet another element—classical mythology. . . . But Watteau, by depicting the lovers on the point of departure, has added a poignant touch. A sense of the fleeting nature of happiness pervades all of Watteau's pictures. . . . His figures . . . recapture in Baroque form an earlier ideal of "mannered" elegance.[10]

These comments could as easily describe *Love's Labour's Lost*.

Moshinsky's *Love's Labour's Lost* is heavy on mannered elegance, light on both naïveté and earthiness. Almost everyone is sophisticated, and the banter, the linguistic elegance in which the play is so rich, gives a patina and a glibness to the action. Nothing can quite be credited; everything is subject to sportive repartee or rationalizations. With the emphasis on the manner, the style, and the language, no romance or deep feeling comes into play, which is just as well, Moshinsky believes, since he insists *Love's Labour's Lost* is not about love anyway but about comedy.

The mannered style is far more pointed with the exterior sets than the interior, therefore more with the ladies than the men. Not only are they often lit by footlights, but in their entrance scenes they were asked to play far more theatrically than naturalistically, as if they were on stage: listen but face out. When Maureen Lipman, the Princess, asked if that would not seem artificial, Moshinsky explained, "not with the pink lights" in these painterly shots. There must be tableaux, he added; that is the style for this set. In the library, the style is very different. And in that way he constructed the production's contrasts, once again casting for different acting styles to enhance that contrast, in this case combining comedians and actors. Maureen Lipman, the Princess, is a well-known British television personality, a comedienne, and John Wells, Holofernes, was also playing Mr. Thatcher in satiric sketches in the West End while doing *Love's Labour's Lost*. The one objection to Moshinsky's casting, in fact, came from literary advisor and Oxford professor John Wilders, who was very upset by having an adult play Moth, who is consistently referred to as a "boy" and a "juvenal" in the text. Moshinsky, wanting to use John Kane, turned those references into another of Armado's verbal eccentricities, but Wilders was never assuaged on the matter.

In starting his television work in 1980, Moshinsky had planned the details of *All's Well* meticulously and varied very little from that plan in the studio; in *Love's Labour's Lost* in 1984 he was exuberant and playful, and excited by the set and by the wealth of props provided by buyer Magda Olender, he quickly invented business to use them, as with the small silver statue of Atlas holding a globe, the top of which lifted off, just perfect for stuffing a crumpled sonnet into, as Moshinsky discovered. In the studio he also added the crystal sphere for Dumaine to use in that scene, the cupid on the cornice behind Berowne atop the ladder, and Longaville's suddenly thinking of a line for his poem and adding it as he reads, and he entirely changed Longaville's blocking from under the table to behind the easel and picture, which Moshinsky moved over for that purpose. As Holofernes and Nathaniel read Berowne's love letter in IV.2, Moshinsky asked Nathaniel to remove his wig and later built in his bustle to put it back on at the scene's end. In the library set and in Armado's room Moshinsky was continually dressing the backgrounds of his shots with a chamber pot or rearranging bookcases and pictures with designer Barbara Gosnold while joking about the action. During rehearsal while watching Armado in eyeshade awakened by Dull, for example, Moshinsky offhandedly joked that it was too bad the eyeshade had no tassels. In the last camera rehearsal he looked at the monitor and discovered it did have tassels, temporarily, thanks to the infinite resourcefulness and humor of props buyer Magda Olender.

Much of the direct address to camera developed out of that extemporaneous air as well; in beginning to rehearse his "And I, forsooth, in love" soliloquy (III.1), Mike Gwilym asked Moshinsky about delivery as if it had never been finalized, "Can I do it to camera?" and was answered, "Yes, but use the room." So they began exploring the set to refine movement, Gwilym building in direct address to the large classical statue as well as to camera. Moshinsky later gave the same kind of last-minute "to camera" instruction to the King during camera rehearsal of his opening speech.

On the other hand, some effects planned through rehearsal went by the way in the studio—Holofernes's cat, for one. In his first scene, standing atop the library ladder, Holofernes originally carried a small book and a large cat, directing any number of lines to the feline, patting it, and generally making the most of the living prop. The cat warmed the character of Holofernes, and on his exit he casually handed the animal to a most perplexed Nathaniel. But the tractable cat was black against Holofernes's black coat and was scarcely visible (all three cats the trainer had brought were solid black), besides which it was thought distracting and disturbing to the actor, so it was omitted for taping.

As in Jane Howell's productions, members of the camera crew for *Love's Labour's Lost* were very supportive of and helpful to the actors, explaining angles and problems or making suggestions. Camera supervisor Garth Tucker had worked with Moshinsky on *Coriolanus* and so understood the nature and rhythm of his shots. Unlike Howell and other directors who arrange camera shots to be able to tape long sequences or entire scenes unbroken, Moshinsky more often breaks action once or several times while taping some scenes to reposition the cameras, going back a line or two to get a running start. His final emphasis is on getting the pictures, for the acting will accommodate to the demands of the medium, especially when the bottom line in television is being seen. Some sense of Moshinsky's camera values became apparent, for instance, during rehearsal of the end of the lords' eavesdropping scene, when Berowne rationalizes their shift from scholars to lovers. Seated behind the small table, Gwilym told Moshinsky he felt very off camera during the scene with the men to his left and the camera to his right. Moshinsky responded that the slight profile was a much stronger shot, less interviewlike. Then, reviving his devices from *Coriolanus*, he told the camera crew he wanted all the close-ups off center. As a result, here as in his other productions the visual composition of the camera shots is unlike usual television fare; there is a concern not just for good shots but for carefully defined artistic and aesthetic shots.

Ask Elijah Moshinsky about the value or achievement of the BBC Shakespeare series and he is quick to respond. When he joined the series, he stated, it was artistically in disrepute, and elsewhere he asserted that "it was only Jonathan Miller's appointment that pulled the BBC Shakespeare series out of its artistic nosedive,"[11] but by the time he made *Love's Labour's Lost* the BBC productions were seen as superior to the RSC's. The televised productions reversed the idea of what Shakespeare could be, he felt; not mannered shouting nor overly theatrical, these Shakespeare productions could be psychologically valid. And in addition to providing a major alternative in producing Shakespeare, he continued, the series is permanently accessible and offers good performances.[12] If his view is correct, he can be justifiably proud of his part in the series's achievement.

6   Jane Howell's
         Approach

The visual lushness of Moshinsky's productions complemented strong performances and directorial interpretations, but representationalism was not the only successful method of televising Shakespeare in the BBC series. Jane Howell stylized every one of her productions in the BBC Shakespeare series, basing her decisions as much on theatrical assumptions as on those of television. Of all the directors in the series, Howell seemed most receptive to and most creative with stark settings, not by having no set at all as in the RSC televised tragedies but by an inventive use of unit sets. As she explains, in doing Shakespeare on television she knew the rules were to have one set, a theatre set such as Shakespeare's, by which she means one that suggests rather than one that duplicates. In *The Winter's Tale*, the *Henry VI–Richard III* sequence, and *Titus Andronicus* the setting for each was one predominant structure—the wedges, the wooden stockade or "playground," and the amphitheatre respectively.

The rules she follows are the original production rules—not strict Elizabethan staging but the fact that one scene follows another immediately and that the focus must be on the actors. They are the essential reality,[1] not the set, for Howell believes a production must give the audience a chance to contribute with their minds, their imaginations.[2] "I don't see the point in a lot of explicit scenery or filming on location," she says; "if you are going to do Shakespeare filmically, then you've got to do it like Kurosawa in 'Throne of Blood' and go the whole hog. What you need in television is a space which can be inside or outside and which leaves you free to create. Once you start having all those palaces, it takes away from people's imagination and ties it down."[3] (Even so, she thought the location work of the BBC *Henry VIII*, for instance, worked

Jane Howell in camera rehearsal for a scene of 1 Henry VI with Alencon (Michael Byrne, left), Reignier (David Daker), and the Bastard of Orleans (Brian Protheroe, right). © BBC

very well.) Hers is obviously not a view limited to the television-must-be-real belief.

Using one set, however, does not mean the setting is static or unchanging. In all six of her productions, a number of design variations are wrought on the basic circular unit: in *Winter's Tale* it is color and textural changes as the huge wedges go from Sicilia's winter white to gray and stony for Bohemia's coasts, golden for Bohemian fields, and a creeping spring-green verge back in Sicilia. The stockade or adventure playground of *Henry VI–Richard III* experiences the wear and tear of the Wars of the Roses; the bright colors fade, more doors appear, and the set looks charred and chipped by the end of the sequence. In those plays as in *Titus* with its gray brick amphitheatre, Howell is also able to effect changes by having small pieces added: in the histories, a dais and canopy for a throne or a green and brown shag rug and some stylized trees for a garden; in *Titus*, a table, curtains, a plank-roofed colonnade, or a single tree and a vast net to shroud the set and suggest the murky glade. The technical challenge—to vary a given set so that it seems interior or exterior, new or old, public or private—brought out the best in the BBC set and lighting designers.

The most noticeable aspect of Howell's productions, however, is their strong conceptual basis and visual imagery, more noticeable perhaps because the plays are not rendered realistically, so the concepts show. For instance, in the Wars of the Roses plays, "it struck me," Howell observed, "that the behavior of the lords of England was a lot like children—prep school children."[4] Howell underscores this view of the nobles' behavior in *1 Henry VI*, I.3, where Winchester and Gloucester challenge each other from hobbyhorses while their men brawl, after which Howell cuts to three French boys fighting over a weapon at the start of I.4. Just as the juxtaposition of these fights comments on the nature of the former, having the men riding hobbyhorses undercuts their concern for power and precedence. Howell uses much the same kind of transitional comment in *2 Henry VI* where, after the lords have plotted the fall of Duke Humphrey and his wife, as II.2 opens, we see several boys, the sons of the Duke of York, bowling; the pins knocked down in the foreground of shot are painted like a lord and a lady. For Howell as for the RSC televised plays, the visual element of a production complements the text and often works to interpret it, as it can and should in the medium of television.

Winter's Tale was the start of Howell's experience with the Shakespeare series, and of all her productions it has the most highly strung cast and the most abstract set. "It looked wonderful in the studio," she reflected, implying that the effect may not have fully transferred to the television screen. Amid the seasonal changes of the script—the winter, the harvest, the spring, all suggested in production by a lone tree—she sought an image for the eternal, rendered by the huge wedges arranged against a monochromatic,

The Winter's Tale *unit set registered colorful seasonal changes on a series of wedges and a tree. Young Shepherd (Paul Jesson).* © BBC

Designer Oliver Bayldon's unit set for the Wars of the Roses tetralogy began 1 Henry VI *in pristine condition painted with bright reds, blues, and yellows. Talbot (Trevor Peacock) and Joan of Arc (Brenda Blethyn).* © BBC

evenly lit cycloramic curtain. This geometric abstraction may have taped a bit coldly, and it does leave a great deal to the audience's imagination even if it does change color. *Winter's Tale* also displays her use of the camera, which is not just there invisibly to record movement and dialogue, but which is consciously an eye, a perceiver that some characters, especially Autolycus, address, raise an eyebrow toward, or glance at knowingly. Howell frequently engages that camera eye and its accompanying sound-boom ear in every production to provide inside information or private reaction, whether verbal or facial, giving the camera the role of confidant in these productions, a technological adaptation of an age-old theatrical tradition. Howell says she likes seeing faces on television and direct address to camera, as her productions reveal.[5]

Howell's focus, like her productions', is on the actors and their performance because she believes the power of Shakespeare's work is in the words. They have to communicate clearly, and the audience must listen.[6] This belief affects her view of acting, which is

By 3 Henry VI *the unit set shows the ravages of the long conflict in its worn, charred doors and chipped, weathered boards. Richard (Ron Cook) and Young Clifford (Oengus MacNamara).* © BBC

firmly antimethod in its traditional sense. You cannot just work yourself up to an emotional crisis and then do a scene, she says; in Shakespeare you must let the words lead you to emotion.[7]

Howell works supportively with her casts, which become almost familylike, and as a result she likes to work with actors she knows. For instance, Paul Jesson, David Burke, and Peter Benson all appear in *Winter's Tale* and in the *Henry VI–Richard III* sequence; Brian Protheroe, Trevor Peacock, and a number of other actors are in *Henry VI–Richard III* and in *Titus*; Anna Calder-Marshall in *Winter's Tale* and in *Titus*. In fact, the spirit of repertory is evident with all the directors during the Miller years, an unofficial and loose experiment in the company approach to production used by both the Royal Shakespeare Company and the National Theatre in England, here adapted to television.

Howell's predilection for such casts manifested itself most strongly in her approach to the *Henry VI–Richard III* sequence of history plays, for which she established a full-scale repertory company. The plays demand huge casts, both of speaking characters and warriors, but rather than work with deMille-sized ensembles, for practicality she insisted on casting a smaller number of actors in multiple roles carefully selected for thematic effect. Because the audience was intended to recognize the repetitions, Howell chose them thoughtfully, as when Trevor Peacock who plays chivalrous Talbot in *1 Henry VI* is also cast as rebel Jack Cade in *2 Henry VI*; when David Burke plays Humphrey, Duke of Gloucester, then Dick the Butcher and Catesby, ever the man supporting and advising the leader; when Peter Benson as priest sings the eulogy for Henry V that opens the sequence before he appears as a pious Henry VI and finally as the priest who meets Hastings in *Richard III*; and when Ron Cook, later to be seen as hunchback Richard, early on appears as a messenger, a villager, and a hunchback porter. After seeing these faces in various guises for three plays, Howell says, "*Richard III* should be like a nightmare,"[8] an idea she developed even further in the production.

Planning the sequence and its casting became a months-long, intricate affair. For Howell the plays are director's pieces, individual aspects of which the actors realize, for whatever the production limitations of budget or time, the quality is up to director and cast. The director must give the production staff and the actors a "signpost," she says, to indicate a direction. At the first rehearsal for the *Henry VI–Richard III* sequence she talked for two hours setting the direction for their endeavor ("I've never talked so long"), and one of the actors later told her if she had done nothing else during the productions those comments would have led them.[9]

In terms of these specific plays, however, Howell felt no production limitations; there was enough money and enough rehearsal time. The underwriters' brief describing production style was another matter, though, since "leeway softens things," she says, and the period insistence can be slightly limiting since in directing a play "you must do it about today; we live today." The set for the tetralogy was a modern structure "that said something to us today—but also had a medieval flavor" for Howell. Based on a British adventure playground, a "multi-level [jumble] of doors, ropes, platforms, catwalks, walls" made from salvaged or surplus lumber,[10] the set provided adaptable, open, multilevel space that could be either interior or exterior and also supported the idea that the action of the play had the nature of an elaborate, increasingly vicious and violent game, a cult game, something along the lines of American football, and the costumes, especially in *1 Henry VI* and *2 Henry VI*, reflect some of this sense. Armor only appears later in the sequence; at first the quilted leather battle garb and protective pieces are visual cognates for football pads, and even the helmets have metal face masks so actors sometimes look like quarterbacks barking signals. The shift of values over the course of the Wars of the Roses also seemed very contemporary to Howell:

What I was concerned about in the first play . . . was that for a long time, the code of the people had been chivalry. But with the death of Talbot one starts to see a demise of chivalry. . . . When times change and codes vanish, people don't realize for a long time, so one still has the remnants of chivalry in Part

Two, as upheld by Gloucester. With Gloucester's death, anarchy is loosed and you're left with a very different set of values—every man for himself. You're into a time of change in which there is no code except survival of the fittest—who happens to be Richard.

What interests me is that I think we are in that sort of state today, a time of change.[11]

For *Titus*, however, she felt the best setting of that intense struggle for honor and revenge would be Northern Ireland, but such a contemporary setting was beyond the series's brief, so she opted for quasi-historical togas and Roman armor. The BBC gives admirable care to such production detail; even Tamora's bright red hair and huge bead-and-bone jewelry, a contemporary punk look, was "very tribal and historically accurate. The tribe we based the Goths on in the production did dye their hair red," Howell noted.

Even a single show by Howell can be intense, as *Titus* indicates. Attracted to the play, as a number of directors said of their choices, "because I didn't know how to do it," Howell confessed that making sense of or finding a route through the violence was not easy. Amid all the slaughter, it was actually the killing of the fly and the presence of a young boy amid all this trauma that first caught her attention. To him, Howell realized, it would be a nightmare, as it also seemed to her, and she drew support from Titus's desperate query, "When will this fearful slumber have an end?" So she shaped the production around the boy and the idea of dream, making him a silent observer to much more of the action than is scripted, accentuating his watchful role by having him wear glasses.

The production quite appropriately opens with a close-up of a skull beside which appears young Lucius's face as the camera pulls back to reveal him at the funeral procession for the Emperor. Using superimposed images, soft, slow two-way fades (one image coming into view as the other vanishes), and wipes (one image moving in from the edge horizontally or vertically to replace another), Howell builds the dream effect through her editing, including not just the skulls at opening and close but for transitions flames (as when banished Lucius leaves Rome), smoke, or a dog barking (before the hunting scene). Even in mid-scene she superimposes an empty tribune's mask over Titus as he pleads for his sons, actually showing the hard, unresponsive quality Titus speaks of. The accretion of images and the number of scenes that open with a close-up of young Lucius's face both contribute to the dreamlike or subjective sense of the action.

In addition to including young Lucius in extra scenes, Howell rearranged and divided the action in the long and action-packed I.1 so the play would open with Titus's entrance to Rome and a separate burial scene before the political dispute erupts: "It makes no sense if it opens with Saturninus and Bassianus yelling at each other; an audience just wonders, 'Who are they? What's up?' It's better to see a power vacuum." Also Titus was a surer hook for a viewer, Howell thought.[12] Thus to give a stronger narrative effect we see Titus in action rather than simply hear how he usually sacrifices a prisoner upon his return.

Howell uses the visual element to show the political crisis wordlessly. The Emperor's garland and scepter are ceremonially removed from the dead body by the tribunes, and the body is carried out with the two sons following; they pause and drop their handheld masks long enough to glare at each other and to clarify their contention. The masks on the rest of the procession give them an unchanging, unresponding face; however, the masks Saturninus and Bassianus hold up indicate the difference between their public appearance and private intents. As that procession passes, Titus's military procession enters—the enshrouded bodies of his four slain sons, the war trophies, the Goth prisoners, and finally Titus, who enacts a ritual libation and lights the ritual flame, as the action overlaps political and military, home and abroad, war and peace. By the end of the scripted morning's action, the war, too, has masked itself but continues, no longer on distant battlefields but right in Rome, which becomes its own "wilderness of tigers."

The public ceremony makes way for a private family ceremony; as the Andronici proceed to the tomb, Titus pauses by one son's body, his staunch Roman code mastering paternal grief. The camera catches the look, then moves in for a close-up of the corpse's face (which during camera rehearsals had been stained with dried blood). The crypt, dark and cavelike, lit by candles and torches, is hung with shrouded skeletons or mummies, the first of several scenes that involve death and things hanging. Soon we see, for instance, Titus's sons Quintus and Martius raised from the pit in a net where they hang with Bassianus's trapped, dead body. The death/hanging pattern develops again late in the play not only with Saturninus's judgment on the pigeon-toting clown and Lucius's threat to hang Aaron and his son, but even more vividly in this production in the next scene where Tamora and her sons, disguised as Revenge, Murder, and Rape, appear against a background of sides of meat hung on poles (the prop meat was from the movie *Oliver*, the props buyer said). It seems a strange setting, as if Titus were by avocation a butcher, but recognizing that makes the thematic point that he indeed has been a butcher and that butchery is the subject of the play. The raw meat becomes all too apt a context when Titus hangs Chiron and Demetrius upside down next to real animal carcasses (kosher lambs from an Arab butcher) and slits their throats as in ritual slaughter.

The development of that hanging meat pattern, of course, joins with the series of banquets that culminates in the meat pie containing her sons' flesh being served to Tamora. That series of meals begins in Howell's *Titus* as in the script with III.2, the fly-killing scene at Titus's family dinner, but Howell adds another dinner scene in IV.2, which opens with Tamora's sons sprawled on a food-cluttered table—the central dish is a meat pie—a scene that develops into a food fight just before young Lucius's entrance with Titus's gift of weapons. (In the first camera rehearsal, Demetrius's hand was actually in the meat pie as he lay across the table, a grisly and ironic serendipity, for the next meat pie we see, as Hamlet would say, is not the one where they eat but where they are eaten. Note that Titus, when he eats, eats soup.) Meat, both raw and cooked, abounds at the end of the play. Not only do the pieces of the pattern fit—the bodies, hanging, slaughter, devouring—but Howell intends them to fit. She often chooses a symbolic visual element to express meaning; such a pattern in production does not occur by chance.

Just as she divides the opening scene for television, Howell also divides the last scene: the banquet with its bloody vengeance is separated from the selection of the next Emperor, which thereby becomes more formal and also more disturbing for our having watched the effects of power on Saturninus and knowing Lucius's cold, ruthless nature, his having perfected the public mask. We see the figurative mask in action in this ceremonial mourning and also the mask of his politically manipulative uncle Marcus. Only young Lucius shows real concern, real grief at the deaths, the violence, and the betrayals he has witnessed. Howell also balances scene against scene through the middle of the play, as with IV.4 and V.1, the Roman meeting during which the pigeon-carrier is sentenced to hang and Lucius's scene with the Goths during which he nearly hangs Aaron. In each the assembly is masked (if Roman) or hel-meted (if Goth), and one speaker is on high opposite them, Saturni-nus on his throne, Aaron on the ladder. Howell planned the paral-lels, intending a parodic relationship.

Not only is the scenic presentation of the action and its interpre-tation carefully shaped and controlled but also the casting. With Trevor Peacock as Titus, the other principals were selected to com-plement his stature. The look of the show also results from many considered, interpretive decisions about the design for the space and lighting, the actors, their costumes, their movement, and the camera angles and interplay of shots, enhanced by editing and by music, especially the music for Aaron's plotting and the rape. Al-though Howell says a director's job is not to be noticed, in their thoughtful arrangement and tight development her productions testify to her invisible guidance.

To appreciate the effect of the *Henry VI–Richard III* sequence, then, we must realize that the power of a single production is multi-plied, the production is four times larger, the patterns varied, some within a play, some across the sequence, demanding greater control and offering greater possibilities. Howell exhibits many of the same strengths, the same effects, in the tetralogy as in the later *Titus*. She had developed her own solution to some of Shakespeare's chal-lenges and used what she learned. For instance, when the actor playing Alarbus in *Titus* later shows up as the third Goth meeting with Lucius, when Titus's kinsmen also double as Goths, we can see her continuing the repertory casting she used so effectively and on a far larger scale throughout the histories. Those reappearing faces establish the repetitiveness of events and attitudes in the sequence—the ambitions, the efforts to protect, the promises, the betrayals. Consequently, the historical sequence is not just a welter of faces in a power-mad struggle; it is a study of the hunger for power itself.

Amid its very serious theme, however, the historical sequence is also a celebration of performance, and Howell incorporates this aspect, too. Especially in *1 Henry VI*, she says, "a lot of it is very simply based on good, old-fashioned theatre gags." So along with the unit set and her affirmation of the dynamics of Shakespeare's plays in theatrical performance, she also affirms the inherent theatricalism of the material and even works the title into the opening of each production: on a banner over the door in *1 Henry VI* (at I.2) and *2 Henry VI* (at I.1) and on a shroud for the pile of dead bodies in *3 Henry VI*, while Richard himself chalks the eponymous title on a board at the start of his play. Proclaiming the performance as performance, the actors proceed to confide to the camera and audience, to glance at the camera to emphasize a response, and to enjoy the potential of theatre and television in combination. We see this impulse in the treatment of the witchcraft/entrapment scene in *2 Henry VI* (I.4), where the props are set, the sound effects readied, the book laid out, and we see a carefully planned spectacle with thunder sheet, drum, horn, recitation, "inspiration," and pyrotechnics; the presentation is self-consciously theatrical as Howell uses her material and blends her mediums.

In content the histories share with *Titus* an interest in plotting and revenge, public forums and private talks. The challenge of the histories, as producers of the BBC Shakespeare series knew from the very start, is the battle scenes. On Shakespeare's stage a battle is a scene "Where—O for pity!—we shall much disgrace / With four or five most vile and ragged foils, / Right ill-dispos'd in brawl ridiculous, / The name of Agincourt" or Shrewsbury or St. Albans, for it is, as the Chorus in *Henry V* insists, an action that must be enlarged by the audience's imagination. On film, of course, a director rents several thousand extras and marches Harry to Agincourt,

Napoleon to Moscow, or Genghis Khan anywhere he wants to go. But in a television studio, with a nonrealistic unit set, how does Jane Howell stage a battle—or rather, the seemingly endless series of battles comprising the Wars of the Roses? By making choices, developing a pattern, and hiring a special second company of twenty-eight fighters along with a good fight arranger for all four shows, in this case, fight manager Malcolm Ranson, one of the best. The progression of battles, which begins with the French soldiers' comic, almost Keystone Kops charge through the set's double doors and their immediate flight back through them early in *1 Henry VI*, gets bloodier even in that first play, as with the treatment of the cannon shot explosion killing Salisbury. Now we are seeing weapons and their destructiveness—and blood.

Using camera and editing potential, Howell frequently builds battle montages—quick shots of particular exchanges and deaths amid a larger fray to give a sense of scope—and also uses slow motion to focus on specific confrontations and blows. In *2 Henry VI*, for instance, York and old Clifford finally meet at St. Albans; each admires the other's courage but challenges the other's allegiance. They fight all over the set, a long sequence in which a drum beat underscores the action; several times Howell switches to slow motion so we see a turn, a grimace, a violent slash, or an exchange of blows that seems much more powerful at this slower speed. The drum beat also slows, sounding more like a heart beat or a death knell. With the slow motion we actually become more involved; we can better see the strategy of the combatants, their thrust and counter. We also gain a sense of subjective time, for what seems fast paced to an observer has, with the total concentration of a mortal risk, a longer duration. We sometimes see principals fighting in the midst of a skirmish, but more usually, as with York and old Clifford, we see a single combat on an otherwise empty set. Additional variations occur in weather—they fight in bright light, in smoke, finally in snow—and in weaponry, as Henry Fenwick reported following a conversation with fight arranger Ranson:

In *Part 1* [there were] "romantic swords and shields or single sword"; *Part 2* had a few more maces and Cade's rebels used an assortment of brutal though everyday implements for kill-ing—pitchforks, sickles; in *Part 3* a lot of maces and axes were used, as well as bows and arrows, and halberds and spears were introduced "and shields started being used as an offen-sive weapon." The spears that the soldiers use against this feared figure of Richard, keeping him at a distance, had there-fore been carefully placed in advance so that they were not totally new. The ball and chain which was the only possible weapon for Richard to use if he were to fend off large numbers of attackers was also introduced earlier. "I introduced a ball and chain in *Part 2* for Richard. He didn't fight with it, but you did see him with it. . . . You can keep quite a few people away from you with a ball and chain. . . . The idea of that was to get the feeling still of fear of the soldiery for Richard."[13]

If the weaponry was carefully orchestrated for Richard, so were the confrontations leading up to the fight at Bosworth. In *1 Henry VI* Ron Cook, who later plays Richard, is a hunchback porter to the French countess; after she leaves with Talbot, Talbot's men cir-cle around the servant and stamp at his feet, tormenting him and making him jump, so that having soldiers surrounding a hunch-back becomes a visual image. In *3 Henry VI* when Richard's father, the Duke of York, is captured by Margaret's forces, a host of sol-diers encircle him with spears and swords, an entrapment that fore-shadows Richard's at Bosworth. Richard, too, finds himself sur-rounded but refuses to be captured, fighting to the death through spear thrusts and sword gashes. His death is carefully staged so that he dies on his knees impaled on Richmond's sword; he remains in this posture while Richmond gets the crown, so that as the sol-diers kneel in allegiance, Richard also appears to be kneeling at the fore of the group, a startling visual irony.

In portraying the seemingly incessant battles in France and En-gland, Howell does not celebrate violence, nor does Shakespeare. The dying speeches of mortally wounded characters are lessons on fortune, evanescence, and life's endeavors. For those without speeches, Howell lets them silently attest the destruction; at the close of *2 Henry VI*, for example, King Henry kneels before the body of a dead soldier, and later Salisbury pauses before the same synecdochic corpse, recognizing the cost of the wars. Howell extends this confrontation with death from the participants to the audience: the last shot of 2 *Henry VI* is a montage of bodies covered with wounds and blood, all left from the battle at St. Albans. The images are forceful and also preparatory, linking the plays, for the next play opens with a stack of dead bodies, as if to say there is more to come. Captures, killings, and bodies subsume the action. Before the set piece of the father who has killed his son and son who has killed his father, young Rutland and then York are taken and killed; after it, Prince Edward and Henry are killed. But Henry's death is not on the battlefield, and with Richard's blow in the Tower the action of the sequence shifts from the rites of war to subterfuge and murder. If bodies abound in 3 *Henry VI*, only Richard dies on camera in *Richard III*, though the play is full of murders and deaths. Yet to culminate the sequence, the long wars, the lives they have cost, it is not enough to have Richard's corpse and Richmond crowned; the action of the tetralogy is much larger than the figures who terminate it. Acknowledging this fact, Howell concludes the sequence with a long pan up a stack of dead, maimed, shirtless bodies to wild-haired Margaret, a Queen of Death, who sits atop the pile laughing and cradling the mangled body of Richard in what Howell called a "reverse Pieta." It is a stark and horrifying image, reminiscent of those in Resnais's *Night and Fog* and designed for the same mnemonic purpose.

In the histories as in *Titus* we see Howell using processionals, not just for spectacle, though they are effective in that regard, but to develop a pattern, as in the opening of 2 *Henry VI*, Margaret's triumphal arrival at Henry's court. The white carpet is rolled out, confetti flies as it had for Joan la Pucelle in I.5 of *1 Henry VI*, and Suffolk proudly introduces the woman he has chosen as Henry's bride, a woman who is quickly disappointed. Her pride hardens her in this foreign court; the Margaret of 3 *Henry VI* starts to evolve. Later in 2 *Henry VI* during Cade's rebellion Howell sets up another processional entrance carefully arranged to reflect the initial one: Cade comes in to his followers (IV.6), and they strew his path with stolen brocade—red, blood-colored brocade—to make a carpet for him, and a pillow has burst so the air is full of small feathers, confettilike. We see Cade speaking from a chair on a raised platform just as King Henry does, and that seat gains importance through the play since the throne is the subject of the wars. York carefully sits on the dais steps and leans on the throne in 2 *Henry VI*. We expect another procession as 3 *Henry VI* opens with a shot past the throne down the formal carpet to the door. We get an ax head breaking through the door, followed by York, his sons, and their party, and York does finally process up to take the regal seat from whence he confronts the startled Henry, a move that sets up the later shot of Richard as crowned king led by Buckingham in a procession to the throne.

Howell also supports her view that the action has elements of a violent sport by the way she incorporates chants and cheers in the production. In *1 Henry VI* it is reported early on that the English troops rally to the battle cry, "A Talbot!" (I.1). In Howell's production it serves again as their battle cry at Orleans (I.6 and II.1). As Talbot rouses his entrapped forces at Bordeaux (IV.2), they gather round his raised figure, swords and lances extended, and shout, "A Talbot!"—a tableau we see in both medium and long shot, so we see the triangular shape of the tableau, which Howell reiterates by cutting to a torch flame of the same shape. Much is made of the tableau, of course, because Howell is returning to it before IV.5 where, just having heard both York and Somerset deny Talbot aid, we see the troops turn from their chant to face outward into the darkness, and of course the name echoes throughout the exchanges of Talbot Senior and Talbot Junior. Also, in *1 Henry VI* we see Joan la Pucelle carried on the shoulders of the French soldiers like a winning coach after a big game, a move repeated in *2 Henry VI* by the rebels (perhaps more like international soccer fans in this case) with Jack Cade, whose name they chant (IV.3). Later we see York's sons carried on their followers' shoulders. And the fires Cade's rebels start are not the controlled theatrical spectacle set to entrap Gloucester's Duchess, though they share an element of witchcraft with that scene, especially once we see the close-up of Cade's demonic grin. Law, literacy itself, the order of the commonweal are engulfed by their consuming flames and harsh injustice, just as the monarchy and country are consumed by the nobles' ambitions.

Besides flames, 2 *Henry VI* is full of heads, in close-ups, certainly, but more especially the disembodied heads of Suffolk (we hear two strokes off camera; history tells us it actually took six strokes with a rusty sword to behead him) and of Cade's victims Lord Say and Cromer. Seeing Gloucester's head convinces Warwick he was murdered, and Winchester's death raving is all head-acting (besides, his head gains visual prominence against the white shirt and white sheets). There are a few grace notes to the heads, both involving Cade's head. As Iden drags the slain rebel from his garden, Cade's head lies on his wide outspread collar as if on a platter, and later as Iden brings the head to Henry and obligingly kneels to be knighted, he offhandedly passes the sack containing the rebel's head to York, sweets to the sweet. York's own head ends up on display in *3 Henry VI*. Iden's treatment of Cade's body, of course, parallels Richard's unceremonious dragging away of King Henry's body at the end of *3 Henry VI*, where the King's arms spread into an outstretched crucifixional position to complete Howell's image of sacramental slaughter (there are, she points out, bread and wine on the table, and lighting designer Sam Barclay lit a crossbar amid the darkness to the rear "as a little gift").[14]

To build a pattern with the three York sons at the end of *2 Henry VI* and opening of *3 Henry VI*, Howell adds Clarence to five scenes: in *2 Henry VI* to V.1 and V.3 (and also Edward here) and in *3 Henry VI* to I.1, I.2, and II.1. Thus Clarence enters with his brothers to support his father before the battle of St. Albans, then helps to celebrate the victory, stands by the throne after his father assumes it in *3 Henry VI*, and helps convince his father to claim his right to the throne, not abide as heir. Aside from gaining a sense of "we band of brothers" with these additions, Howell works toward II.1 of *3 Henry VI* for the vision of three suns with all three sons present. With a single-camera developing shot, she arranges the actors' movements carefully so that during dialogue Richard breaks across toward camera, Edward steps up beside Clarence, and when Richard turns and steps back they are suddenly all in line angled across the left of frame to have the vision of the suns. It is deftly achieved.

As this action indicates, Howell is very good at blocking for extended single-camera sequences, keeping actors and camera moving in an intricate exchange that appears effortless but is actually a precision movement for all concerned, like jets flying in formation only inches apart. Those single-camera sequences and long takes occur frequently throughout the histories; as she told Henry Fenwick, they are "part of the production's fundamental approach."[15] That means extra planning and concentration for the cameras, for those in front of them, and for the designers behind them, especially with lighting. Since everyone is moving, angles are changing, and nearly everything can be seen, the lighting designer's primary concern amid all the choices and rigging is to avoid shadowing. Even with the best lighting, though, shadows can transpire amid movement, and it is useful for a viewer to watch a scene just to observe how the actors trained not to steal another's light deal with shadows. The alert, experienced, and sensitive ones will instantly make small compensatory adjustments; some will never see or acknowledge the shadow. Only a high degree of concentration allows an actor to move naturally, speak convincingly, respond appropriately, and amid many other actors hit his mark open to the camera and without casting shadows on others' faces.

Because Howell is careful throughout the histories to use television's visual capability to show what stage cannot, she regularly adds battle scenes before or after the scripted battlefield dialogue; thus we see bits of the action at Bordeaux before IV.5, IV.6, and IV.7 in *1 Henry VI* and Cade's rebels at work before IV.3 in *2 Henry VI* as well as several different aspects of the battle at St. Albans during V.2. We see men fight, we see men killed, we see the carnage after a battle. Yet *3 Henry VI* is the most battle-filled play of the tetralogy, and here Howell inventively varies the presentation. Rather than just showing more bodies struggling, hacking, thrusting, and falling, for some conflicts, as at Wakefield (II.3), she gives the sounds of battle, the trumpets and the drums, and shows the white-rose and red-rose banners of each side overlaid on shots of moving soldiers, a somewhat more metonymic approach to battle. At Towton there is a formal mirror sequence, the cannons, banners, drums, troops, lancers, archers each drawn up left or right in apparently endless lines. The troops advance, the arrows fly, they land amid the shields, and then the shot cuts to the dialogue that attests the ardor of the fray. We see swift bursts of violence, as in the sequence called "the holocaust";[16] we see the battlefield taunting of York, of young Clifford, and finally the taunting of Prince Edward and Margaret after the battle in the snow at Tewkesbury. As Howell and Ranson have orchestrated them, we know we are watching different battles, ever more vicious. They become a vital part of the narrative, a complementary interpretive vehicle in these productions.

Howell bridges the action between 3 Henry VI and Richard III very tightly. At the end of 3 Henry VI King Edward proclaims an end of war and begins the festivities; after kissing his heir and having his brothers symbolically kiss the babe, he starts a dance that develops into a large ensemble affair in two circles. But peace and war are indistinguishable to the ambitious, and Richard, finding himself amid these celebratory circles, breaks through them and limps to the door. His exit concludes the play with a note of dissent. The opening of Richard III picks him up coming through the door from the other side; we hear the muffled stamping and chanting of the King's dance as from the next room. Thus juxtaposed, the pace of events is very fast. There is no peace; there is menace.

One of Howell's finest exploitations of the television medium in Richard III is the dream sequence before the battle at Bosworth. On stage, because both leaders are sleeping we get no reactions to the ghosts' curses and benedictions except sometimes a twist or turn from Richard; the sequence is a long, sinuous procession of intoning spirits. On television, Howell takes us into Richard's nightmare and gives us subjective images: as Richmond's dark-haired head settles on his arms for a nap, she cuts to tight close-up of dark hair, then the head turns and it is Richard's. As we hear the Duchess of York's curse repeated, Richard's eyes open and the shot moves in to an extreme close-up of Richard's right eye, in the pupil of which materializes Richard's figure in the dream sequence. Images appear and disappear quickly, Richard cannot grasp them, objects transform before his eyes—it is an effective rendition of the alogical and symbolic reference of the dream state.

Howell actually prepares us for the unexpected a few shots earlier when we see Ratcliff leave Richard's tent; Richard sits alone, then looks up. She cuts to two figures entering, but when Stanley kneels and throws back his hood, we realize the scene has changed to Richmond's tent, as the shot then reveals. This trick of context is played on us here and also between II.4 and III.1, where Queen Elizabeth, fleeing Richard and Buckingham, flies to sanctuary through double doors opened by servants, and the shot cuts to double doors opening as Richard and Buckingham cheerfully greet the camera and entrant, Prince Edward, like spiders to a web, though for an instant we think it is Elizabeth who has walked right into a trap. These "gotcha" shots fit the mood of surprise attack in *Richard III* and prepare us to appreciate the dislocation of Richard's nightmare, a warped memory sequence of all the people he killed to gain the crown.

The order of ghosts is textual and chronological; the suggestive details and visual transmogrifications as the ghosts appear as well as Richard's sense of having someone behind him give the scene its disconcerting effect, as when Prince Edward is seen amid Tewkesburian snowflakes; when Clarence looks up with liquid streaming down his face as if fresh from the malmsey butt, though when he approaches sleeping Richmond suddenly Richard and the camera watch through a sheet of water; when Rivers, Grey, and Vaughn, the chop lines of beheading on their necks, are seen through a fisheye lens greeting Richmond; when Hastings appears seated at a table scattered with low-burning candles and strawberries that turn to bloodstains as Richard snatches the cloth, a cloth that sprouts pillow feathers as the little princes appear. Far more subjective than it could be on stage, the nightmare sequence uses both props and camera craftily. The figures continually appearing from behind prefigure the kind of encirclement Richard faces on the battlefield. As she planned that dream sequence, with care and artistry, so

Howell planned all four histories, and they too have a powerful cumulative effect.

Howell uses the medium of television confidently to serve and enhance her material. Like most directors, she has her own predilections and style, such as long takes and single-camera sequences. And there are other technical habits. In the histories and also in *Titus*, unless a character is alone on the set she rarely frames a 1-shot without someone in the background; she maintains a sense of group presence, of action and reaction, so that even close-ups catch other carefully chosen figures fuzzily in the distance. The technique binds the action together, keeping us aware of the others as we would be in a theatre and giving depth to the field of the picture. She also believes in creating images, especially for transitions between scenes, because "cutting points are very important in television."[17] Cuts, fades, and mixes all work purposefully in these productions, as do sound bridges (where the sound of one scene overlaps the visual of another) as we see in *Titus* between I.1 and I.2 with Aaron and in *1 Henry VI* between IV.7 (with its amendment from V.2) and V.1, where Lucy is left to cross himself before slain Talbot's body as we hear the chant of a mass as for the dead, then the scene cuts to King Henry kneeling before a crucifix, the priests just finishing the chant (Howell uses a similar death-to-mass shift in *Richard III* after the murder of Clarence). While juxtapositions and sound bridges are far from uncommon editing devices, Howell uses them meaningfully in her productions.

In his early plays, Shakespeare's rhetorical set pieces and balanced emblematic action can pose problems for theatre or television, and some scenes, such as the choral mournings of the Yorks or choral curses of the former queens in *Richard III*, would challenge anyone's ingenuity; the usual response is to cut them. Howell keeps the scenes and rivets the camera on the words and speakers, even if the pace is necessarily slower; it is, after all, the pace Shakespeare built for these plays. Pace is certainly the only major criticism of Howell's shows by those who like all action to be at "television-speed," that is, fast moving, and it is a criticism shared by the American videotape editor who worked on the series and viewed these slow fades and developing shots impatiently. Finally whether the pace works well is a matter for the viewer. Though some directors do not, Howell asks the viewer to wait for effects. And she certainly takes her work seriously and builds a similar commitment in those she works with; artists usually do.

7   A Study in Diversity

THE TELEVISED

SHAKESPEARE CANON

The director's care in melding text and camera work, an essential conjunction for televised Shakespeare, shows in the productions of Miller, Moshinsky, and Howell. Their choices differ, but their individual styles reveal how potent an interpretive device televised production can be. The series is richer, in fact, for their very diversity of approach, their particular technical interests, which are more easily seen when considering their plays collectively. Certainly no single method of televising Shakespeare is guaranteed to bring success; stylization can be exciting as in the controlled effects of the RSC televised tragedies and the BBC *Henry VI–Richard III* sequence or distracting as in parts of *King John*, and a representational or realistic emphasis can be enriching as in *All's Well That Ends Well* or *The Merry Wives of Windsor* or irrelevant and intrusive as in *As You Like It*. Nonetheless, the visual element of the productions was a major concern of the directors working with this visual medium; some directors considered creating the world of the play their essential interpretive contribution.

With the two on-location productions the first season, there was admittedly a bias toward realism or the representational early in the series. But this exploration was not limited to the initial productions; directors throughout the series were drawn to representing reality, to attempting *trompe-l'oeil* studio work. Nonetheless, these productions vary in their approach to and definition of reality, for some are more obviously studio-bound or stagey than others. Even filming reality itself varies in effectiveness, as *Henry VIII* and *As You Like It* demonstrate.

One major difference between *Henry VIII* and *As You Like It* is that, despite the elegance of the settings chosen for filming locations, *Henry VIII* did not become a production about castles, whereas *As You Like It* very nearly became a production more about Mother Nature than about Rosalind, Orlando, or the dukes. The characters in Arden were dwarfed by their green environs as members of the Tudor court were not by Leeds, Hever, or Penshurst, although *Henry VIII*'s director Kevin Billington thought the location work was a vital part of the production: "I don't think the play would work in a studio. . . . I wanted to get away from the idea that this is some kind of fancy pageant. I wanted to feel the reality: I wanted great stone walls."[1] (Compare the walls of *Henry VIII* to the walls in *King John* to survey the difference in effect between real stone and stylization.)

Billington, his designer Don Taylor, and his production manager chose historically apt sites for taping: "We shot at Hever Castle, where Anne Bullen lived; at Penshurst, which was Buckingham's place; and at Leeds Castle, where Henry was with Anne Bullen," Billington explained.[2] Moreover, Billington found opportunities to use place to clarify narrative, as when we see the King and his party of maskers arriving by barge at Wolsey's palace (I.4) rather than simply hearing a drum and a trumpet offstage. Television also solves some practical problems, as script editor Alan Shallcross pointed out; the only scene cut was the one with the commoners preceding infant Elizabeth's christening: "You have to have the scene in the theatre if for no other reason than that people have to change clothes,"[3] a need taping obviates.

Henry VIII greatly benefited from being taped on location. In the hands of the BBC, the history closest to Shakespeare's own time, his only work treating Renaissance historical figures, proved how effective reality itself can be. In the context of the Shakespeare series, several small details exemplify the difference. From the opening shot of *Henry VIII*, for instance, we see the ceilings in the castle rooms, and only by registering their presence are we aware of how often rooms are ceilingless in the rest of the series, since ceilings would block out lighting in the studio. In *All's Well* the camera had to shoot through a pane of painted glass to provide the appearance of a ceiling in the French king's hall, and in *The Comedy of Errors* any shot from the piazza up into the second story of the

Phoenix had to be very carefully arranged to avoid shooting off the set and into the lighting grid because there was no roof over the structure.

Moreover, because *Henry VIII* was taped in winter (late November until early January), it was cold, and we often see the characters' condensed breath as they speak, both outdoors as in I.1, the arrest of Buckingham, and indoors, as in II.4, the divorce trial. This effect is lost in the studio, for while one might easily shiver in a BBC control room since all that equipment likes to be frigid, the studio lights and activity usually keep anyone from getting a chill on the floor; Imogen and others play several scenes of *Cymbeline* in studio snow, but we never see their condensed breath. The climatic realities of *Henry VIII* were not just visual grace notes, however, but sometimes serious impediments to the production, since frozen cameras cause major problems and production expense.

Surrounded by Tudor architecture and sporting elegant costumes that look like Britain's National Portrait Gallery on parade, the actors succeed in bringing the political intrigues of this Tudor court to life, the whisperings of lords, the observations of gentlemen and commoners, the grantings, the public rituals and private confrontations. Billington's cast gave fine performances: the exercise of will in both Henry and Wolsey matches Katherine's firm dignity, Anne's willing but thoughtful acquiescence, and Cranmer's un-Wolseyian humility in their reactive roles. Billington knew the production was a success because this neglected, musty play proved exciting before the cameras: "It's a play that deserves looking at again. I'm hoping that this production will set people off trying to see how they can do it in the theatre. That would be a wonderful thing for television to do."[4] The ability to capture both physical detail or surroundings and psychological detail of character portrayal proved the advantage of televising Shakespeare, though the expense of this production prompted the BBC to mandate the rest of the series as studio-based, a victory for the play but something of a defeat for the options of putting Shakespeare on television. In the rest of the histories, Giles's selective stylization and frequent representationalism and Howell's carefully planned stylizations are responses to taping in the studio.

As You Like It, on the other hand, by literalizing the pastures of the pastoral mode, diminished Shakespeare's effect, his playfulness with conventions and attitudes. If *Henry VIII* ran into winter chills, the gnats of summer plagued *As You Like It*'s actors—realism with a vengeance. The idea of doing the play on location was producer Cedric Messina's; as he pointed out, "Ninety-five per cent of it takes place in the forest," so using real woods seemed perfect, and he thought "*As You Like It* fitted completely beautifully into the bucolic setting."[5] Basil Coleman does get the benefits of nature's rich colors, the estate's wooded vistas, and beautifully dappled summer sunlight, but planning for location work differs from designing for studio work because instead of building to order or to concept, one uses the locale. As director Coleman explained, "Everything tends to begin from the location." Oak woods, beech woods, an ancient chestnut tree became taping sites, but there were no meadows for grazing sheep at Glamis, and they had to construct a shepherd's cottage (twice, since cows ate the first one).[6] The location often determines the effect, for, as set designer Don Taylor added, "normally what is there dictates, or heavily influences, the way things get done."

In location work there are explorations, discoveries, compromises, rethinkings, and even surprises, as when the pine woods, selected months ahead for the scenes with the banished Duke because of their wintry quality, were three feet deep in ferns when taping occurred in June.[7] Consequently, the hardship and inclemency mentioned in the text never threaten these woodland visitors; their time in the forest appears to be more an upscale camping expedition than exile, as when chic campfire entertainment is provided by two cellos, a flute, and a zither and later an impromptu masque poses no difficulties. Being set in a real park prompts an audience to ask questions and make demands of the action that would never occur in a theatre because there an audience accepts the limits of theatrical realism. The acting had trouble getting momentum; though Rosalind and Touchstone had moments and Richard Pasco's Jaques was eloquently morose, the overall production never quite sparked into sustained life in its woodland setting.

In the studio, along with Elijah Moshinsky's efforts, both John

Gorrie and David Jones also sought to create realistic worlds for the camera and the plays. Consider Gorrie's work. His productions, *Twelfth Night* and *The Tempest*, are based on the belief that the places shown need to have a real geography, that spaces need a definite physical relationship visible on camera. Hence in *The Tempest* we see the trees on one side of the island's cliff face and the shore on the other, and in *Twelfth Night* we could draw a blueprint of Olivia's house. The *Twelfth Night* set for the country manor was especially lovely; years later those involved with the series still fondly recalled that vine-covered estate. Gorrie developed the viewer's familiarity with the house and its forecourt and then capitalized on it. Not only do scenes go back and forth through the gate and the doors, but when she is inside, Olivia helps the viewer be aware of the outside by looking for Cesario out the window.

In many scenes Gorrie was careful to show the environs, using long shots of the courtyard or the main hall with its fireplace, and often pulled the camera back at the end of a scene as the characters exited. At least once Gorrie played off that geographic familiarity; he divided the long III.4 into five smaller scenes yet took care to relate them. Olivia sees the newly cross-gartered Malvolio in a side room, then leaves to greet Cesario in the courtyard. Malvolio lingers in self-satisfaction, then proceeds the length of the corridor to the main hall. There is a cut to action with Sir Toby in the hall, into which Malvolio strides. Since the audience just saw him approach that room from the other angle, his appearance binds the scenes and establishes simultaneity. The rest of III.4 is united in a similar manner as Sir Toby and Fabian incite the unwilling combatants to a duel; the composite set lets camera cuts suggest parallel action on each side of the wall.

In this production Gorrie also used point-of-view shots quite well, especially regarding Malvolio. When the steward makes his yellow-stockinged entrance to Olivia, the shot cuts from her amazed face to pan up his body from feet to head, following the angle of her gaze. Later we peer into the cell at Malvolio, always, like Feste, on the outside. The most complicated shots, however, are in Malvolio's letter scene. Theatrical eavesdropping scenes are notoriously difficult for television, but Gorrie succeeded admirably in this complex exchange by presenting a series of reverse perspective shots. After an establishing shot with Malvolio foreground walking past the tree and the eavesdroppers rear in the arbor, there is a reverse so Malvolio is seen from their perspective, as when he leans on the arbor where they are hiding so Sir Toby and Fabian can whisper in the foreground of shot. Switching perspectives and moving the listeners from arbor to tree keeps fresh the suspense and humor of this improbable scene. The rest of the scene's effect is due to the quality of the cast, for Alec McGowen is a delightfully self-absorbed Malvolio. The casting is strong throughout the production, in fact, for Felicity Kendal and Sinead Cusack provide strong leads, and as roisterers and tricksters Robert Hardy, Robert Lindsay, Trevor Peacock, Ronnie Stevens, and Annette Crosbie fully realize their characters.

The Tempest shares Twelfth Night's sense of geography without its rich, warm characterization and zest. Tempest's magic changes the equation, for a play with a monster and spirits and spells begs the realistic. The balance of physical and spiritual wobbles in the various groups on the island; the drunks are successfully physical as is very hairy Caliban, but the nobles are a bit pristine and low-key, Prospero and Miranda almost disembodiedly ethereal, while the spirits are uncharacteristically physical, with all the focus on virtually bare, writhing bodies. Most of the magic comes from television technology rather than Shakespeare, for frequent invisibility makes the production full of technical tricks, although it does not take long for a viewer to predict just where and when Ariel will disappear. Thus, this production has a full geography of place without a full geography of spirit.

Many directors of comedy seek a naturalistic environment and consider casting the key to comedic success. Gorrie certainly did, and so did David Jones in Merry Wives. For that play, of course, he wanted to suggest not just a country house or a section of an island but the entire village of Windsor. Not able to work on location, he wanted a naturalistic studio setting. Although "you never get total reality in a studio," as set designer Don Homfray said, he gave Jones almost that by building interiors based on Tudor structures associated with the Shakespeare family; Falstaff's room is based on the home of the author's mother, Mary Arden, in Wilmcote, and the wives' residences on Hall's Croft, Stratford home of Shakespeare's daughter Susanna and her husband John Hall. He also had a toy village of miniature Tudor houses built of Plasticine for the distant view, shifting them in the background to provide different vistas.[8] Within that setting Jones provided the bustle of a village, Mistress Page stopping in the street to buy produce from her Renaissance greengrocer and Pistol making advances to Mistress Quickly behind the Garter Inn.

Jones's camera work also complements the detail of this lovely set with a series of crane shots that establish Page's yard, the village across the roofs, Dr. Caius in the glen at dawn ready to duel, and Herne's oak in Windsor forest. At Dr. Caius's house the camera work parallels the wariness and suspicion in the early scene there, for Jones initially shoots into the room through the doctor's cabinets past vials and bottles, alternates shots into and out of the closet where Simple hides, and always catches Dr. Caius on the other side of the balustrades peering in, a perspective the camera work had foreshadowed.

In addition, Jones carefully differentiates the characters so that George Page becomes a warm and well-rounded role, and the wives are not clones but different in nature and social status, Mistress Page a well-established bourgeois and Mistress Ford nouveau riche.[9] This texturing makes the action more credible and also feeds the comedy, which is built out of character, not incident, as Jones recognized:

> I said right from the beginning . . . I'm not concerned at all if the play is not funny. I've seen it happen time and time again with *Merry Wives*. People think it has to be terribly funny and they go into funny walks and trips and all this goes on and the comedy of it, I think, lies absolutely in character observation and confrontations of characters that don't mix. I said, "If we tell the truth we will be funny; if we try to be funny by a short cut we'll be in a lot of trouble." So there's never been any

pressure on anybody to be other than that genuine person in that genuine situation. I think therefore, hopefully, a lot of it *is* very funny.[10]

Such a disclaimer goes with a script that begs for certain standard comic bits, and Jones did not miss many opportunities: as when Falstaff must continually negotiate a low beam in his attic room, when the closeted Simple hands out the green box before Mistress Quickly opens the closet door, when Mistress Quickly coos over Fenton and the purse of money, when Dr. Caius in practicing for the duel runs his rapier between Jack Rugby's legs and Rugby responds in fearful falsetto, when Falstaff almost climbs Mistress Ford in fondling her from foot to breast, when on his second visit he gets her on his lap but dumps her onto the floor when he hears Mistress Page's voice, when Master Ford assaults the buckbasket—this is not a conscious avoidance of what we know to be funny. It is confidently seizing the gauntlet of comedy that the play hurls down. With Master Ford, the wives, Mistress Quickly, and the duellers (Ben Kingsley, Prunella Scales, Judy Davis, Elizabeth Spriggs, Michael Bryant, and Tenniel Evans), Jones has a surefire comic cast who recognize comedy when it greets them on a Tudor platter. *Merry Wives* is a fascinating collection of comic types; Jones, however, succeeds in rendering them as more than just types. Only Richard Griffiths's Falstaff, the visitor in Windsor, seems a bit dour, as if he never quite catches the energy of the rest of the cast.

When David Jones turned from warm village comedy to the challenge of romance with *Pericles*, he could not have a Tudor village built for that tale of voyaging in the ancient world. Yet we see many of the same directorial impulses at work; he maintains a sharp definition of place and uses long shots during the action to establish locale. The peregrinating plot of *Pericles* necessitates a world more of the imagination, and while the settings are specific and often detailed, they are not real in the sense that the Tudor village was. The geographic movement of the tale means that for clarity and efficiency place must be readily recognizable, a demand designer Don Taylor met, especially by means of color and versatile lighting. Antioch is a lush, flora-filled atrium and a city gate; Tyre a set of rooms lit blue in the night scene; Tharsus an arid square, sun bleached and barren; Pentapolis much warmer, like its inhabitants; the brothel a more fetid enclosure; the beaches open sandy stretches with rock outcrops, dunes, and sea grass. Like the costumes, the settings are not strictly real but suggestive enough of place that they provide an appropriate context for the action.

The audience's awareness is aided by the long shots Jones uses frequently in this production to open and close scenes and also for perspective within scenes. The camera at times works subjectively, as when Pericles suddenly realizes the meaning of Antiochus's riddle and we see quick glimpses of incestuous embraces, half in long shot. Likewise, the situation at Tharsus is told as expeditiously by the long shots as by the dialogue. Mike Gwilym, playing Pericles, found the long shots also worked as interpretive devices: "I think David [Jones] has cleverly used a lot of long shots so it is a small person looking round a very big world, trying to take it all in."[11]

Jones often puts Gower into these settings with the dumb shows that illustrate his narration: the camera picks him up speaking at the empty fountain in Tharsus, for instance, then pans to show the revitalized town square as Pericles takes his leave; Gower is on the beach just before Dionyza arranges for the murder of Marina; he is in the street in Mytilene as Boult finally leads Marina out of the brothel. By placing him within or near this action, his presence serves to unify separate pieces of action rather than isolating his narration from the drama (David Giles treats the Chorus in *Henry V* in much the same fashion). *Pericles* is always a retrospective, a tale told by one who knows its ending as he begins, as with Shakespeare's other choral figures.

Even with this traditional distancing device, the individual scenes have great focus and power. The two tour-de-force scenes of *Pericles* rise to the occasion in this production: the storm scene in terms of technology with the rocking ship above deck and the synchronized rocking camera below deck (and thus a very expensive scene in this already expensive production) and the recognition of Marina in terms of performance. Jones lets some of the magic of the romance tradition settle over the production, not trying to explain away the peculiarity of this dramatic creature but letting it work. Mike Gwilym agrees: "I've just come more and more to trust in the wonderful nature of the story."[12] Jones himself also believes "it's helped enormously by being done on television."[13]

These productions and most of Moshinsky's insist on representing a complete world in or out of the studio, and they show their quality in their treatment of exteriors, for outdoor scenes reveal studio work far more quickly than interiors, as can be demonstrated in a number of productions.

Alvin Rakoff with *Romeo and Juliet* and Herbert Wise with *Julius Caesar*, both productions juxtaposed to the *As You Like It* filmed on location in the first season, opted to work toward a close representation of reality. Verona and Rome are given the environments usual in many attempts at studio realism: the interiors more successfully suspend the viewers' disbelief than do the exteriors, which almost inevitably stylize the reality to some extent, since in form they are so closely related to theatre sets. In the sunny, weatherless clime of the studio, these buildings are actually at most a week old, and their pristine newness shows, all sharp angles and smooth, clean surfaces, even if a bit of debris is thrown along the edge of one Roman street. Moreover, the terrain is remarkably smooth and flat, obviously a painted studio floor. In a fanciful comic world such as Ephesus in the BBC *The Comedy of Errors* these considerations scarcely arise, but in tragedies, especially when based on historical subjects and done on a quasi-representational set, they may.

The representational quality of the BBC *Romeo and Juliet* cannot brook comparison with Zeffirelli's film in which his huge public square could accommodate a considerable brawl, the balcony could overlook a lush park, and night scenes could appear truly dark. In the BBC studio the square is a modest intersection of two streets, the balcony overlooks a domesticated arbor, and the night scenes appear to be generously moonlit. Film and good locations do wonders for authenticity. Though Rakoff might have preferred to work on location had that been offered, his production seeks a representational environment in the studio but ends up seeming stagey, giving the actors a set to pose in front of rather than places for characters to live.

Within these comparative confines, Rakoff works to establish a sense of larger space, most obviously in the duels at the center of the play, Mercutio versus Tybalt, then Tybalt versus Romeo. The conflicts move rapidly, and so do the camera shots and angles. As the sequence showing Romeo pursuing Tybalt builds, the sharp angles and quick shots, the blend of long shots and close-ups strive to imply that the young men have been running far and wide rather than almost in place. The Capulet ball, too, uses the open studio space and a two-level staircase to suggest a great hall, and the director keeps long shots in evidence.

Rakoff also works for representational action, for the dynamics of real households, real families, real friendships, so we see the bustle in the kitchen, Capulet in the market, and Benvolio's indulgence and disapproval of Mercutio's broken-rhythm taunts as they kill time or search for Romeo. In terms of realism, however, casting a fourteen-year-old as Juliet is the production's most striking example of the doctrine's limits. Rebecca Saire appears adolescent without always having the emotion to match the poetry, while Patrick Ryecart's Romeo registers as decidedly adult by contrast, not a boy but a man. In the production's Veronese context, the lovers are the coolest elements, though Rakoff brings the camera very close for their passionate outbursts. Each is absolutely still while speaking, as if transfixed by emotion. Except for Romeo's explosion for the duel and his death scene, these can seem surprisingly static moments in the play.

In *Julius Caesar* Herbert Wise and his actors and cameras turn such private or intense moments into stronger psychological studies; they may also thereby demonstrate that *Julius Caesar* is a better play for television. Cassius's opening temptation of Brutus is a case in point. The colonnade makes an effective setting, a backdrop that also affords more distant views through the archways as the men move. Cassius stalks Brutus and moves in to him confidentially, what we come to see as conspiratorially; we watch Cassius's face past the back of Brutus's head. Until Cassius circles his auditor, we do not know for certain how Brutus is responding. As positions shift, Wise gets an extreme close-up of Brutus's face; we see his eyes as an eyebrow lifts. Casca's interruption provides incubation time for Brutus to consider Cassius's words. Once Casca leaves, the camera returns to study Cassius as Brutus departs; again the camera moves in to a close-up of the actor's face, to his narrowed eyes, while his thoughts are presented as a voice-over on the sound track.

The close-ups, extreme close-ups, and voice-overs establish both style and interpretation in this tragedy of thought. The voice-overs, for instance, are widely used: Cassius, Brutus, Artemidorus, Portia, and Mark Antony all have lines presented as thoughts, thoughts that range from scheming to contemplation, concern, distress, and self-congratulation. Brutus sometimes combines thought and speech, as during his deliberation in his garden, when in the midst of a voice-over considering Caesar's ambition he says aloud, "Then lest he may, prevent," as if taking a position; the thought becomes word and is on its way to becoming deed. Such a distinction between thought and speech in the production enhances the subjective element and differentiates private and public, individual and group. It also lets Brutus, a man of much thought early on, noticeably become a man of speech during and after the deed, while the role of primary thinker shifts to Mark Antony, who has most of the voice-overs in the second half of the play. The icily calm Octavius, interestingly, has no voice-overs; we are left like Antony to guess at his thoughts. Thus Cassius succeeds in involving Brutus, Brutus succeeds in accomplishing the assassination, and Mark Antony succeeds in barring them from victory or glory in the deed.

Part of the difference in effect between *Romeo and Juliet* and *Julius Caesar* is that Rakoff develops interpretation in action and then lets the camera capture it, whereas Wise uses the camera and sound track as part of the interpretation, as thematic and technical elements in the production. Both productions have varying degrees of representationalism and are less successful with the large outdoor civic spaces (if the extras were not so clean and neatly clad and carefully positioned and mechanical in action, it might help as well). But because the public action in *Julius Caesar* uses one speaker rather than a combat (whether with words or weapons), the focus is at times tighter and the result more powerful, a more successful set of rhetorical manipulations and responses.

The battlefield in *Julius Caesar* is a step closer to realism than its Rome, and since the action switches from one to the other, the seam shows. Yet more is also out in the open between the characters late in the play; they are embattled, Cassius angrily against Brutus, Octavius silently against Mark Antony, each pair against the other, and finally Cassius and Brutus individually against despair and defeat. Wise uses his rock outcrop not just as backdrop but as an open-air space divider; at times the camera stays before it tracking characters who are moving behind it, a technique especially effective for Brutus's approach and discovery of Cassius's suicide.

If the studio setting was not necessarily an asset to *Romeo and Juliet* and *Julius Caesar* in the first season, that was largely because of the staginess (as opposed to theatricalism) of the sets and their use. Many of the BBC Shakespeares gained from their studio worlds and from the television artistry a director could bring to the plays in this medium. With another play produced during the first season, *Measure for Measure*, Desmond Davis provides a better demonstration of how to use television for Shakespeare. He explored a number of allusions in his setting and camera work, from Shakespeare's stage to modern film. Most of the Viennese settings are detailed, but the references of the scenes' atmospheres vary: the Duke's audience hall is formal and furnished with elegant restraint, while the brothel has the clamor and activity of a saloon in a western, which is exactly the allusion Davis sought, just as he wanted the prison to have the torch-lit, scream-filled grotesquerie of a horror film.[14] With both representational and aesthetic references, Davis then staged the last scene on a platform as a reference to the Globe, an exterior scene that nonetheless suffers the same limits of stylized realism as the first season's other studio exteriors.

Within these spaces, Davis used the camera thoughtfully and for effect. For instance, the arrest scenes of Claudio and of Pompey, both done in long tracking shots, clearly establish a sense of the city, as Davis explained: "I hope it looked as though we were going down endless streets, but what we were really doing was going round and round the studio. Poor Stuart [Walker, the set designer] had to provide set all the way round. The camera actually went eight times round the stage in a continuous track."[15] Always Davis's camera shots support the action, as when Lucio, the creature of the streets, is seen through the small opening in the convent door when he seeks out Isabella; after their conversation in the courtyard the camera moves with him back to the street, where the door bars him from that other world and through the aperture we see Isabella inside. Opening the first interview scene between Angelo and Isabella with a close-up of Angelo stamping a document gives the proper sense of his officiousness. In both interviews Davis develops the action from anteroom to the Duke's audience chamber, focusing part of Angelo's II.2 scene-closing soliloquy at the empty chair of state and then answering that shot by placing part of Isabella's II.4 final monologue in the same room and toward the same chair. Throughout the interviews, in fact, the camera work is careful and impressively tailored to the action: "It was just shot very simply," Davis said; "Two cameras the whole time, two opposed cameras that did the whole thing—a very simple piece of shooting that looked rather complex. It was a visual idea; he was rather large, shot from waist level, and she was a minute figure, shot using the whole depth of the room. Then slowly they come together."[16] Such interpretive simplicity is the art television lends the productions, the advantageous use of cameras to provide meaningful visual images.

Davis knew the nature of these effects:

If it looks filmic I think the secret is in using space more. . . . Any idiot can do close-ups against three feet of flock wallpaper, but if you have a great set it's really stupid not to use it, use the whole depth. I think there's a slight tendency in television to work too much in close-up and you get head upon head upon head. While it's very clear it doesn't express the poetry of movement, and I find after a while I lose the geography of a scene. . . . I think you've got to choreograph your shooting and think very carefully before you get into huge heads.[17]

Davis deservedly won an award for the direction of this production, which was strongly cast and well performed. He also expressed some terms that distinguish this and other work in the series: "geography" and "the poetry of movement" when setting, action, and television cameras work effectively together to present Shakespeare's plays.

A similar use of more representational interiors and less representational exteriors occurs in the productions directed by David Giles, all histories. Giles directed *Richard II* in 1978 as an individual play, with no thought of beginning a related set of productions, yet he was subsequently asked to finish the tetralogy in 1979 and arranged those three productions as a series with consistent casting throughout, also managing to retain Jon Finch, his Bolingbroke from *Richard II*. Rehearsals for *1 Henry IV* began in February 1979; *Henry V* came out of the studio in late June. Even these, however, he approached as separate plays with shared casts but individual design concepts and settings, unlike Jane Howell, who knew she was tackling four plays at once and approached the entire sequence as a unit, four integral parts of one big picture.

Messina chose David Giles to direct in the series because he is an experienced Shakespeare director and a television director well known for his BBC work with *The Forsyte Saga* and other shows, including a 1974 televised version of *Twelfth Night*, produced by Messina and filmed at Castle Howard. *Richard II* was selected for the first season because as a history play with no battles it posed comparatively few major production problems, or so the theory ran. Giles protested that *Richard II* held plenty of challenges—a confrontation from a castle wall and a combat in the lists, which he called "an absolute swine" of a scene for television,[18] both of which are noticeably more stylized and studio-bound than the interior scenes, which more successfully convey the size and texture of castle and hall.

In directing *Richard II* Giles incorporated the image patterns of Shakespeare's script into the visual element of the televised play. For instance, ups and downs are the thematic core of the play, and throughout the action Giles has Richard separated from the court, above them, at first seated on dais or platform with the occasional steep camera angle for effect. Repeatedly Richard is seen atop steps—in Gaunt's chamber, at the dock, at Flint Castle, a superior position always followed by a subsequent descent. In using his camera work as an interpretive device, Giles also balances shots and scenes, as in the shot across the bathtub that opens and closes the cronies' gathering in I.4 or the matched pair of balcony shots for three lords conspiring, Northumberland and two others against Richard and in defense of Bolingbroke early on, then Aumerle and two clerics against Henry later.

Using the camera in close-up on Richard for his shifts of thought and mood, his insights and manipulation, also allows Giles to break up scenes, as in the long deposition scene, presenting private moments between Richard and Henry among the public pronouncements, moments when the animosity carefully guarded in assemblies becomes evident, for if Henry usurps the crown, Richard usurps the scene. The best sequence of collaborative script and camera work, however, is the dividing of Richard's prison cell soliloquy into separate camera shots that imply the passage of time, an ongoing meditation. One image fades into another; drumming fingers indicate his boredom or his head against the barred window his languor and longing. Two shots open with the crucifix, reminding us of Richard's hope for spiritual justification and his own "sour cross" and suggesting his coming death. When he is finally stabbed in the back by his assailants, he throws wide his arms, visually linking his death with the crucifix. Throughout this production Giles demonstrates care in selecting the focus for our camera-aided eyes.

The text is also full of "sun" imagery, for as Giles noticed and used, the play's movement is "from Richard's night to Bolingbroke's fair day." He very consciously moves *Richard II* from day through dark to day, putting Bolingbroke's direct challenge of return, Richard's arrival from Ireland, and the Flint Castle exchange all in the dark of night, the dark doings of the power play thus appropriately enshrouded. The Flint Castle confrontation is juxtaposed to the bright sunlight of the Queen's garden for the news of Bolingbroke's victory, so that the only remaining nocturnal scenes

are Richard's night—his leave-taking from the Queen and his murder—while Bolingbroke's are all fair day.

Giles also uses reactions to Richard as commentary. In Richard's
initial entrance to hear the case between Henry Hereford (Bolingbroke) and Mowbray, he readies himself confidently at the door,
nods for it to be opened, and strides formally through the lords to
the chair of state as trumpets sound and the lords all bow; we see
the pompous entrance of a proud king. This ceremony contrasts
with all the rest of Richard's entrances, especially Richard's return
from Ireland, which is to an empty plot, only Aumerle and Carlisle
to attend him, and his appearance on the walls of Flint Castle,
which evokes no sign of tribute or reverence from those below;
they only kneel after the concessions and on Bolingbroke's signal.
In contrast to the first scene, in the deposition scene the camera
waits for Richard, not with him; the doors open and in he comes,
slowly, hesitantly, to a silent room of unbowing lords who have just
kneeled to Henry. Not even the page delivering the mirror acknowledges Richard; the boy kneels to Bolingbroke. The loss of
place and of public identity is underscored by the television treatment of these entrances. In his cell at Pomfret, he is kneeled to by
none except a groom. But Richard has one more entrance in the
BBC television production, in a coffin. Giles makes the most of that
entrance, completing his pattern. Once the body is identified as
Richard's, Carlisle and Aumerle kneel on either side of the casket,
King Henry steps off the dais to kneel at the far end, and everyone
follows suit until Richard in death once more gains the tribute of
his subjects' knees.

In *Richard II* Giles contrasts a formal, taciturn Bolingbroke with
a spoiled, quicksilver Richard. By retaining the York family scenes
with Wendy Hiller's broad comedy as Duchess rather than cutting
them as is sometimes done in the theatre to save time and to keep
the focus on Richard's fall, Giles completes the contrast between
Richard and Henry as arbiters, judges, and subjects of plots. It is
still Richard's play, but Giles generally trusts the symmetry of
Shakespeare's structure.

With the next plays in the tetralogy, Giles could plan for the sequence as well as the single play. The two *Henry IV* plays contrast tavern and court, plot and policy, meetings and battles; they are, as designer Don Homfray indicated, "Social Histories."[19] Giles wanted to keep these productions as realistic as possible, even the battlefield, because they are "more private—it all happened in rooms."[20] We get low, enclosed wooden spaces for the taverns, high, open, stone spaces for the court, a hummocky hillside for Shrewsbury, large tree trunks and fallen leaves for Gaultree Forest. The exteriors still pose the greater challenge, and like a number of other directors in the series, Giles had the camera lens support the effect he sought by using a long lens that would focus on the actors but slightly blur the backgrounds. Some scenes, such as those outside Henry's tent at Shrewsbury, still have a strong look of the studio, but other exteriors begin to represent more effectively a realistic environment for the historical rendering.

Richard's character was more verbally indulgent than any character in the rest of the sequence, though sheer wit and imagination abound in Sir John Falstaff and in Hal when in his company. Thus the action, like the rebellion, is split onto several fronts and must keep moving. Because appearance is a dominant theme, especially in *1 Henry IV*, Giles blocks for reaction shots, as in II.4 when he brings Hal into the foreground to think as Falstaff behind him announces the rebellion; we see the serious resolve in Hal before he turns with a quip to Falstaff. And Giles takes advantage of his historical sequence to signal Henry's skin disease with elaborate hand washing and medicating in *1 Henry IV* (III.2), long before any mention is scripted.

Giles moves toward a more stylized concept with *Henry V* and *King John*. The realistic settings in *Henry V* are obviously part of a larger, more stylized production. If he cannot switch from the Globe's stage to film, that is, to "reality," as Olivier did in his rendition, Giles can use the studio space forthrightly by placing realistic facades against a flat white cycloramic background; he lets long shots give the vista and its limits, then moves in closer. In the opening sequence, the Chorus steps into shot from the surrounding darkness, speaks, and as he begins to move forward the lights come up; "Suppose within the girdle of these walls / Are now confin'd two mighty monarchies," he says, and walks between the banners and assembled figures of each court in tableau, French to his right, English to his left. His "supposition" is made literal; we see it. The light fades as he moves beyond the figures, and he ends once more in darkness, steps to his left to exit, and nods to two clerics entering. The BBC script notes that the scene shifts, and it does in the studio (these were two different tapings and settings), but the experience for the television audience is of unbroken action. Continuing this style, the clerics, too, are surrounded by darkness; as they leave their prayers Canterbury walks back, the lights come up, and he is suddenly seen to be in Westminster Hall with the court. He bows, takes his position, and begins I.2. Again the action moves seamlessly to the tennis ball toss that links I.2 to the Chorus's next speech. The Chorus is apart from the action yet a part of it, for here as the camera pulls back to reveal Bardolph's proximity, the figure of Chorus jumps, startled, and then exits as the next scene begins with Bardolph's entrance to Nym. Thus, like Olivier, Giles finds a way to show the Chorus's exhortation of the audience's imagination, the confession and celebration that all they will see is appearance and art, not reality.

And like Olivier in his film, Giles's battlefields are the most realistic part of the production, a naturalistic picture in a stylized frame. At Agincourt we are no longer watching actors play on the undisguised flat of the studio floor against a white cycloramic curtain; there are ground and grass, campfires, and a perspective view of distant fields. The Chorus appears to walk the ground between the camps thanks to another action-binding camera cut, and the French lords, always in a setting more stylized than the English (compare the stone walls of Henry's palace to the blue, fleur-de-lys bedecked drapery of the French court), share with the English the more realistic fields of France. The battle of words continues—and, of course, in a play the only real battle we can have is the verbal one—but we see the effect of and reaction to the slaughter.

Appearances notwithstanding, *Henry V* is not necessarily a play about a battle, and not even a staged battle with alarums and fierce exchange of blows between six or eight men is scripted, though Shakespeare does that often enough in other plays and Olivier made the armed conflict the high point of his film. Giles keeps the focus close up on Henry, so that on television we clearly see those moments of reaction we strain to see in a staged performance—his berating and sentencing of the traitors at Southampton, his face at news of the crime and sentence of Bardolph, his meditative soliloquy following his talk with the soldiers before the battle, his reading the list of the English dead—in all of which we perceive the effective play of David Gwillim's eyes and mouth as well as hear his tone and pace of delivery. The production is a portrait of the young man as king, whereas *1 Henry IV* and *2 Henry IV* were portraits of the king-to-be as a young man.

Giles brings his effects full circle in the production; at the close we are in an admittedly staged setting, with cycloramic curtain lit deep blue and the towers hung with the tapestries we now associate with France. Everyone even takes the positions we remember, Burgundy in the center, the position formerly taken by the Chorus, with the English on his left and the French on his right—the arrangement of the play's opening tableau. The lights fade on this background as the action moves forward into a gazebo, reminiscent of the columned alcove Olivier used, for the wooing of Katherine, but the lights come up again to reveal her father's re-entrance and the flags flying above the towers, after which we get a second tableau, the marriage, as the Chorus steps forward to conclude the play. The balance of theatricalism fore and aft in the whole production as well as in that last scene is not just the accurate visual rendering of Shakespeare's style as Giles sees it but a strong commentary on the action and title character, on pose and appearance throughout.

Therefore, as a general rule Giles will be realistic when he can in televising Shakespeare's histories, and when the playwright himself stylizes, Giles follows, creating as in *Henry V* a stylized frame in which smaller, more realistic scenes appear. This choice has to do with both the medium and the nature of the play; histories, even literary ones, open up to a quasi-documentary approach (designer Don Homfray called *1 Henry IV*'s style "semi-documentary,")[21] asserting that "this is the way it was" or at least "this is the way it looked." With Giles's tetralogy the television audience gets a visual perspective on the Middle Ages that Shakespeare's audience had in name only, not complemented by costume or set; consequently on television we get the referential reality rather than the artistic or Elizabethan reality. The Chorus, the least realistic of characters, often speaks from the environs of the action, a treatment we also see David Jones use with Gower in *Pericles* and Alvin Rakoff with the Chorus in *Romeo and Juliet*. The underlying philosophy determining these decisions, it would seem, has more to do with the director's belief about television than with Shakespeare, even when emphasizing the theatricalism of a production.

Giles faced many of the same challenges he had in *Henry V* with the script of *King John*, a play with another choral character, the Bastard, and some highly stylized and formal rhetorical exchanges. He used the same approach in *King John* as in *Henry V*, direct address to camera for choral comments and a number of stylized settings, but here the use of setting is less effective. *Henry V*'s scenes at the French court, that bright blue, gold-trimmed sea of fabric swathing a set of risers, ask greater indulgence from the audience than do the play's other settings and work on a slightly different basis of stylization than the rest of that production, but since they seem to be in the spirit of poking fun at the French that is so much a part of Shakespeare's play, a viewer tolerates them. *King John*, too, follows Giles's principle of visually stylizing where Shakespeare does, so Giles and designer Chris Pemsel mix gaudy Byzantine interiors of John's castle and some semistylized scenes in the fields (such as a few tree limbs and a sunset) with highly stylized, seemingly cardboard castle exteriors.

Yet much as a viewer tries to exclaim that the scenes at Angiers look like a medieval painting—lines of figures against sketchily representative environs on a decorative background—or to heed Giles's claim that the setting is "emblematic" and "heraldic,"[22] the setting ends up looking flat and more fake than stylized. Perhaps in terms of stylization the contemporary eye is more willing to credit empty space as place than too intricate a nonrealistic visual pattern. The gold fleur-de-lys scattered over the blue backdrop in France and the painted floor, painted tents, and shelf of gray rock make the setting appear to have been exhumed from an early

1950s stage production. Nor does the stylization provide Giles with the same visual excitement that most of the stylizations in *Henry V* do, and in shaping the action he does not respond as interestingly to the environment. "Heraldic" becomes heavy, even with a strong cast and some fine performances—a sassily confident Bastard from George Costigan, who has the depth to portray the character's principles along with his irony; Leonard Rossiter's erratic and disturbing John; and the talented mothers, Claire Bloom's Constance and Mary Morris's Eleanor. The pieces do not fit: visually it seems an outdated storybook, in performance a sometimes moving portrayal.

This halfway house approach, partly representative, partly stylized, can leave an audience unsatisfied because of the disjunctures. Giles comes close to making it work in *Henry V*, but the all-or-nothing rule seems dominant in judging the effect of the BBC productions. Yet directors who chose a detailed foreground with more stylized background or a fanciful world for the dramatic action did so in response to their sense of the nature of the play, whatever the success of their choices.

Stuart Burge, for example, working on *Much Ado About Nothing* in the studio, recognized the artifice of the play's rhetorical structures and chose his stylistic approach accordingly:

> I don't think a play like this works if you try to do it with a naturalistic background or on location. You can do a *version* of it, just as Zeffirelli did a *version* of *Romeo and Juliet*, but I think the subtleties and sophistications of this play require some kind of stylized setting. I did think at one time of doing the whole thing against tapestry, but it's not that kind of play either—you've got to have a real arbour to hide in, etc. I think Jan [Spoczynski, the set designer] has succeeded very well in merging a stylised background and a real foreground.[23]

Such a combination gestures toward a representational world into which the costumes and action fit, but it does not insist on a totality; it is what one set designer called "stylized realism." The environment of *Much Ado* is carefully suggestive of Sicily and the cultures influencing it in the sixteenth century, North African,

Turkish, Spanish Moorish. And the foreground of the production is rather dense with representation—the courtyard with its columns and plants; the abundant arbor with its vines and orange trees; the rose window, grillwork, and altar in the chapel; the elaborate staircase and hall. Many of the scenes used the same painted floor and simply moved new set pieces in and altered the lighting: the hall where the dance is held in this way transforms into the chapel for the wedding and later into the family monument for the mourning scene; the same floor is used for the streets of Messina. A number of productions wrung variations on this approach to give a representational context close to the actors with a more stylized presentation of distance. It is a staple of the BBC Shakespeare series, especially among the comedies.

Several directors, however, put all the representationalism in the costumes and kept the entire setting stylized, so the actors stand out against their spare environment. Jack Gold made this choice for *The Merchant of Venice*: "If you imagine different planes, the thing closest to the camera was the reality of the actor in a real costume—the costumes were totally real and very beautiful—then beyond the actor is a semi-artificial column or piece of wall, and in the distance is the backcloth, which is impressionistic."[24] His decision, too, was based on his sense of the play: "Having read *The Merchant* I thought: this is not about sitting down and about props. It's about people speaking to each other, relating to each other. It's also a very dynamic piece: I could see it with a lot of movement."[25] Thus his emphasis was on open space and atmosphere rather than detail of place, the same principles he used in approaching *Macbeth* two years later. Jane Howell chose a similar approach for *The Winter's Tale*, abstracting the space to give a universal quality, as did several of the tragedies to thrust focus on character.

In *The Merchant of Venice* set designer Oliver Bayldon obliged Gold by providing a 360-degree impressionistic backcloth for both Venice and Belmont and mounting the scenic pieces on castors.[26] On television, the painted gauze backdrops for *Merchant* imply locale without photographic reproduction; they suggest air and water and distance, city and park, and aptly show their derivation from Turner's paintings. Sometimes the viewer has the sense of definite vistas, sometimes of hazy shapes. Against this airy suggestion Belmont is a gazebo, a set of wide stairs and columns, and some obelisks; with a suggestion of Venice in the distance, the commercial district is a series of archways and walls and columns.

While the set, costume, and lighting designs provide an interpretation of the production's world, a director still must put action in that world and capture it on camera. That challenge may be the greater when the director is working with stylized open space, as Jack Gold was on *Merchant*. Gold liked the freedom to move action around the studio and follow it with the camera. Gerry Scott, designer of *Macbeth*, also commented on Gold's propensity for shooting 360 degrees around the studio,[27] as occurred only rarely in the series (with Gold's productions and with *The Comedy of Errors, Measure for Measure, The Tempest*, the hall on Cyprus in *Othello*, and the Greek camp in *Troilus and Cressida*; most sets are open-ended to allow access of equipment). Gold uses his space, showing figures approaching or retreating in the distance (and there is a lot of coming and going in *Merchant*), tracking movement, framing dialogue against or through archways to gain silhouette. In addition, he builds planes of action, especially at Belmont, where Portia is seen waiting behind a suitor making his choice; we also get the reverse shot with Portia foreground and sometimes a shift of focus from one plane to the other as in II.7. And like Howell and Miller, Gold makes effective use of single-camera sequences, developing movement in front of the camera rather than consistently cutting between several shots. The shifting triangles of blocking in I.3 are a good example; the discussion changes perspective as we watch. With this technique Gold can show the grittier, nastier dealings in Venice and keep the tone of Belmont more placid.

The courtroom is a less spacious setting; it is enclosed and lined with three rows of spectators. It also involves far more camera cuts and significant close-ups, ~~ch as Shylock whetting his knife, Portia for the "mercy" speech, Shylock's response of "content" to the demands, Salerio forcing Shylock to kiss the cross, and finally a view of the scales and knife left on the table at scene's close. The dappled moonlight of Belmont indeed seems like another, more spacious world after the courtroom drama. Shylock having exited alone from the court, as if in answer the production's last long shot is of Antonio left alone on the terrace after the couples depart.

Juxtapose the urban settings of *Much Ado* and *Merchant*. Because Burge has a street set of stylized realism in *Much Ado*, he enhances that effect of real space by starting with a crane shot high above the street, then moving down to catch the entrance of the Watch amid the sounds of a cat fight and barking dogs; the sounds prevent the space from seeming an empty set waiting for the actors to enter. The shadowy, moonlit space works effectively, even if in the dark under the overhanging porticoes two warm beams of light miraculously appear, one for Borachio's face while he brags about his deceptive deed and the other for Seacoal's book during his note-taking (at least the Watch had a lantern). The Watch may be earnest buffoons, but they exist in as real a world as everyone else in *Much Ado*. In *Merchant* we have the impression of Venice from the impressionistic backdrops; moreover, a reflection as of light off water dances under the bridge before which Launcelot debates serving Shylock. The urban meetings, the baitings, and the hagglings lose nothing by missing the actual stones of Venice, especially as we worry more and more about the bond and the actual pound of flesh. Under these circumstances it also seems appropriate that Gold limits the open space for the courtroom; life and death issues are more real at that point in the play.

The different styles and their effect become even clearer by juxtaposing their natural settings, Leonato's arbor and the garden at Belmont. The lesson of total reality has already been learned: real trees in a real park are lovely for Arden, but, of course, that is probably more reality than *As You Like It* requires or can use; it is not ultimately a play about trees. We know Leonato's arbor stands against a painted backdrop in a television studio, but the prop verdure is sufficient (and usually at the BBC vines and plants themselves were real and watered regularly to keep them appearing fresh). Benedick need not be completely obscured by vines; we want to see him hidden and reacting to the tale of Beatrice's love for him. On location a real vineyard would probably have to be pruned to provide appropriate sight lines. At Belmont, what is most important is not the house or the horticulture but those three caskets, and we see them clearly. Thus the very nature of a natural setting can affect audience focus.

As with *As You Like It*, in *The Two Gentlemen of Verona* director Don Taylor also experienced a disjuncture between naturalism and literary convention, but in reverse. Splitting his stylistic elements, he made the casting as naturalistic as he could by tapping very young actors for the leads, then put them in a garden of courtly love, a very formal and stylized setting, thus playing the adolescent impulses against a literary pattern of behavior. The forest, a mass of metal poles that the cast nicknamed "Christmas at Selfridge's," extended that non-naturalistic environment. Such an approach renders the comedy as performance and the characters as actors more than a representational setting would. Taylor had actually begun planning a more naturalistic set; with the sudden inspiration for a garden of love with live cupids and emblematic statues of Amor to embody the courtly love exchanges, he urged set designer Barbara Gosnold to alter plans. Making a literary abstraction literal and visual, however, is not always an asset. Whereas gilded cupids in a garden of love may be elegant images for the imagination in a courtly love poem, they are somewhat disconcerting for the eye when standing next to Proteus or Valentine (despite the symbolic names) in a Shakespearean comedy. Sometimes there can be too much reality, whether one has insects to flick out of one's face or cupids.

For *The Comedy of Errors* James Cellan-Jones decided the unlikely events necessitated a fanciful environment, and so the Ephesus of the BBC studio was generated, the piazza sporting a full map of the Mediterranean (useful in the exposition of the first scene), and the three necessary structures, the Phoenix, the Porpentine, and the Abbey, evenly spaced around the circular market. While Cellan-Jones wanted to view the plight of the play's protagonists seriously, the setting, the action, the physical gags keep the production firmly within the bounds of farce. Don Homfray provides a complete world with detail in the foreground, but overall it is a fairly stylized comic context for the twins' day of confused identities.

The productions of *Hamlet* and *Macbeth*, by contrast, stylize the sets far more, never claiming to provide more than figurative space but especially in *Hamlet* making that space complement the play's themes. When every set is suggestively consistent and the approach enhances the action, a viewer can quickly adapt to the stylized visual world. For *Hamlet*'s exteriors, the studio floor is unabashedly the setting, a flat, open expanse with only a small ramp in the distance against the cycloramic backdrop. Interiors are more varied but obviously suggestive rather than realistic: walls may be painted with vistas, but they are always painted walls. Some rooms are cubicles; we sometimes see the tops of the partitions (therefore no place is really private or secure), although in the great hall windows and walls continue out of frame. Gertrude's closet is entirely hung with curtains. Only the theatre set for the play-within-the-play has a forced representational perspective. The castle setting, especially those spaces related to Claudius, Gertrude, and Polonius, establish a sense of being covered over, of false perspectives, of surfaces that disguise actuality. As a setting for *Hamlet*, it is significant when it needs to be, as when Claudius and Polonius hide behind a painted panel to overhear Hamlet's talk with Ophelia, but otherwise unobtrusive and simple enough that two thrones can take focus and gain import.

For the ramparts, of course, not much set is necessary, a Ghost and a bit of fog for atmosphere. In fact, open space implies there is nothing in the world except this mysterious shape in the dark. Used also as port (I.3), the plain crossed by an army (IV.4), and a graveyard (V.1), the open space is associated with farewells and messages of remembrance, and silhouetted figures of sailors, soldiers, or mourners at times walk the ramp in the background.

Rodney Bennett has a strong cast and uses them with strength. Derek Jacobi confides his thoughts to camera in the soliloquies, not only as a means of thinking aloud but as a means of self-expression and self-explanation in a world where he must hide or obscure what he thinks, what he feels, what he suspects. His only other friend and confidant is Horatio, for when Hamlet first sees Rosencrantz he stumbles on his name; clearly they are but acquaintances. When Hamlet first sees Horatio at the end of I.2, on the other hand, a focus shift from Hamlet foreground to Horatio rear makes it seem as if Hamlet can scarcely believe his eyes as he turns. As in *Julius Caesar*, another conspiratorial play, television brings out the manipulations in *Hamlet*, the anglings, the looks of suspicion or distress. The psychological study is also subtler because it is intimate and not projected to the upper galleries or hurled over sixty yards into a stiff wind at Kronberg Castle, as Jacobi recalled doing on tour: " 'To be or not to be' may have been said better but it's certainly never been said louder."[28]

Nothing gets in the way of the actors' performances in *Hamlet*; everything enhances it. That was Bennett's goal; having seen Shakespeare productions work with open staging in a small theatre, he knew the value of a spare or minimalist approach and the significance gained by whatever is included. Doubtless using that theatrical approach—three boards and a passion—gives these stylized productions their power. Having space also helped. Like the set designer of *Macbeth*, Don Homfray of *Hamlet* reveled in the size of studio 1: "It's a wonderful volume to use and one can so rarely get a chance to use it as a totality."[29] Space and images, not real place, were the key to the design of both these tragedies.

In *Macbeth* Jack Gold got performances that explode on a shorter fuse than the long wait in *Hamlet*; that is the nature of the plays and the characters. In *Hamlet* a series of feints and sleights postpone the fatal blows until the end; the awful doing of the Scottish play begins much earlier and sustains itself throughout the play, murder on murder.

For *Macbeth*, director and set designer quickly discarded the idea of realism; though they wanted the barbarism of eleventh-century Scotland, they wanted space more, space divided only by steps, platforms, and various massive wall pieces that could be rearranged scene by scene. So a stylization began, and against those thick stonelike surfaces much of the action takes place. The heath is murky, the castle is dark, with a threatening portcullis hanging at the end of its tunnel entrance; in the scene of Duncan's arrival at

Macbeth's castle the camera moves past the spikes of the portcullis to greet him and shows the slow descent of that gate to ominous music at scene's end. The chthonic witches appear to emerge from the ancient ritual stones, stones that are the squat, northern cousins of Stonehenge. Against this spare, stony setting, powerful, destructive human forces begin to work. Nicol Williamson growls and pants and keeps the thane's tortured psyche visible, close to the surface so it can be observed by the camera. And the camera moves in for close-ups and back to use the dramatic backlighting provided for the first murder scene.

Compared with a film version such as Roman Polanski's, Gold's *Macbeth* emphasizes what it does not show rather than what it does. With Polanski's film, in addition to panoramic vistas and details of castle life, we see the spectral dagger before the murder, the ghost Macbeth sees at the banquet, and the visions he has at the witches', so that the subjective element is real to us; we share the torment. We see Polanski's Lady Macbeth linked to the coven of witches by nude scenes. We also see the death of the first traitor Glamis, the rape and murder and pillaging of Macduff's household, and the fight to the death at the end, with a shot that tracks Macbeth's severed head as it rolls down a flight of stone steps, a grisly but fascinating business throughout.

Gold's witches and thanes' wives are amply clad. We see no visions with Macbeth—no dagger, no ghost, no pageant of future kings; we only hear voices and see Macbeth's spellbound face over the fumes of the brew. Rather than share his horror, we watch its effects. And we do not see the final death blow or a severed head; instead, the crown is removed from the whole and supine corpse and presented to Malcolm. The murders we see are Banquo's ambush in the dark, several more thrusts by Seyton to insure the murderers' silence, the toss of Macduff's son onto Seyton's waiting sword, and Macbeth's slaying of young Siward. Where Polanski interprets the play as a relentless and universal yearning for power and its concomitant destructiveness that will continue after Macbeth's death, as we know when we see Donalbain limp through the rain to the witches at the end, Gold's is a study of the moral collapse of one man and its costs to society. Thus his production choices keep focus on the characters, not their context, and especially on Macbeth.

Looking at the different approaches used in presenting Shakespeare's tragedies in the BBC series offers us a basis for examining production and stylistic options for Shakespeare on television. Six of the ten tragedies were given straightforwardly stylized productions—*Titus Andronicus, Hamlet, King Lear, Macbeth, Timon of Athens*, and *Antony and Cleopatra. Romeo and Juliet* and *Julius Caesar* leaned toward representation. *Othello* and *Coriolanus* more fully succeeded in turning the studio into a full-scale world, even though one is representational and the other stylized. *Othello*'s set for the interior scenes in Cyprus is carefully based on period architecture, a palace in Urbino, and the dark street in Cyprus based on a real street,[30] while *Coriolanus* is a pastiche of the Elizabethan era and Etruscan Rome, in no way representational of one era. Yet its weather-faded surfaces and opulent lighting convey a rich, somehow believable visual context for the action.

Whatever its basis, some degree of stylization, often total, was the most common response to producing the histories and tragedies in the studio. Comedies and romances usually got more representational treatment. Because of their very natures the genres may tend toward these respective approaches; tragedy plumbs the individual, and comedy emphasizes the society. As a result, the social fabric may benefit by its visibility in those comic plays that affirm it.

Another way of describing this distinction between tragedy and comedy is that while Shakespeare wrote only one so-called domestic tragedy, *Othello*, he wrote only one nondomestic, affairs-of-state comedy, *Troilus and Cressida*, the only erstwhile comedy with battlefield scenes. All the rest of Shakespearean comedy is domestic, and domestic with a focus on the manors and homes of aristocrats and wealthy merchants, including their necessary servants and accoutrements. Only *The Taming of the Shrew*, of all the comedies and romances, contains no titled character, no "sir" this or "duke" that, no prince of Arragon, no king of Bohemia or the fairies. Outside the dwellings, Shakespeare's comic world usually involves the civic environment with its constabulary forces and street vendors, pimps and prostitutes, inns and abbeys. Only four of the thirteen comedies have action in a forest—*Two Gentlemen*, *A Mid-summer Night's Dream*, *Merry Wives*, and *As You Like It*—and only in *Dream* and *As You Like It* does that action extend for more than one scene. Most of the natural world in the comedies is not wilderness but tame, a series of gardens and courtyards, very civilized. The wilder areas of Shakespeare's comic geography are the shores, appearing briefly in *Twelfth Night* and more frequently in the romances, *Pericles*, *Winter's Tale*, and *Tempest*; *Cymbeline* moves to the mountain terrain near Milford Haven. Thus while romance may run to extremities of nature, comedy as Shakespeare writes it is usually within civil bounds.

Given these attributes, it is no surprise that the most representational or realism-oriented plays in the BBC Shakespeare series are the comedies and romances. Not *all* are representational, of course. *Winter's Tale* and *Merchant* are completely stylized, as is the forest at the end of *Two Gentlemen*. The courtyards in that play are partly stylized as well; so is the Ephesus of *Comedy of Errors* and some of the settings for *Shrew*. In *Troilus and Cressida* Troy is a set of schematic openings. We can judge the effects of these varying degrees of stylization as environments for comedy and romance, but far more noticeable are the detailed representational settings or foregrounds of most of these productions. The manors seem sumptuous, the houses livable, the streets peopled and busy, the gardens pleasant. The stunning aesthetic worlds of *Love's Labour's Lost* and *All's Well*, where Shakespeare's characters walk through scenes that seem like three-dimensional Watteau and Vermeer, are matched by the architectural charm of the Windsor of *Merry Wives* and the Illyria of *Twelfth Night*.

The decision about production style is a major aspect of televising Shakespeare, and with its numerous directors and designers the BBC Shakespeare series explored a variety of approaches. Yet for the most part its production style for comedy also parallels television's own general attitude toward comedy. On television, action shows such as police and private eye dramas involve location work; most comedies of situation are taped in the studio. Stylized reality, it would seem, is the major mode of televised comedy, and while classic drama uses style as part of the interpretation, this approach proves an especially useful means of conveying Shakespeare's plays on television when reality can be as artfully stylized as it is in many of the BBC's productions.

Moreover, not only David Jones but many of the directors for the BBC Shakespeare series thought their plays were helped enormously by being done on television, for television let them pay attention to the action in ways that do not occur in the large houses of the well-known Shakespeare theatre companies. The lesser-known (and in some cases perhaps just lesser) plays often got a care and scrutiny that argued their value, as occurred with *Henry VIII, Measure, All's Well, Cymbeline*, and *Titus*, among others. The more famous and widely beloved plays could be rendered with a fresh psychological power of performance due to the intimacy of the camera and sound boom; histrionics proved unnecessary.

In addition to directors, actors also found the televised Shakespeare series to be full of challenges and opportunities. Building emotionally through a great Shakespeare role on stage means discovering a definite rhythm for performance. The technical aspects of television taping therefore posed a special challenge to actors who were performing some of the world's greatest plays piece by piece—sometimes breaking scene by scene, sometimes couplet by couplet—but never in the Shakespeare series giving an entire, unbroken live performance before the camera as in the theatre, though that, too, has been tried on television. As compensation, a number of the directors in the series worked for long takes to enhance performance, among them Don Taylor of *Two Gentlemen* (who has been known, after meticulous camera rehearsals, to tape unbroken runs of a play, a somewhat unorthodox approach to studio work), who said he was

> a very fervent advocate of continuous performance—most of this was done in great long chunks, twenty-minute chunks. I think that the film-making approach to television is ludicrous, it's a waste of resources. . . . You can do other things in a television studio—you can get that dangerous element of performance. . . . It seems to me far more important in a play that was designed for the theatre to go for that rather than

for very carefully arranged pictures and very carefully angled lighting. . . . You destroy the actors' performances when you do that.[31]

Some directors did occasionally work filmically, shot by shot, through sections of a play, but Taylor was more concerned with what a production loses as a result of that approach; with his long takes, for instance, he said "there were at least two occasions in this play where an actress did things in the heat of performance that were far beyond anything she'd reached in rehearsal: insights and perceptions that only performance can achieve."[32]

For the actor, therefore, studio work poses a different set of performance considerations than does the theatre. Because every scene is treated in isolation, there is no natural build, no natural restraint, no natural demand for pacing from scene to scene as in a theatrical performance (not forgetting that all those "natural" elements are the result of weeks of careful rehearsal). All that must be internalized and for television each piece performed as if it *were* in context. As Michael Hordern pointed out, "You've got to be extremely careful to hit the right level a day later. . . . In the theatre there is the natural progression of the evening to keep you in check."[33] Even the breaks within one day can prove challenging; Derek Jacobi spoke of trying to hold consistency and concentration when the first two lines of his descent speech at Flint Castle in *Richard II* were taped on the battlements, then the rest of the speech was taped on another set after a thirty-minute lighting change. The rhythm of studio performance is continually interrupted or strained, as Jacobi noted: "In the theatre Shakespeare gave you time off, little breaks before your crescendos. Here we were doing the big scenes one after another. The orchestration of an actor's tempo is thrown out of gear—but it always is with television."[34] The demands that television taping makes on performers can be formidable. Kate Nelligan (Isabella in *Measure*) proclaimed, "If you can act on television, you can act on water," and went on to explain, "The difficulty with television is that technical considerations come first. It's no good the actor being excellent if the cameras or lights are wrong. And you've really got only once or twice to get it right; if you do badly, you can't go back and do it again as you do in film. For me, it's the most difficult medium of all."[35] Jacobi expressed a similar feeling: "The freedom that you get on stage when the juices are really flowing, you don't get on television. There are too many technical things to worry about."[36]

And performing Shakespeare on television means all the intimacy and proximity of the close-up medium are focused on lines usually delivered with grand theatrical flourish, which gave some actors concern, as Leonard Rossiter (King John) observed: "I think there is a great danger, when filming Shakespeare for television, of subduing everything in an effort to make it more real. The problem is, then you have nowhere to go when you get to the soliloquies. . . . I'd rather shout than miniaturize the action into nothing. Shakespeare's plays were meant to be performed theatrically, and there is no reason to bend Shakespeare unnecessarily, or tone them down, for the sake of the medium."[37] Thus to some degree television as a medium for Shakespeare can be defined negatively, by what it is not, by what it prevents. The basic charge or implication here is that it is not theatre, that the performance conditions are not theatrical, both of which adversely affect or alter the result. For theatre lovers—performer or audience or critic—television never entirely overcomes this truth.

The tradition of theatricalism, that is, of grandness, as Rossiter's comment suggests, is strong; it results from centuries of performance in cavernous theatrical houses. But there are other possibilities for performance. Michael Hordern, in talking about *Lear*, added, "I enjoy acting Shakespeare on television. People are always talking about how it diminishes the size and power of a performance, but you rarely hear anyone praise the way it enables an actor to vary the size, the tension, and the intimacy of his work. One simply doesn't have to project all the time. . . . And if you're really not happy unless you're playing to a live audience, there are always all the people in the studio."[38] A number of other performers in the BBC Shakespeares agreed; during *Much Ado* Robert Lindsay (Benedick) said, "I think the subtleties, the subtext, which are difficult to project on stage, you can do on television. Just the fact that you can stand next to someone and say one thing, while your eyes are saying something else, is wonderful."[39] And while working on *Henry VIII* Timothy West (Wolsey) felt the medium and the play were well suited: "Most of us think it's a good play for television because it isn't a play of enormous rhetoric. It's a play where thoughts change very rapidly and there's an awful lot the television camera can help you with, which perhaps would need a lot of work to get over on stage."[40] Thus, television also lets actors and directors explore aspects of Shakespeare that theatre cannot, providing insights that can enhance understanding.

In assessing the demands the medium makes on an actor, Elijah Moshinsky during *Coriolanus* explained both sides of the challenge: "For the camera you don't perform, you have to expose yourself in front of the camera—you get nothing back and it's a very difficult and unnerving thing to do. To be entirely open at the moment of the take—that really is the trick," and yet he continued, "[*Coriolanus* is] a cold play, there's very little warmth about it. . . . That's why it needs phenomenal technique, like Alan [Howard]'s got, to do it—you can't just say the lines and identify with the character or you'd end up crying all the time."[41] Honesty and openness and consummate technique necessitate a delicate balancing act, but one that many of the actors relished.

Casting is crucial in televised Shakespeare, requiring actors who could handle verse as well as prose and present the character fully for a camera; everyone involved in the Shakespeare series knew casting was the key to the productions. Looking back at the series, many critics question the casting first, usually asking why the great actors from the British stage were not used or not used more often.

Such a question may seem strange, for surveying the casting in the series is like a roll call of great British actors and actresses, those with long-established reputations—John Gielgud, Wendy Hiller, Celia Johnson, Cyril Cusack, Claire Bloom—those who have led the Royal Shakespeare Company—Alan Howard, Richard Pasco, Michael Pennington, Patrick Stewart, Ben Kingsley, Nicol Williamson, Jane Lapotaire, Mike Gwilym—in addition to the well-known stage figures Derek Jacobi, Helen Mirren, Timothy West, Irene Worth, Anthony Hopkins, and Jonathan Pryce; those with as much television fame in Britain as stage experience, such as Felicity

Kendal and Donald Sinden; and established younger actors, such as Juliet Stevenson and Anton Lesser, who had also starred at the RSC and the National Theatre. These performers all delivered the goods; their characterizations gave depth and power to the series. Thus the void that critics perceive is partly an illusion. To the extent that some notable British actors were not included, the series is answerable and can answer: it was a matter of the right roles at the right time at the right price. Between stage, television, and film commitments, many fine actors were simply unavailable for the specified five-week rehearsal and taping period when directors in the series sought them. Some may have disdained the project or its reputation early on. Some may have demanded a fee beyond the production's budget or may have been uninterested in the offer. These are the usual problems of casting, not specific to the Shakespeare series. On the other hand, some directors may not necessarily have wanted only big names but instead may have sought compatible actors familiar with their techniques, known quantities. Furthermore, many actors whose names are not widely known gave fine performances in the series.

Much of the criticism of the casting in the series focused on casting in the famous tragic roles such as Romeo and Juliet, Lear, Othello, Antony and Cleopatra, where the performances were not deemed the equivalent of memorable stage renditions. Of course, were these roles not difficult they would not be held in high esteem. The standard theatre wisdom about Romeo or Juliet, for instance, is that by the time you know enough to play the role you are too old to play it. Casting very young actors in the roles is always a risk, and the play was not helped by the perverse delivery Anthony Andrews used as Mercutio. Though Celia Johnson shone as the Nurse, that role alone cannot sustain the tragedy. Lear, Othello, and Antony and Cleopatra open a different issue, for here the performers gave exactly what the director, Miller in all three instances, asked; the actors were cast on purpose for their nonheroic qualities, since Miller wanted to go against the grain. To attack the performer is not altogether just, since the difference of opinion is with the director's interpretation, not the quality of the rendition itself.

There were, admittedly, a number of disappointing performances in the series. *Romeo and Juliet* and *The Tempest* are almost universally considered losses, with only a few comic spots to redeem either from deserved oblivion. Much of *Julius Caesar* remained wooden despite the efforts of Richard Pasco. *The Winter's Tale* needed a Leontes to spark it, and Jeremy Kemp never found the flint, nor did some of his cohorts. Richard Griffiths's lethargic Falstaff seemed a bit off-key in an otherwise sprightly Windsor. Other factors also took a toll, as when Ron Cook's hunchback king showed the fatigue that Jane Howell's mini–repertory company felt by the time they had fought through the Wars of the Roses and gotten to *Richard III*; Howell herself admitted they were all probably too tired to do the play justice. Critics differ in their assessments, but some criticism is just since problems in leading roles inevitably affect the success of the entire production.

Sage observers in BBC's Drama division did not expect the famous plays to be the hits of the series, but they thought giving care and attention to less frequently performed plays might produce some surprising results, as was indeed the case. Tim Pigott-Smith and Kate Nelligan squared off as Angelo and Isabella in a rousing *Measure for Measure* aided by Frank Middlemass's incorrigible Pompey Bum. Pigott-Smith's Hotspur was equally strong in *1 Henry IV* and stretched David Gwillim's Hal. Derek Jacobi's Richard II was widely admired. All three leads in *Henry VIII*—John Stride, Claire Bloom, and Timothy West—helped to make that play the revelation of the first season. Helen Mirren and Robert Lindsay led a strong cast in a fully realized *Cymbeline*. In *Merry Wives* Ben Kingsley was predictably outrageous as Ford and was supported merrily by Prunella Scales and Judy Davis as the wives. Mike Gwilym brought *Pericles* to life along with rich performances by Amanda Redman and Juliet Stevenson. Alan Howard proved his tremendous power as Coriolanus for the camera just as he had on stage. George Costigan provided a thoroughly insouciant Bastard in *King John*. In the *Henry VI–Richard III* tetralogy Julia Foster was fascinating in developing Margaret of Anjou from girl to bitter queen to cursing crone. These few bouquets only sample work in leading roles; in some productions the entire company cohered in worthy efforts, as was true of Howell's *Henry VI* plays and *Titus* and of Moshinsky's *All's Well, Love's Labour's Lost,* and *Cymbeline.*

Some performers appeared in the series frequently enough to demonstrate their considerable range and talent. Robert Lindsay's five roles—Fabian, *All's Well*'s Second Lord, Lysander, Iachimo, and Benedick—showed him to advantage, as did Trevor Peacock's Feste, Talbot, Jack Cade, Boult, and Titus. Michael Hordern's five roles encompassed Lear, Prospero, Capulet, Jupiter, and Lafew. Mike Gwilym successfully portrayed Pericles's age range and emotional challenges along with assignments as Aufidius and Berowne. Ian Charleson was called upon for three cold fish, Fortinbras, Octavius, and Bertram, and gave differing sangfroid to each. Penelope Wilton was warm, loving, and full of integrity as Desdemona, cold, selfish, and full of spite as Regan. Paul Jesson almost made a career of the series for several years with roles in eight plays, as the Clown in *Winter's Tale,* Clarence through the Wars of the Roses, Cloten, Costard, and *Coriolanus*'s First Citizen. Thus, although the BBC Shakespeare series did not work from a repertory company, in some cases the effect is the same, offering extra rewards to the series's viewer.

Moving Shakespeare's plays from stage to television demands accommodations and ingenuity, technical insight into how best to use the camera to enhance play and performance and how to capture energy and nuance, passionate outburst and quiet glance, for the small screen. Directors, designers, and performers all labored to make the transition not just workable but exciting and effective. Occasionally there was a larger claim, as Elijah Moshinsky's statement that "television is the ideal medium for the serious performance of Shakespeare" exactly because "it frees performances from a static stage" by providing "an endlessly flexible frame for the action" and also "has the great filmic capability of the close-up." Citing the efforts of William Poel, Tyrone Guthrie, and Peter Brook to gain flexible intimacy and freedom from stagey pictorialism, Moshinsky argues that "in many ways, television is the logical and obvious heir to the modern movement in Shakespearian production."[42] Many of the best televised Shakespeare plays prove

Moshinsky's point. With theatrical stagings or filmic effects, studio realism or a variety of stylizations, voice-overs, close-ups, intricate developing shots, exceptional lighting, and some strong performances, the BBC offered Shakespeare's plays a wealth of experience and artistry, proving as had the RSC that Shakespeare *can* be produced effectively on television.

Three

The Exigencies of Production

How was it?

Well worth the seeing.

—Henry VIII

Break we our watch up; and, by my advice,

Let us impart what we have seen.

—Hamlet

8 *Troilus and Cressida* and Jonathan Miller

SUMMER 1981

*I*n approaching *Troilus and Cressida* for the BBC Shakespeare series, Jonathan Miller felt the modern echoes of this Shakespearean drama, just as Shakespeare had felt a contemporary resonance in his classical subject matter. The layers of the play interested Miller; he chose to set it firmly in the Renaissance rather than the classical world (although both settings distance the play from a modern audience, there is somehow an extra degree of distance by having Achilles with a codpiece and Cressida in a snood), saying as he did so that the Renaissance could only view the classics as a reflection of itself, as its art demonstrates. Yet through nuances and allusions Miller simultaneously linked the play to the modern sensibility:

> I feel that Shakespeare's plays and all the works of the classic rank, of literary antiquity, must necessarily be Janus-faced. And one merely pretends that one is producing pure Renaissance drama; I think one has to see it in one's own terms. Because it is constantly making references, one might as well be a little more specific about it. Now that doesn't mean that I want to hijack them for the purposes of making the plays address themselves specifically to modern problems.
>
> I think what one wants to do is to have these little anachronistic overtones so that we're constantly aware of the fact that the play is, as it were, suspended in the twentieth-century imagination, halfway between the period in which it was written and the period in which we are witnessing it. And then there is of course a third period being referred to, which is the period of the Greek antiquity.[1]

Miller's idea of anachronistic overtones as well as his own style for the BBC Shakespeare productions was apparent as he described the sets and costumes to the cast the first day of rehearsal, 29 June 1981. Troy was to give a sense of urban decadence, the clear, almost abstract lines of the set reproducing one of Jan Vredeman de Vries's Renaissance architectural exercises in perspective, so that the set itself would have a deep perspective with the towers, stairs, colonnades, even a loony bin for Cassandra, all made of treated plywood (Miller's favorite building material for his productions), and there would be pools of light from apertures in the set, not just light in general. The costumes, to be made of rich fabrics in bright colors, were inspired by Cranach and Dürer; Miller displayed open art books on a nearby table. Cranach was chosen, Miller later said, because he was poised on the edge of a new world, halfway between the Gothic world of Chaucer's and Henryson's portrayals of the lovers and Shakespeare's Renaissance world.

In establishing Troy, Miller wanted a sharp contrast to the Greek camp, which Miller and designer Colin Lowrey based on the faded, patched tents of an indigent travelers' camp near the BBC Television Centre in West London. As Miller described it, the Greek camp was to be a cluttered, squalid tent city, after seven years infested with rats and dysentery, ennui and bickering, and built, Miller envisioned, on the ruins of an earlier Troy, devastated in some even then ancient campaign—bits of roof would jut out amid the camp, and there would be a chunk of fallen statue, a twelve-foot face with water collected in the eye (perhaps people would even be doing their laundry there, he added). The camp would stand amidst great pools of water, adding to the malarial atmosphere, and on one side would appear the beginning of a leg of the Trojan horse, never to be mentioned or explained. (The horse leg is clearly visible behind Cressida in the photograph on the back cover of the BBC *Troilus and Cressida* script.) Overall, the camp was to give "a tremendous sense of everything running downhill," Miller said, with the men bored, drinking, or doing exercises to keep fit. The army was to be clad uniformly in khaki-colored Renaissance garb, a military effect purposefully suggestive of *M.A.S.H.* (or early *Apocalypse Now*, he added) with a Gothic-lettered name tag on each officer's garment and, as later became apparent, a wardrobe characterization of Thersites as the Corporal Klinger of the classical world.

Miller's enthusiasm for the project was evident in his descriptions, but he made no general comments about the play itself and, contrary to usual practice, had no read-through the first day. He surveyed his cast, pleased, then sent most of them home and began work with the few needed to begin blocking the opening scenes.

Rehearsals were held five, sometimes six, days a week from 10:00 A.M. to approximately 4:00 P.M., but they were run according to Miller's preferred rehearsal schedule, with no big break for tea or lunch when the cast would disperse; instead he had tea and sandwiches brought down to the rehearsal room from the cafeteria. Four weeks of facing luncheon meat, cheese, or egg on a hard roll got a bit grim, but the strategy paid: the cast stayed together, ate together, and never really broke concentration, never came back sluggish from relaxing at lunch over wine or a pint. When the afternoon session began, everyone was sharp, and Miller did not have to build momentum again. Miller always runs his rehearsals by this schedule, but it proved especially useful in this case as a subtle way of giving the cast a sense of siege—being in one place for a long time with the same people—which is good background work for *Troilus and Cressida*.

In working on scenes in this play the cast inevitably became two casts, the Trojans and the Greeks, rehearsing on separate days. One Greek, Diomedes, goes to Troy, while a number of Trojans—the warriors and Cressida—go to the Greek camp for a scene or two, for the contest or in exchange, but some characters stay in one place and so have knowledge only of that environment. Curiosity grew, and well into rehearsals some members of one group would ask if they might come to a rehearsal for the other locale to see what was happening.

Miller's approach to casting is, as he says, to give the piece life, to cast "interesting people" in the roles, and by "interesting" he means interesting to him, which because he often has acute insight into literary character and acting ability can create some startling effects, effects that are right in unexpected ways. The two casts in

The streamlined plywood set for Troy in Troilus and Cressida *was a three-dimensional version of the steps, columns, and archways in one of Jan Vredeman de Vries's perspective exercises in Renaissance architecture. Hector (John Shrapnel, left), Troilus (Anton Lesser, rear), Andromache (Merelina Kendall), Priam (Esmond Knight). © BBC*

By contrast, the Greek camp in Troilus and Cressida *was full of khaki tents, period props, restive soldiers, camp whores, and quiet allusions to the Trojan War, as with the start of the Trojan Horse, one leg of which is visible behind the barrel. Diomedes (Paul Moriarty, left) and Cressida (Suzanne Burden, second from left).* © *BBC*

Troilus and Cressida were remarkably different in temperament and in professional disposition. The Trojans worked with a family feeling or a sense of Musketeers, usually very smooth and quick in taking notes and working out action. The actors of the Greek camp were to a greater extent every man for himself, demanding attention (though a few were so cooperative and quick as to be honorary Trojans by these criteria). The focus was always on clarifying and giving the best performance, but the questions and the crablike suggestions of alternatives were most prevalent in working with the Greek camp.

Throughout the production Miller obviously strove to achieve

Miller's sportive allusions to M.A.S.H. *in* Troilus and Cressida *included costuming Thersites (The Incredible Orlando, Jack Birkett) in a whore's castoff gown to suggest Corporal Klinger while Ajax (Anthony Pedley) lounges with his pin-up girls created from copies of Cranach nudes.*
© BBC

naturalness and to cut staginess, declamation, and histrionics. At times, in trying to gain naturalness rather than pose, he would describe a character's attitude or response with vivid, deft contemporary stories to help an actor. Through such explanation and analogies Miller gave the actors a clear, full sense of action and intention. Miller would also regularly break a cardinal rule of directing by showing an actor what he had in mind, especially in comic bits, and since Miller is an accomplished mimic and fine sketch performer, he would often give a brief, perfect rendition no one else could subsequently match. In fact, the spontaneous Miller vignettes, anecdotes, asides, and lectures made *Troilus and Cressida* rehearsals the best free show in London.

In rough-blocking the scenes, Miller's thoughtful and thorough analysis of the action and his preparation of the play were apparent. He described the atmosphere and the nature of the characters and their interactions to the actors and began developing moods and discovering bits of byplay he wanted. The first week's rehearsals covered most of the scenes, but the emphasis was on the Greek camp. Of the first seven rehearsals, only one dealt with Troy, and then only with the lovers' major scenes together, though rehearsals for the Trojan scenes evened the balance later in the schedule.

Miller's descriptions of the scenes as he worked on them provide his rough overview of the play. In dealing with the early scenes in the Greek camp, he wanted all to be aware of the seven years they had already been fighting; even the officers in council are war-weary, bored, almost distracted or forgetful of purpose, except Ulysses, who calmly reasserts the point. Miller described Ulysses as orderly and sharp, with a "word-processor mind," like a government under-secretary who knows everything and advises soundly. Nestor and Agamemnon, however, do not listen to each other much any more; Agamemnon spends much of his time reaching for the wine goblet in the early scene. Diomedes, competent and watchful, serves as discreet secretary of the group. Miller also said he wanted many of the Greek camp scenes to be done from the camp beds, to which everyone has consigned or resigned himself.

In Troy Miller was most discursive about the leave-taking scene. Troilus, he said to Anton Lesser, here shows his first signs of maturity. The sight of Cressida's hysteria calls forth his need to be a man in the situation. Cressida, on the other hand, is self-concerned and flawed, yet with the sort of flaw many never discover in themselves, Miller added, like a house that can stand 120 years cracked from eave to floor. Moreover, she likes attention, especially the attention of older men; the Greek camp will seem very glamorous to her, he told Suzanne Burden. For Cressida, he said, leaving Troy for the Greek camp will be like leaving a girls' school and seeing a steel works—all those men stripped to the waist.

The contest between Hector and Ajax in the Greek camp is a strange affair in which the enemy becomes guest and the rival males—here face to face, as the actors were well aware—must avoid confrontations about their women. Under Miller's hand it took on a framework of comedy. He set up the duel as a prizefight, with a ring built in the center of the Greek camp. Throughout the early part of the scene, Ajax takes practice thrusts at a straw dummy, and the contest itself is done in rounds, complete with Diomedes and Aeneas as trainers with stools, buckets, and towels. The polite geniality inevitably shifts into challenges; as earlier between Diomedes and Aeneas in Troy, here the banter between Hector and Ajax, then Hector and Nestor, leads to the confrontation and challenge between Hector and Achilles. But during the greeting period, in addition to all the bad Menelaus jokes in the script, Miller built in a comic identification process; like an aide to a political figure, Aeneas leans back to whisper the Greeks' names to Hector as he meets them.

During work on the long series of short battlefield scenes that end the play, Miller explained that he had purposefully excluded the fighting, especially the fight between Hector and Achilles (V.6.13–21), leaving only the killing of Hector. Traditionally, he said, the end of the play on stage is one long, sporadic battle. Instead he wanted an emphasis on the words, a sense of the confusion, since most of the battlefield deeds are only reported, with the action itself offstage as in Greek drama. His idea of the scenes was to show some dim skirmishes in the background, soldiers passing by, cannon being hauled; he also discussed having the scene lit as if by flares to give a World War I effect, his favorite analogy for the battle. In working through these scenes, actors began negotiating for the reinstatement of certain lines cut in the rehearsal script, John Shrapnel (Hector) for the pursuit of the golden armor (V.6.12 and 27–30) and Kenneth Haigh (Achilles) for the carrying in of Patroclus's body (V.5.44–47), both of which Miller considered and later accepted.

Simultaneously with the rough-blocking of these scenes, the fight rehearsals began with fight arranger Bill Hobbs, starting with the Ajax-Hector contest. Though only part of the fight would be shot as the central action, as Miller told Hobbs and the actors, it would always be seen in the background, so they began working out a sequence of moves and pauses to fit the scene. Miller said Hector should be deft, bullfighter quick in parrying Ajax's blows; Ajax, the mad bull, would do real damage if he connected. The idea was to show that he would hurt a lesser opponent, Miller added. In the first rehearsal, round one was fought with swords, then as round two developed Tony Pedley (Ajax) took up an ax, at which point he and Miller, kindred comic spirits, began spinning possibilities for Ajax—perhaps he might kill someone in the crowd by accident on a backswing or when the ax slipped from his grasp; then, they added, he could do in another bystander with a cudgel out of sheer frustration. Later, of course, the weapons changed and these ideas faded, but for that afternoon the duel proved unexpectedly lethal.

By the second week, as Miller and the cast began repeating and developing scenes, almost all the actors were off book; their quick study gave Miller far more effective rehearsals for everyone could feel the shape and movement of the scenes. In explaining movement, Miller always worked with the model of the set, showing actors their positions and the production staff the camera angles. As he proceeded, he described how he wanted to shoot the scenes, though he always left himself open to changes during camera rehearsals in the studio. He calls this method "discovery," and while he practices it, he adds that the BBC hates it, considering it "bad planning"; every move, they feel, should be set in advance and proceed like clockwork. Miller shrugs and admits he does not work that way; he changes, and designer Colin Lowrey does not mind (though, Miller pointed out, some designers do). An instance of such "discovery" occurred early in rehearsal when, in working with the leave-taking scene in Cressida's bedroom, Miller rearranged the rooms and moved the bed. There was then much scurrying by the production staff to adapt the rehearsal set, change the tape on the floor indicating position of walls and doors, and call the designer. In the same way Miller leaves his camera script open, discussing scenes and shots with the production staff before and during the rehearsal process, indicating angles with his own sign language (two fingers held in a horizontal "v") during scenes. Then he later compiles the shots for the studio camera script, a move that separates him from those directors technically trained to television, for whom creating the camera script is primary, a personal achievement.

Miller also chose to work with Jim Atkinson, one of the BBC's most experienced, creative, and forthright head cameramen, whose opinion he respected. When Atkinson appeared at rehearsals, as he did several days the third week, he discussed shifts in groupings to tighten shots, sighted potential troubles, and suggested reworking some elements. The duel and greetings, for instance, were reblocked for the cameras, which could only shoot around the edges of the Greek camp; Calchas's tent was moved six feet to help camera movement, and Agamemnon's bed was put on blocks to help the camera shooting into the tent under the side flap. As in this case, Miller tried to surround himself with the best production and technical staff he could so he could draw on their expertise to complement his ideas while he concentrated on performance.

Work on scenes in Troy focused on the Trojan council, which Miller emphasized was a *family* council. He wanted to keep the scene from being, as it too often is, a series of independent proclamatory orations. He insisted that with so many family members present all the arguments are familiar; they have done and said it all before, yet, he added, in this day's discussion there is tension, a potential division. John Shrapnel (Hector) had many questions about his motivation, especially about his apparent change that is the climax of the scene. Miller explained that Hector does not change his mind; he says what he says as if for the record, here is the truth. He does, however, change his *decision*, to fight rather than send Helen back. Also Miller pointed out that Cassandra seconds Hector's opinion, displaying the irony of madness. He added that Cassandra does not seem raving mad in Hector's later arming scene and would not be played as such. Here they tried toning down the screaming madness of the standard stage Cassandra, all volume and little sense. Cassandra (Elayne Sharling) approached the table intently and earnestly but speaking in a normal voice; the men rejected not her but her words, and as Hector backed her up to the cell or cage built into the set she entreated him in an intense whisper all the way, keeping almost hypnotic eye contact. It was a stunning version of Cassandra because suddenly one was *listening* to her, hearing her words as Hector heard them, while everyone else at the table tuned her out in annoyance.

In the third week, like magic, many other scenes started to take definite shape. The early Ajax-Thersites scene (II.1), for instance, had gone through the gamut of languorous beating to boisterous blows to almost entirely verbal combat, with Miller thinking through each variation overnight and at next rehearsal saying, "That's not quite right." Every version that Tony Pedley and Jack Birkett did was fully rendered and had its own possibilities; they trusted Miller to choose the best. He ended up letting the text's insistence on physicality dictate the action, so that the two shoved and slapped each other, just like small boys, Miller commented, pleased that even Achilles gets sucked into their clamor.

The Trojan council scene gained a slightly new approach to Cassandra. Mad with truth, she now played the whole scene locked in the cell; she cannot get to the table to tell them what they need to hear about their stupid course of action, so she cries out, Miller told the actress. When Hector walked back to the cell to calm her, she spoke in that effective, intense whisper, crying out again as he left her; then, unheeded, she paced defiantly until she let out one great deep laugh as her brother gave in at the end. Miller was still trying to create a mood in the council like that at the end of a long board meeting—chairs and table disordered, everyone tired. He told the actors to move around, get up, sit on the table, pace, think, look at each other silently in annoyance or support—and also to break up the speeches so each part had color. The brothers began to slouch and lean and grimace, all of which helped the scene, and to show little respect for Priam, whose grip on consciousness grew more slender at every rehearsal.

But the big scene of the week, and perhaps the single most remarkable moment of rehearsal, was the leave-taking scene, which had been discussed, walked through, tuned, but never done full blast. One day Miller drew his chair close to the rehearsal platform "bed," from which proximity he always watched that scene with rapt look, and told Lesser and Burden to cut loose. The scene began, hushed and tense, but as Burden sobbed, threw herself on the bed, and with cracked voice and the anger of victimization cried, "I will *not* go from Troy," the usual businesslike undercurrent and shuffle of the rehearsal room ceased. Everyone was breathless and engaged in the action, the only sounds her choked words and sobs and Lesser's broken attempts to console her while needing consolation himself. As the scene ended, there was silence, a pause of tribute. Then Miller bounded up, whooped, and danced a jig around the platform—the perfect nonverbal response for what everyone felt: "this is a *scene*." Then he went to work. He added the comic moment of Troilus and Cressida standing on each side of the door as Pandarus passed between them teasing, and he asked Burden to give varied tone and volume to her denial of the news, shaking her head before she spoke, the sort of body language Miller is very good at clarifying to make a moment right.

By week's end Miller was refining the scenes after the contest in the Greek camp. After the fourth or fifth run-through, the drunken approach of the Greek officers bringing Hector to Achilles' tent began to get the jovial, boisterous, rapid pace Miller sought; "Otherwise," he commented drily, "the scene begins to take on a significance it does not have." The betrayal scene Miller continued to reblock, bringing more and more of the action outside the tent. He asked Cressida to fetch the sleeve and bring it out to Diomedes so Troilus sees it. Then she can return to sit on the bed while Diomedes kneels over her ("Much more of a rape position," Miller told Paul Moriarty, "like the painting of Tarquin ravishing Lucrece") instead of sitting beside her. Miller also felt their exchange needed some physical contact at the end, a kiss or preferably a bite on the ear; the scene must be violent and lusty, very sexy, he told them. He also discussed Troilus's pressure-cooker response as the tension builds, blowing only once in anger at Diomedes and once in tears at Cressida, his only breakdown; afterward he is grim, cold, hard, another side of his immature inflexibility.

As the lovers' meeting developed in Troy, Miller pointed out that Cressida half teases Troilus, feeling in control, but breaks as Troilus's force releases her emotions and she is caught up. The "true as Troilus" speech should begin seriously, rhapsodically, then Troilus should play with images to delight Cressida, ending again in seriousness. Cressida is innocent, Miller asserted, continuing that he thought the sluttish portrayal of Cressida is all wrong. She tries to convince herself that she can and will be true, as if realizing she may not be. After all, he said, the play is a tragedy: innocence is eradicated. Both Troilus and Cressida are young, Miller reiterated, and are not given time to get to know each other; Pandarus hurries them off to bed before the relationship has a chance to grow. They never work through a day-to-day togetherness. Troilus is left with a religious fanaticism about his love; once that is shattered he becomes a fanatic about the war, Miller observed.

After three weeks of rehearsal, with much of the play performance-ready, Miller still concentrated on the Trojan council scene, perhaps the play's most difficult scene to put into production. In the last week Miller introduced all the women to the scene, not just Cassandra but Helen and Andromache as well, a move seldom if ever seen on stage (where it usually has the atmosphere of high-level commanders meeting in some smoke-filled room), a move with remarkable effects on the scene's dynamics. In fact, Helen's presence just behind Paris radically altered the scene: Hector found it doubly hard to say, as it were, "Send her back; she's not worth it" to her face, while Troilus and Paris had a focal point for their gestures, an example, a "pearl." Miller told them he wanted to get the feeling of a Kennedy clan meeting overlaid with the atmosphere of a *Dallas* family discussion. Much new movement occurred, new tensions and pacing. Miller encouraged Troilus to be more biting, more ironic and sarcastic, in his remarks to Hector and said that Troilus's line "What's aught but as 'tis valued" may be the focal line of the entire play, prompting him to emphasize "valued" in delivery. It is an idea very like Hamlet's "nothing is either good or bad but thinking makes it so," Miller added, since this scene and much of the play concerns relativity. Then Troilus goes on to give Hector a concrete example. The whole scene, Miller said, should be like a string of Chinese firecrackers going off, one brother sparking an eruption from the next.

As a result of a joking suggestion by production manager Peter Stenning, Cassandra's part was changed yet again. Sharling (Cassandra) was asked to do the whole scene at a rip, all shouted, starting out of the cell so two large goons, male nurses, could grab her and lock her in as she raved. All the dignity and fascination that the character had earlier is lost in such a rendition. Because it is also entirely opposite to the later Cassandra scene, it provides a schizophrenic pattern. The outburst was shocking as they rehearsed it and disrupted everyone at the table; Helen paced, Paris shifted, others stirred and turned. Miller left Cassandra with this interpretation, later adding a rocking, hair-chewing preliminary to it modeled on the outbursts of a schizophrenic patient Miller knew. Her explosion suggests the near explosiveness of the discussion in the Trojan council, although the earlier version of Cassandra had been refreshing and clarifying to the role and the council scene.

The Thursday before the first day in the studio (Tuesday, 28 July) was the technical run, a day with the atmosphere of a sporadic cocktail party amid the scenes, with the production staff and all the designers and their assistants present with notebooks, sketches, and blueprints checking plans against realities. The lighting designer and his assistant had been in rehearsal several previous days to plan lighting angles, but the sound supervisor, Derek Miller-Timmins, had seen almost none of the play; therefore, concerns about sound were paramount. The greatest problem he foresaw was in the lovers' meeting scene, which was blocked in and around the arches of the colonnade. Meanwhile, other deals were being made between actors and costumer and make-up designer. The cast did all the Greek scenes in story order, then all the Trojan scenes; it was as close to a performance of the whole play at one time as they ever got. And the actors, aware of a new audience, were superb.

The last days of rehearsal after the technical run were an elaborate holding pattern; the technical run had been a strong performance, and everyone knew it. It let Miller see clearly what he had asserted from time to time along the way, that the play—at least in this production—was a tragedy, an insight he reiterated during the last few days of rehearsal. There was no sense of urgency in rehearsals, but instead an air of satisfaction. Slowly they worked on the battle scenes, long unrehearsed, Miller reminding them there was to be no nobility, just groveling and grappling. To accommodate the reinclusion of Hector's pursuit of the golden armor, Miller had given his production manager the task of finding a "Darth Vader" (as the character was always referred to, even in the actor calls on the camera script), and Stenning obliged by engaging an actor almost seven feet tall. The scene at the command tent after Hector's death, Miller said, should be a stunned silence and a great sense of anticlimax, a "well, that's a wrap" feeling. The script editor David Snodin added that he thought, given the mythic sensibility of the play, Achilles ought to be seen rubbing his heel, which unleashed a barrage of heel jokes.

A zany exuberance at times punctuated the closing days of rehearsal. When asked who would do the voice-over of the prologue, Miller said he might, though what he wanted, he jested with a wicked sparkle in his eye, was to get a famous British newscaster to be seen in Renaissance clothes wandering about Troy with a microphone doing the prologue, then handing the mike to a passing courtier who would look at it dumbfounded, while someone would be heard muttering, "I didn't think those things had been invented yet."

With so much in place, Miller began to work on the sense of ensemble in certain scenes, to build the texture or to "embroider," as he called it. Miller is committed to ensemble acting, to a realistic sense of humans communicating, not of one actor speaking while others wait for a cue. Rather than using literary convention or theatrical expectation, Miller shapes his direction by the human element and tries to come to each play afresh, striving to make the words, ideas, and exchanges meaningful.

He bases much of his ensemble direction, he says, on the work of social psychologist Erving Goffman, the well-known teacher and author, on whose views Miller instructs every cast, stressing ideas, loaning books, explaining behavioral responses. By the end of the first week of *Troilus and Cressida* rehearsals, Miller took advantage of a lull to discuss and expound Goffman's theories with the cast of the Greek camp, for whom ensemble was crucial. Miller told them Goffman has the greatest influence on his work as a director and proceeded with a short commentary on theories of behavior. Whereas Konrad Lorenz and others believe humans interact as animals based on impulses of aggression and accommodation, he said,

Goffman believes humans are moral (a view Miller sanctions) and respond to a sense of social audience because they enjoy being accepted or admired. Life, according to Goffman, is an endless series of social wrongdoings, "crimes," arrests, trials, acquittals or convictions, as we act before others. Because we are not perfect, when we err we quickly make a remedial display to differentiate for others between our obvious fault or slip and what we want them to believe we are really like. If while walking down a sidewalk, for example, we realize we have forgotten something, Miller said, to cover our sudden reversal of direction we make a show of snapping our fingers or hitting our forehead with our palm to indicate our forgetfulness. We will overact a verbal stumble or make an awkwardly late entrance with a funny face. These ideas help an actor by illuminating the complexity of interactions in any scene, allowing a director to get at not just the verbal thread or the obvious business but also more of the secondary strands too often missed. All those little gestures, nuances, and intonations are very important to good acting, Miller believes.

These Goffman effects were ever present at rehearsal, not by name so much as in tiny moves Miller would include to finish an exchange, the body language he was so aware of, which is also influenced by his training in neurology. The cast, too, was aware of the ideas; after struggling every lunch break to eat the hard sandwich rolls politely, without squishing egg out the other side or trailing bits of meat after taking a bite, they promptly nicknamed them "Goffman rolls" for the duration of rehearsals. But only at the end of rehearsals, when all the primary strands were in place, did Miller shift his attention almost exclusively to the secondary or Goffman strands of the ensemble.

Nestor became Miller's focus, the most thoroughly Goffmanized character in *Troilus and Cressida*, especially in public or private exchanges with Ulysses. As Ulysses unveils his plan to gall Achilles by praising Ajax at the end of I.3, Miller guided Nestor to try to interrupt unsuccessfully, bluff when he is unsure of Ulysses' meaning, and rephrase Ulysses' speeches as if the ideas were his own (a perceptive move since Shakespeare's Nestor is often a case study in redundancy). After Hector's contest with Ajax, amid postcombat introductions and welcomes and as Menelaus pauses to glare at Paris in the background, Nestor starts long-windedly telling tales of days gone by; Ulysses strategically moves forward and interrupts him, as Miller set up the exchange, but Nestor tries to recover his place as speaker, gesturing and trying to interject until he finally settles for a role as second, nodding and reemphasizing all that is said. Ben Whitrow (Ulysses) once casually asked if Miller was trying to reorient the scene; Miller jovially retorted it was only revenge for all of Ulysses' long speeches. Miller wanted a great conviviality among the men, the storytelling such as "I knew thy grandsire," then the sudden refrigeration of Achilles' presence, the menace. As they rehearsed the Greek camp scenes, Miller added verbal "ahems" for Nestor in nearly every scene, also building a pattern of repetition whereby he would echo a catchy phrase of another speaker, usually Ulysses, as was planned at the end of the Greek council scene, when he exited chuckling "Achilles' plumes" to himself (a nice effect lost in the studio due to an awkward pause and the actors' exit too close to the camera).

Rehearsal had brought individual scenes and performances to clarity and fullness so that each piece locked into place—a Pirandellian modern-dress version of *Troilus and Cressida* in a sixth-floor rehearsal room of linoleum tile, cinder block walls, and metal chairs. In the studio, however, that same action at first seemed strange, as if transfigured, with actors now in early Renaissance tights, slippers, capes, and codpieces, moving about in the vastness of BBC television studio 1 on a large three-dimensional set instead of hopscotching around lines of tape on the floor. As is usual when any production finally gets on the set, the vertical aspect and the very substance of the Trojan set altered everyone's perspective and changed the actors' movements; the set became the missing character that arrives only in time for taping, rehearsals having been conducted with a stand-in, the taped dimensions and a miniature model. Later in the week even the Trojan set seemed empty and austere compared to the wonderful clutter of the Greek camp, a set that filled the studio ankle deep in peat, a collection of large, tatty, faded tents, and a wealth of period props—leather wash basins, small caskets, barrels, stools, swords, toilet articles, bowls, cups.

There was stuff everywhere, some of it lost in the camera shots, but walking that set was a treat. It was also a strong argument for Miller's method of "discovery" despite the occasional liabilities of such an approach. Finally seeing the production all in place—actors, costumes, set, props, lighting—makes a director want to use it to advantage. Miller simply admits that typical directorial response and gives it a name.

Taping for this as for all the BBC Shakespeares proceeded by the "rehearse/record" method, whereby a scene is meticulously camera rehearsed, shot by shot, a number of times and then recorded, so the scenes of the play slowly accumulate. Scenes using the same set are scheduled on the same day so that set changes can occur efficiently, either overnight or on the day off, which falls in the middle of taping. The BBC expects a production to record thirty minutes of its show every day in the studio (so the early 2½-hour Shakespeare productions had five studio days; the longer plays, such as *Hamlet, Othello,* and *Coriolanus,* had eight, not including the day off). A day in the studio appears long; an actor's call may well be an hour and a half or more before active studio work begins at 11:00 A.M. (The BBC taping times are a holdover from live broadcasting; they run from 11:00 A.M. to 10:00 P.M. with breaks for lunch, tea, and dinner.) While eleven hours a day (minus meals and breaks) might seem luxurious to record thirty minutes' worth of action, it is in fact quite a demanding schedule, for out of that time must come camera rehearsals, set-ups, takes and retakes, breaks, and any delays. BBC old-timers brag that the BBC production units are the most efficient and some of the most cost-effective on earth.

The first day in the studio for *Troilus and Cressida* was entirely given over to camera rehearsals. The first two scenes, both with long single-camera sequences, worked smoothly with only the addition of the extras until the pass-by of the returning Trojan warriors. At that point it took much work to find the best camera positions and angles to cover both the balcony and the incoming men. For instance, what began as a level shot from the right side of the balcony to cover Cressida and Pandarus became a shot up at them from below left; two cameras were needed. Miller positioned the extras to watch and cheer the entry from the colonnade below, giving directions for their placement from the control room to his production manager on the floor. "It makes you feel like God," he ad-libbed as the extras took their places, "let there be 3,000 people in Mesopotamia . . . and put in *giraffes*, and. . . ." Timing of the warriors' pass-by for cameras and dialogue had to be meticulous, and in rehearsing it Miller was thrilled by the way the warriors' translucent banners floated across the picture, wiping the frame so Miller could use that as a cutting point back to the balcony. He also built in a shy wave by Cressida trying to attract Hector's attention as Pandarus praises him, though on the best take, the one used, a banner carrier masked that lovely gesture.

While the early scenes were camera rehearsed on the set, Colin Lowrey sat in the control room watching how the set looked on the monitors, going down to make adjustments as vision dictated. The plywood set of Troy, he explained, had six layers of paint and/or plaster treatment over the raw wood; they had tried to use wood from other of Miller's Shakespeare productions, such as the dark wood from Desdemona's bedroom in *Othello* for Cressida's ante-room. Watching the Trojan heroes' entrance and pass-by, he nodded approval, admiring the shots, adding quietly that it would have been even better with the longer colonnade he had planned, which was shortened for budgetary reasons. Later the Trojan council scene was extensively reblocked to accommodate camera movement. The extras Miller added on the stairs and nearby gave a public air to what is often staged as a private meeting. At the end Priam gave a mindless giggle (to which Miller responded, "I love it now that he's completely ga-ga") and as various courtiers passed by the cell he added a camera shot of Cassandra laughing.

Taping the next day provided the usual unexpected glitches. Scene one went off very smoothly, with each of the three takes stronger than the one before. The pass-by of the second scene, benefiting from the careful rehearsal, proceeded without hitch, with one take for the close-ups and one take shooting down the colonnade. But in the earlier and later sections of the scene camera and boom shadows appeared, and because these were single-camera sequences with no cutting points, they necessitated additional takes. As Cressida finished her monologue on the shadowless third take and moved off left, Miller sat back briefly and sighed, "Beautiful, that empty frame there." Only in the studio does the director's visual sense clearly manifest itself, and Miller was full of careful observation, as in setting up the opening shots for the prologue with the camera moving through an empty Troy: "Very enigmatic, that," he said, pleased at the effect.

The real challenges and problems posed by a single-camera scene were demonstrated the next day in the lovers' meeting scene. Miller likes single-camera sequences as a break from the constant cutting between camera shots of most television work. In a single-camera scene, as the name indicates, one camera follows all the action, moving with the actors, as with Pandarus and Cressida for part of the second scene, or remaining fixed while the action develops on different planes within the frame, actors moving in and out of fore- or background, with focus sometimes shifting between these planes, as in Hector's arming scene. Everything has to work perfectly in such a scene, every line, every movement of actor and camera, every detail of lighting and sound, because there are no cutting points. Consequently, everyone tends to watch the monitors anxiously as such scenes progress. The first scene of the play worked flawlessly on its single camera; the second caught a large camera shadow on Pandarus's shirt due to the "bright morning" lighting effect, but even this flaw seemed minor compared to what happened with the lovers' meeting scene.

This scene was the longest, most complicated single-camera scene in the script. They shot eight takes of this eleven-minute scene, only the first of which was scratched due to an actor's error in movement; otherwise, the actors were letter-perfect. But, just as the sound supervisor had foretold, boom shadows plagued the scene, often occurring only at the very end, which, of course, canceled the entire sequence. By the eighth take, the tension was palpable in the control room; everyone knew no more time was available for this scene since other scenes still had to be recorded, but none of the previous takes was technically acceptable. As they taped no one breathed during moves in which shadows had appeared earlier; just once, near the end, as Cressida moved through an archway and turned, a boom shadow flitted across her forehead. Spirits sank, but Miller said, "The performances were strong. That shadow is acceptable. We move on." These are the pressures and choices one must weigh in studio production even with generous limits of budget and time—technical perfection against quality of performance. Like most directors, Miller later said he would choose performance every time under those circumstances. And although reaching for effects, especially single-camera effects, sometimes pushes the limits of sustained studio capability, the technical level at the BBC is quite high. Shadows occasionally will occur, but not because of using a single camera; there are, for instance, at least as many boom shadows in the finished tape of *The Comedy of Errors* with its constant cutting as there are in *Troilus and Cressida* for all its single-camera scenes.

Single-camera scenes not only challenge the technical crews; they also challenge the actors' rigor and patience. Throughout the retakes in Troy, the performances were of consistently high quality and were repeated without comment or complaint. In the Greek camp later in the week, however, a major single-camera sequence had to have a cut-in shot because after muffing a line two or three times an actor protested that the pressure to give a sustained flawless performance was simply too great, as some other actors agreed. In any creative work, the same challenge affects different temperaments in varying ways; as evidenced here, the contrast in Trojan and Greek cast attitude seen in rehearsal carried over to the studio.

Partly because of the time taken to get the lovers' meeting scene, the time pressure for taping the remaining scenes in Troy intensified. The studio schedule called for three days in Troy, a day off to strike (remove) that set and erect the Greek camp, four days in the Greek camp, an overnight strike to clear the tents, then one day on the battlefield. Were time to prove a factor in Troy, contingency plans called for shooting the leave-taking scene last, out of order, since Cressida's bedroom was a small separate set piece that could, if necessary, be reset on a later day, whereas once Troy's set was gone, getting it back would mean a major production overrun. So they proceeded with the other Trojan scenes, hoping to get to the leave-taking at the end.

The arming of Hector was a straightforward single-camera sequence using actors' movements to give depth of field, one of Miller's favorite techniques. But during camera rehearsal as he watched how Troilus's exit and talk with Pandarus worked, Miller had an inspiration; he mobilized all the extras dressed as soldiers, who were standing in and near the studio waiting to tape the play's last scene, and sent them jostling past Troilus and Pandarus to give a sense of chaos. Miller commented that this was very nice as an elegiac scene, against the flow, and told Charles Gray (Pandarus) to be lost in the crowd at the end. The soldiers streaming past made the scene more effective as transition to the battlefield scenes and also provided a stark contrast to the soldiers' return down that same colonnade in the last scene, which was taped immediately afterward.

The decision to set the play's last scene at the gates of Troy in the colonnade was made early in the rehearsal process, partly—with the usual irony of planning—because it seemed there would be more time to do it there than elsewhere (this setting necessitated one script change: "to Troy" became "through Troy"). Having the night scene in Troy rather than on the battlefield gave it new potential; not only is Pandarus at home in Troy instead of wandering strangely about on the plain, but the context of Troy allowed Miller to finish the story, as one might consider it, by showing Hector's body brought in and the family mourning, a moment important to feel the full impact of his death. In discussing the appropriateness of that concluding shot, Miller said he liked Pandarus staggering past the mourners, ignoring the genuine tragedy, the real loss.

In setting up the first shot of the last scene, Miller asked the soldiers to be weary, beaten, to limp and moan as they passed down the colonnade. They obliged; they all limped and all moaned on the first take. Derek Miller-Timmins came out of the sound suite to say they sounded like sheep; Miller agreed and added, "or like tuning up for someone's Concerto in A Minor." He then began to orchestrate the moans, diversifying pitch and rhythm; later he told them they need not all moan, and the production manager on the floor helped vary the limps with falls, staggers, dragging walks, men being carried or supported. At one point Miller from the control room told the extra on the stretcher, "Let us hear a scream as you see the camera lens," to which Peter Stenning, the production manager, replied, "He can't—we've got a blindfold on him."

By the third take the soldiers were convincingly varied in fatigue and pain, and the countercurrent of townspeople crossing the stream of soldiers created the turmoil Miller sought. He told Charles Gray (Pandarus) just to grab a passerby and deliver part of the last speech to him, a move that served to break up the speech as well as to show how delirious Pandarus is. Miller also carefully set up the delivery of Hector's body on the stretcher and the family's entry to it. Just before the first take he went down to the floor to supervise the make-up on Hector's wounds, quickly becoming actively involved in the process. John Shrapnel (Hector) lay with a cloth over his face; Miller said, "Now, John, I'll have to cover you with blood," and he and make-up artist Eileen Mair squished various tubes of liquid and goo over the actor's supposedly crushed cranium, then reaching for another container Miller explained, "now a bit of cerebral cortex." Miller's concern for detail is thorough, whether the situation be verbal or medical. As several people in the gallery turned away from the graphic close-up on the monitors during this preparation, someone quipped, "Is this *Troilus and Cressida* or *The Body in Question*?"

The last Trojan scene was so grim and effective in establishing the air of tragedy that coming into the Greek camp after the set change felt like a reprieve. Not only was the set fascinating to look at, so different in color and visual texture from Troy, but in addition to props and extras it had dogs moving about and caged chickens and rats for domestic atmosphere. The clucking provided noticeable background noise; during camera rehearsal of the first Greek scene, the Greek council, one actor broke off and asked, "What is that awful noise? The hens? Will that go on throughout?" The answer from the control room was, "Yes." That break typified rehearsal and taping in the Greek camp where, unlike Troy, the technical aspects were smooth but some of the actors a bit competitive, a factor not affecting the finished product so much as occasionally making studio work trying and tense.

Part of the tension among some members of the Greek camp was no doubt due to the ensemble effects, as Miller realized. He reemphasized the importance of conversational orchestration, of talking and listening. Too often, he said, production is merely a series of bravura performances, but the effect is so much better when all are acting together, even with overlap of speeches. The success of such an effect, he added, depends on trust of each other and of the director, who must control the overall result. Actors must not feel they are competing with or upstaging one another; they are not. But trust is hard to foster when it challenges training; while most actors adapted to Miller's method smoothly, a few had trouble, so studio work at times became an exercise of cross-purposes.

One reason for this difference is that in the studio a director's perspective changes. After weeks of rehearsal where the major, the *only* apparent concern is actors' performance, much more is involved in the studio. The director is not on the floor with the actors; the director is in the control suite between sound and lighting rooms, facing a bank of monitors and of necessity concerned with the shots, the cuts, engineering and taping, editing points, the text, the time—always the time. The actors *are* the focus and as such are accommodated to great lengths, but the overall production often demands more attention from the director than does the individual performance.

Quibbles recurred throughout the second day in the Greek camp, with actors balking briefly at necessary changes. During taping some actors even suffered bruised shins and crushed toes in group shots as others vied for visibility on camera in anti-ensemble fashion. Camera rehearsals extended with questions and discussion, and takes became re-takes in an effort to get the right pace and liveliness when the dialogue was repartee.

Yet the Greek camp scenes also offered Miller endless opportunities for invention. His comic spirit delighted in the background details, such as the long-planned golf element, a joking tribute to the *M.A.S.H.* allusion. In the background among the lounging soldiers, one is practicing his putting while another makes golf balls according to the standard Renaissance method—stuffing feathers in a small leather pouch and pressing them down against a spike on his armor breastplate. This business never gets camera focus, but it is there. The jokes rarely get focus, in fact, for Miller subscribes to the theory that the comic should be concealed at the edge of the action, never placed at the center (his criticism of much staged comedy is its forced centrality). One should catch the comic out of the corner of one's eye.

Any number of such comic effects occur in the Greek camp of *Troilus and Cressida*. In I.3 during the walk through the camp before the Greek council, not only do the staff officers pass many characters who will prove prominent later, but they also pass a poor soldier squatting in the thunder box dutifully saluting as the officers go by; then on the next camera shot Agamemnon nearly pauses by a whore who gives him a hitchhiking sign. Along with the period props in the command tent was a large easel on which rested pages of engineering drawings for the Trojan horse, a scale model of which sat on the table nearby. At one point in a long speech Ulysses stops and gazes contemplatively at the drawing of the horse's head before continuing—a moment carefully built in— but otherwise these elements are just there to be caught in passing by the camera. In the same spirit, one may notice a copy of Cranach's Eve pinned on Ajax's tent flap like a medieval centerfold as he flips through a series of smaller pictures, period nudes, before attacking Thersites in II.1. Such details inevitably make moments of a Miller production a version of Shakespeare Beyond the Fringe.

Another benefit of close observation, though one only evident in rehearsal and the studio, not on the final tape, was watching Jack Birkett, whose stage name is The Incredible Orlando. Incredible indeed—a blind professional dancer who learned his lines from a tape recorder and his positions by counting his steps, Birkett was not new to Shakespeare productions, for in addition to dancing in Shakespeare-based ballets, he played Caliban in Derek Jarman's film of *The Tempest*. He has the uncanny ability to simulate eye contact without seeing by locating the voice and adjusting the angle of his face accordingly. Miller made the most of Birkett's athletic prowess by switching his costume for his imitation of Ajax from the ragged red dress Thersites had worn earlier to only a pair of trousers so his musculature would show; Miller then urged him to take body-builder poses as he spoke.

One of the significant interpretive changes between rehearsal and studio occurred with Cressida's entrance to the Greek camp. As rehearsed, her entrance with Diomedes was a flirtatious dialogue, a half embrace with her laughing into his shoulder as they moved between the tents. In the studio, however, the two had to pass through a crowd of leering, taunting, grabbing soldiers—no laughing matter. Their entrance turned into a small-scale battle for self-preservation, Cressida clinging to her guide more out of fear and Diomedes shoving their way through the jeering men. In fact, that entire section of the scene altered; meeting the officers became much less her teasing them than their responding to her with only slightly more courtly physicality than had the soldiers. That development gave a new edge of veiled nastiness to the whole scene. As in the last scene at Troy, the extras sometimes made a startling difference in the effect of scenes in the studio. Thirty leers and grabs at a woman's clothing, thirty boos and hisses at the Trojan nobility as they enter, and an atmosphere is instantly created.

The contest in the Greek camp was the most complicated Greek scene to tape, having as it does a number of miniscenes within it— Cressida's arrival, the contest, the introductions, Achilles' challenge, Troilus's asking for Calchas's tent. It was long to rehearse, Miller commenting that it needed many more shots for speed and to capture all the bits of action. Complexity breeds tension when working against the clock, so that once taping began everyone felt the pressure. The opening shot was Ajax practicing his sword thrusts against a dummy, and on the first take Tony Pedley (Ajax) swung so hard he knocked the straw man flying. Amid the laughter and the reset, everyone relaxed a bit and work proceeded smoothly. The last half of the scene ran faultlessly on its first take; Miller went for a second just to have a choice, and it proved even better.

Yet later that second day in the Greek camp taping again was time limited. Because it took almost forty-five minutes to light the brazier and get set between camera rehearsal and taping of a night scene at Achilles' tent, there was no time to retake the scene in which Achilles enters with the bloody body of slain Patroclus (V.5), only sketchily camera rehearsed due to time pressures. In the first take a blocking problem arose on Achilles' entrance so that the shot was not clean, but with no time for another take that part of the scene was regretfully sacrificed, not by choice but by necessity. Much the same circumstances affected the last scene at Agamemnon's tent, which had been rehearsed but was also cut—all the scenes that night in the Greek camp were pressured by the clock.

And the time pressure of recording becomes even more intense the closer to the end of taping one gets. Every night poses its own deadline since taping stops at exactly 10:00 P.M. almost regardless of what is happening in the studio (unless one makes arrangements in advance or goes into costly but sometimes inevitable overruns), and every last day on a given set poses yet another pressure. Already the leave-taking scene had been postponed and the entire studio schedule replanned because time had run out in Troy, and time was a factor as well in the last scenes taped in the Greek camp. The betrayal scene, for instance, was taped the last evening in the Greek camp, after careful camera rehearsal. Each set of speakers was taped separately, so they ran the scene twice, first with the camera on Troilus and Ulysses, then on Cressida and Diomedes; finally they picked up Thersites' asides as cut-ins. The dialogue inside the tent was just a shade less sultry and intense than in rehearsal, but there was no chance for a second take; it was almost 9:45 and Thersites' lines had yet to be taped. And so some decisions are virtually made for a director rather than by him. The tents had to be struck that night both to set in Cressida's bedroom for the next day and to prepare the battlefield, so that part of the betrayal scene stood as taped.

Yet for all the deadlines, the last scenes were taped expeditiously. The displaced leave-taking scene moved smoothly, the camera angles much of the time favoring Troilus, thus indicating that the speeches and scene are to a large extent his, unlike many stage productions in which the scene becomes Cressida's amid the weeping; here the duality of the shock and grief is apparent. The battlefield sequences proceeded almost one take each amid the smoke and background movement of the soldiers. "Darth Vader" made his appearance, and in his confrontation with Hector, exaggerated high and low camera angles accentuated his height and Hector's having to look up at him. The only involved scene was the murder of Hector by the pool. Much as everyone had heard about the pool during rehearsals, no one was quite ready for the scum across the top of it or the revulsion it prompted. And even knowing the Myrmidons were only hitting a bolster did not mitigate the idea of that brutal murder, nor did watching the make-up crew pour red make-up on top of the water and prepare the back of Hector's head as a gory wound assuage the response to seeing Achilles push Hector's head into the scum with his foot (Miller: "Hold your breath for a count of twenty, John. Ready?"). It is an ugly scene beautifully silhouetted against the fading light and setting sun. And, almost predictably after so much time pressure, the last day's taping finished ahead of schedule, and everyone adjourned upstairs to the cast party.

Editing began four days after *Troilus and Cressida* left the studio. Unlike the immense juggling act in the studio where the goal is to get action and useful visual bits on tape, editing is a colder, more evaluative process of exactly what the production will be, which images, how much, excising what does not fit. Miller, for instance, had still not decided whether to include the prologue or not, mainly because he had not yet decided who should deliver the lines, but since the titles were not ready, he could postpone the decision a while longer. (He ultimately did include the prologue, with Ben Whitrow delivering it.) The first complex bit of editing was the pass-by of the Trojan warriors in the second scene. As he and the videotape editor worked to integrate the long shots that Miller especially wanted as a means to present Hector and Troilus on their entries, Miller commented that it was a scene for stage, not for a naturalistic medium such as television: "I've tried to make it too natural." True, that scene is designed for stage spectacle, but after some meticulous cutting and timing it worked as Miller wanted.

The one scene totally dependent on the stage for its effectiveness was not the heroes' pass-by but the betrayal scene at Diomedes' tent. How easy it is in the theatre for the audience to be aware of all

three sets of speakers/listeners simultaneously and to shift focus
between them. In rehearsal the scene had been strong, partly because in rehearsal everyone saw it from a theatrical perspective, all
speakers simultaneously, and it was usually rehearsed without
Thersites. Miller reminded the actors in rehearsal that in the studio
they should not pick up cues as quickly as they usually did because
he would be cutting virtually every two or three lines and would
need the gaps between speeches to edit. That was all very clear in a
rehearsal room, but in the studio, under performance conditions
and time pressures, the scene had run at full speed every time. In
the editing suite Miller found there was "no room for the scissors"
in many of the exchanges, and so began a long, painstaking process
of compiling the scene. Fully one-seventh of the total editing time
for *Troilus and Cressida* was spent on that scene, trying not only to
make the cuts but to find ways around continually switching between groups of speakers. A few of Troilus's quick short lines were
lost to vision because there was no good way to get back to him
from the tent to pick them up, and some of Diomedes' responses
are heard from afar, from Troilus's perspective, rather than in the
closer shot. The scene as edited is not what it was in rehearsal;
many bits were lost because all the actors were responding continually but the camera picked up only one group at a time. The old
lesson of the different potentials of the various mediums arises—
the power of television's close-ups versus the power of theatre's
ensemble staging.

Miller berated himself for not reminding the actors about leaving
the gaps, but the scene's pace and its simultaneous dialogue demand the kind of performances given. The actors responded to the
nature of the scene; the challenge was in adapting that action to the
medium, a challenge that proved greater than anticipated. In addition to trying to break that sound barrier, Miller found that between takes he had also changed part of the visual element in the
matching shots. In the shots of Troilus watching the tent, the shadows of Cressida and Diomedes inside are clearly distinguishable;
they were positioned as in rehearsal, Diomedes beside and above
Cressida. But later when the camera inside the tent taped their
dialogue, Miller had Diomedes move down closer to Cressida to

258 | Exigencies of Production

frame a tighter close 2-shot, but that move also overlapped the shadows on the tent, a change Miller felt would not really matter even though the inside and outside views no longer matched. Yet as with the dialogue, in editing nothing can be done except to enhance through cuts and pace what is on the tape.

Most of the editing, however, was a process of self-editing on Miller's part—either cleaning up shots by trimming or changing his mind about images that open or close scenes. A number of images he had included in the studio were cut in editing, such as the shot of Cassandra laughing after the Trojan council scene, the whore busy plying her trade in a barrel in the Greek camp as Agamemnon and group approach Achilles' tent, and Nestor muttering "Achilles' plumes." The theory well established by practice is to tape what might be useful; the motto is, "You can always cut." Extra is not the problem, only not enough.

And some bits of takes thought problematic in the studio proved very useful in editing, especially as sound bridges, in other words, running the sound track of the first shot over the cut to the second shot as if seeing from the speaker's point of view and then switching sound tracks when the new character in vision speaks. Such a sound bridge was used for Ulysses' entrance to Achilles in III.3 and for Troilus's entry from the bedroom to Pandarus and Aeneas in IV.2, a sequence that ended up a composite of three sound tracks. The most significant sound bridge, however, came about because at the end of the only really good take of the opening part of II.3 with Achilles, Patroclus, and Thersites, there was a sound crackle. After much experimentation with other takes, Miller said to use the sound from another take as a sound bridge and then cut in the shot of Agamemnon and the generals approaching the tent; so to cover the crackle they used a sequence of take 1 that had been scratched in the studio because it was a bit slow. Editing can change one's perspective on studio work as much as studio conditions alter perspectives on rehearsal.

Miller himself was pleased with *Troilus and Cressida*, pleased with how the production presented the play and pleased with the performances. The combined effect of Anton Lesser and Suzanne

Burden as the lovers delighted him, and he thought John Shrapnel's Hector a strong characterization and Jack Birkett's Thersites a scurrilous joy. So much did Miller admire his actors' capabilities that even during rehearsals he began talking of the possibility of doing *Hamlet* with them, a possibility that materialized the next summer (1982) in a London production at the Warehouse with Lesser as Hamlet and Shrapnel as Claudius.

Any director's economy of television aesthetics is apparent through the rehearsal process, based on the premise that if you take care of the pence, the pounds will take care of themselves. For many, the pence of television are the visual elements, the camera shots; for Miller, the pence are linguistic, since for him plays are more about "linguistic space" than about "civic space."[2] In rehearsal, Miller does not dwell on cameras. Instead he emphasizes meaning and delivery, working to make the statements not only clear but "human," clearly motivated and purposeful, and fully illustrated by body language and group dynamics. For Miller that is the essence of drama.

9   *The Comedy of Errors* in Production

In theatre reviews over the years, critics have called *The Comedy of Errors* a "barren and tedious farce" and a "Shakespearean flop,"[1] a play needing infinite gimmicks and imaginative resources to redeem it in performance. Director James Cellan-Jones approached *The Comedy of Errors* for the BBC Shakespeare series with a few gimmicks in mind and his share of imaginative resources but mostly with an attitude of comic seriousness. Cambridge-educated Cellan-Jones is much experienced in television work, with such successes as *The Forsyte Saga*, *The Golden Bowl*, *Portrait of a Lady*, and *Jennie* to his credit. He came up through the ranks, the preferred BBC method, starting as an assistant floor manager and working up to director and finally to head of Plays before deciding to go independent. BBC scuttlebutt was that if Shakespeare could be done on television, Cellan-Jones, well known for his work with modern material and also for wearing sandals year round, would be the man to do it.

In reading the play for production, Cellan-Jones sensed the play was not just farce—Plautus's characters are flat, Shakespeare's full;[2] it was indeed, as the title indicates, a *comedy* of errors. Approaching the play as comedy meant taking the situation more seriously than simply laughing at dilemmas. The issues of identity raised by the confusion of twins seemed frightening and even dangerous in the experience of the characters, not just such stuff as chuckles are made on. And like *The Merchant of Venice* and *Measure for Measure*, *The Comedy of Errors* shows us a society that for this day puts law and a strict justice before clemency. Aegeon's mortal plight is dire; for Cellan-Jones, Aegeon is "a genuine tragic figure" who has lost his family and now is about to lose his life.

That old man is too often forgotten between first act and last, Cellan-Jones felt; he was determined not to do so himself.

Not only was Aegeon remembered in this production, but his character largely determined the initial design concept for the BBC's *The Comedy of Errors*. Cellan-Jones, aware of how many productions have labored through the opening scene's exposition in Aegeon's long narrative, wanted the scene to be a lively, graphic part of his production. "Graphic" is the key here because Cellan-Jones decided to enact the events usually narrated; he wanted to make the geography of the eastern Mediterranean, the voyages, the shipwreck, and the rescues visual and clear. He needed a map but not just a visual aid Aegeon could point to with his finger—one people could move on to demonstrate the occurrences. Therefore the map had to be on the floor, and with his camera-sensitive eye Cellan-Jones envisioned the opening shot of the production, a camera shot of that floor map taken from the lighting grid of the studio. The entire production, as designer Don Homfray said, was planned and at times even distorted by that one shot.[3] Cellan-Jones's choice was a product of his television experience, Homfray added; in an earlier television drama about Spain called *The End of the World*, which Homfray had also designed for Cellan-Jones, the set had been a bullring, and the production had included just such a high shot to good effect.

The map and the high shot in *The Comedy of Errors* necessitated a 360-degree set, a circular pattern that reminded Cellan-Jones and Homfray of the staging of medieval morality plays with their platforms or "houses" at the edge of a circle and also of the classical stage setting of a street facade. From these associations Homfray designed the piazza and structures for *The Comedy of Errors* with the map on the floor in a mosaic pattern sturdy enough to withstand a week's wear by equipment, actors, extras, and crew and with the "houses"—the Porpentine, the Phoenix, and the Abbey—set triangularly at the circle's edge with the Abbey at the head. Three arches, one between each set of buildings, give perspectives on the port, the town, and the countryside, and the market stalls and shops help establish the bustle of a mercantile community. Then Homfray began to elaborate the play's idea of twinness in the set design, to build on the principle of doubling. The houses seen in perspective through the arches, which are actually small 3-D Plasticine models, some only a foot high, carefully echo the architectural lines of the Phoenix and the Porpentine. The colors from the floor are repeated throughout the production, and the backdrop on the stage cart is painted to replicate the scene in the piazza as seen from the far archway—Abbey in the center, market to the left, stage cart to the right, the mosaic floor map.

Homfray tried to keep a sense of intimacy and domesticity in the set, for although in Shakespeare the play has a Greek setting and therefore lures one toward the classical, it is not a grand, aristocratic action. Instead it involves ordinary folks on an extraordinary day. To keep the air of the classical along with the domestic atmosphere, Homfray used Pompeii as the basis for his brightly colored exteriors, painted interiors, and architectural ornament. He also wanted to keep the scale small, so the houses and arches were low; the overhang of the Phoenix, for instance, was just over 5'8" from the floor. Thus Homfray provided an open public place and a comfortable interior for the action, with enough vistas to be varied and visually interesting out the windows of the Phoenix, into the market stalls, or through the archways in the piazza.

With the set design complementing his idea, Cellan-Jones started planning the other element vital to invigorating Aegeon's I.1 speech, the action on the map. He wanted Ephesus to be a city full of trade, hence the market, and, picking up on the textual references to sorcery, also a city with other sorts of street people, such as fortune-tellers, wandering musicians, traveling players, always eager to ply their trades as well. The traveling players he wanted were a commedia dell'arte troupe; thus their improvisation of Aegeon's tale would be plausible as they listened to the story and acted it out for the crowd to the accompaniment of their artistic cohorts, the street musicians. Such a troupe would also be a link with the tradition of Shakespeare's play, for Italian commedia grew out of Roman farce such as Plautus's *Menaechmi*. The style is closely linked literarily and theatrically to *The Comedy of Errors*, as a number of directors have recognized. Cellan-Jones's mimes were to be another natural facet of Ephesian life, lively and, for Antipholus of Syra-

In an early rehearsal for The Comedy of Errors *in the chilly warehouse, director James Cellan-Jones organizes the arrest of the Ephesian master and servant in IV, 4. Adriana (Suzanne Bertish, left), Officer (Frank Williams), director Cellan-Jones, the Antipholus double (Brian Attree), Antipholus (Michael Kitchen, with ropes), Pinch (Geoffrey Rose), the Courtezan (Ingrid Pitt), and Dromio (Roger Daltrey, right). Photo: Franz Michel*

cuse, at times disturbing in their observant presence, almost menacing in their costumes and masks. But the mimes are not entirely cold-hearted sorcerers; for instance, they alone acknowledge and comfort the wandering Aegeon by sharing their simple lunch with him.

Along with design decisions, Cellan-Jones had to make basic casting decisions early in planning, especially the decision paramount to *The Comedy of Errors*, how to cast the two sets of twins. On stage, nontwins playing twins is accomplished by a series of difference-reducing devices—casting actors of comparable builds and coloring, putting them in similar costumes and wigs and makeup—with the rest done by the willing suspension of disbelief, al-

As the aerial view of the studio set demonstrates, The Comedy of Errors had a rich visual environment centered on a geographic floor mapping the eastern Mediterranean, around which designer Don Homfray placed a street market and the Phoenix, the Abbey, and the Porpentine. © BBC

The visual doubling throughout the production design of The Comedy of
Errors *is evident in the opening scene with the similar costumes on the
Duke (Charles Gray) and his page (Kiran Shah) and in the backcloth on
the mimes' booth, which reproduces a view of the set's piazza (with its
floor map) and Abbey.* © BBC

ways a potent factor in Shakespearean drama involving disguises and twins. (While Shakespeare's company may have included a set of twins at the time *The Comedy of Errors* was originally performed, as some have thought,[4] Cellan-Jones was convinced that Shakespeare left enough time for an actor to exit and dash around to enter from the other door as his own twin.) But Cellan-Jones faced a casting problem unlike a stage director's. While he could certainly cast actors of similar appearance, television is a more intimate, less forgiving medium than the stage; the willing suspension of disbelief is less readily granted. Fortunately, Cellan-Jones had video technology to rely on—one can appear to be two on the screen by means of split-screen taping. So he decided to capitalize on television wizardry and use one actor for each set of twins; whereas stage productions using two actors per set must emphasize similarities, his actors would establish differences in attitude, aided by minor differences in costume (Antipholus of Syracuse wears his collar up, Antipholus of Ephesus wears his down). Thus, as in all television work, both camera and actor are necessary to determine the nature of the final performance.

In planning for the interaction of actor and camera well before the company was assembled, Cellan-Jones considered the action of *The Comedy of Errors* and built in a number of specific comic bits to underscore the idea of twinness. He planned confrontations and near misses for each set of twins, such as a mirror sequence in the market for the Dromios, so that when Dromio of Syracuse discovers the frame has no mirror in it and that the other self he saw was no reflection, he begins II.2 full of confusion. Cellan-Jones also wanted a mirror upstairs in the Phoenix to build in more reflection and doubling. He planned for Antipholus of Syracuse to leave the Phoenix and be observed by Antipholus of Ephesus who is standing on the balcony of the Porpentine; the Ephesian looks twice, then attributes the effect to the wine he is drinking. Initially there was to be another near miss between the Antipholi passing in the market (such an effect is almost irresistible for a director of *The Comedy of Errors*), but Cellan-Jones discarded the idea before going to the studio. At first he thought he would use split-screen shots for III.2 with the Dromios shouting through the Phoenix door but quickly changed his mind, well before rehearsals. Using the dog and dog door in that scene was another early idea, one that stayed. Cellan-Jones's rehearsal script, prepared as usual before casting, indicates the locale of every scene and additionally the mix into it, in other words, how the camera will establish the scene. For instance, the introductory direction for II.1 in the rehearsal script reads:

> Exterior. The Phoenix.
> (Music.
> We mix to the sign above the door and crane up to the first floor window. Adriana comes forward and looks out: the clock says nearly two o'clock.)

And that is exactly the way the scene's opening was taped, except that after the crane-up Adriana was discovered already looking out, tapping her fingernails on the windowsill. Cellan-Jones thinks first and always in camera terms, as the rehearsal script indicates. Kate Bradley, assistant floor manager for *The Comedy of Errors*, commented on how thoroughly Cellan-Jones had "done his home-work" and what a good television director he is, already knowing where his shots will be and where he needs cutaways and reaction shots. Not all directors, she added, organize or know; some just leave such work to the cameramen.

The script also involves dealing with 400-year-old words and jokes. In discussing Shakespeare and television Cellan-Jones ob-served, "You have to be so careful with language. If you could change that. . . ." If you changed that, it would not be "Shake-speare," but it would be television, for television work, especially series and serials, usually involves a great deal of script work and adaptation right up to the last minute. The BBC production scripts of Shakespeare's plays include inverted lines, minor cuts, even some modest rearrangement of scenes or lines, but the guideline remains —as full and accurate as possible.

What changes Cellan-Jones would have made in the script of *The Comedy of Errors* given a free hand he never elaborated. From other remarks he made and the textual changes he introduced, it is obvious he felt that the verbal humor workable in the Renaissance posed the largest problem for the modern television audience. Before rehearsal he cut half the Syracusans' verbal byplay of II.2 (especially the hair versus wit debate) and some of III.1 (the fowl without feather banter), but even of the banter remaining Cellan-Jones said, "The jokes are awful, and the only way to deal with them is just to rattle them off."

As his planning indicates, Cellan-Jones tried to avoid loopholes in *The Comedy of Errors*; the production meeting on 30 September 1983 at the end of the five-week planning period is an example. Nearly the entire production and technical staff was present: the director; the series's production associate (most important because he controls the schedule and the purse strings); Peter Hider, the production manager (who is in charge of the practical aspects of planning and production and who runs the taping on the studio floor); the two assistant floor managers (who order props and watch the script in rehearsal and assist the production manager in the studio); the production assistant (the director's administrative assistant who books personnel, produces scripts, watches continuity, and keeps tape and timing records in the studio); set designer Don Homfray and his assistant; costume designer June Hudson and her assistant; the make-up designer; lighting designer Dave Sydenham; sound supervisor Chick Anthony; and the technical coordinator (who is liaison with engineering in the studio)—everyone except the camera crew supervisor, who was away on assignment. With the tentative taping schedule before them, they all sat in the production office around a cluster of small tables with the model of the set before them and talked through the taping schedule day by day for plans and problems, always referring to the model, using pencils to indicate camera and lighting angles.

In planning for the first day's work on Phoenix interiors, the piece of roof on the Phoenix (necessary for exterior shots) proved a problem for lighting and sound work in the interior; those designers asked Homfray if it could be hinged to flip outward. The chronology of lighting for the play's day in Ephesus was also questioned, lighting designer Sydenham pointing out the difficulties of changing once they had set for the later hours of the action. He later asked about compass points, for if the port is in the west, as it must be in Ephesus, the map on the floor was upside down. As they worked, Homfray explained that he had designed the components of the circular set with movable pieces to help access for lighting, sound, and cameras, which could replug through arches and the market rather than moving entire pieces of equipment. The taping schedule was juggled to lighten the load near the end (a prudent move as studio work turned out). In thinking through the camera work, such issues arose as the height of the safety rail on the upper level of the Phoenix; throughout the meeting the discussion combined aesthetic issues, technical concerns, and the regulations of the BBC and the various unions (such as engineering/videotape schedules in case of the need to pick up extra taping time, how many hours extras can work without overtime, and whether the union-specified time for musicians includes wardrobe and make-up). Later Cellan-Jones and Hider praised the cooperation of the staff and the quality of the technical people working on the production. They also explained how production meetings can indicate the subtle political dynamics of television work: once upon a time engineering ruled production meetings; now it is more often lighting that necessitates changes or accommodation by other production elements.

His production thus as fully planned as possible, Cellan-Jones began the first rehearsal on 5 October 1983 with the traditional read-through and a long talk about the nature of the play and the nature of the production and design. Ephesus, the world of *The Comedy of Errors*, he told the cast, is a world in which there are established rules of conduct—a time for polite behavior, a time for whoring and drinking. This idea is central to the action, he continued; "You can do anything in the right place at the right time. If you do the right thing at the wrong time you look silly and the audience is pleased." The play is built on such moments, he added. Throughout planning and rehearsal Cellan-Jones emphasized the public nature of the private actions; the beating of servants, the fetching of husbands home to lunch or to be exorcised of demons, the arrests happen in the street, for comedy depends on the public setting. And thanks to the clock on the Abbey, he mentioned that in the production as in the text, "we will always know the exact time"; it is a time-specific play. He also developed the contrast between the view of Ephesus that the voyaging twins, the newcomers, have—the dangers of a strange environment, the mime troupe that may not be quite what it seems—and the locals' view of Ephesus as a very familiar environment, even a bit boring at times.

During the read-through, which was lively and full of character, the amount of interpretation Cellan-Jones had accomplished in casting became readily apparent. He had for the most part cast actors he had worked with before: Michael Kitchen, Cyril Cusack, Wendy Hiller, Ingrid Pitt. The one major exception was with the Dromios, played by Roger Daltrey, whose agent for plays had submitted his name and had given Daltrey a script upon his return to Britain after a film-making trip to the United States. Daltrey looked through the first section, read for Cellan-Jones, was offered the part, and proved to be one of the most energetic and generous performers in the cast during rehearsals and taping.

Rehearsals for *The Comedy of Errors* ran the prescribed four weeks; there were actually twenty-two rehearsals, a few of those half days, held in a warehouse roughly a mile west of the BBC Rehearsal Rooms, a cavernous space, the walls of which a BBC crew hung with black stage curtains to hold the sound, for otherwise conditions would have approximated rehearsing in Mammoth Cave. Like the *Henry VI–Richard III* series and *The Two Gentlemen of Verona*, productions that had also rehearsed in the warehouse, the design of the large unit set for the studio meant action had to be placed and plotted in a space with the actual dimensions of the set, at the smallest a fifty- to sixty-foot span that no area in the BBC rehearsal rooms could hold. So on the floor of the warehouse were taped the outline of the set facades and also the shape of the Mediterranean map crucial to the movement in I.1. (Once the mime troupe joined the cast they worked several doors down in a separate warehouse with its own map taped on the floor.) Two small glass-front offices at one end of the warehouse became the production office and the green room. In the warehouse itself the humans were dwarfed by the space, which was also chilly since when the rumbling heater was on no one could hear anyone else speak.

Cellan-Jones was a very congenial director with his leading players, discussing the *Times* crossword with Charles Gray, bantering with others, taking time daily to chat with Kitchen and Daltrey, calling the women "Pretty" and greeting them with a kiss on the forehead. He was open and approachable; he was also a man with a mission, the one on whom the pressure was greatest, trying to satisfy divided loyalties to camera and cast. Throughout rehearsals Cellan-Jones often stood close to the actors, where the camera would be, for in addition to being an audience he also worked as director of cameras, framing shots with his hands, trying out angles, deciding the look he wanted for the action and later writing it down for the camera script.

In planning the rehearsal schedule Cellan-Jones staggered the dates cast members joined rehearsal, as many directors do, partly as an economic measure. The principals (Antipholus, Dromio, Aegeon, Emilia, the Duke, Adriana, and Luciana) started on Wednesday, 5 October, the first day; during the next week (13 October) they were joined by Angelo, the Second Merchant, Balthazar, the Courtesan, and Pinch. A week later (20 October) the Gaoler, Luce, and the First Merchant along with the mime troupe joined, so that the last two weeks were with full cast. After rough-blocking for three days, Cellan-Jones had the principals do a run-through, with the other parts picked up by the doubles for Antipholus and Dromio and members of the production staff. Then Cellan-Jones concentrated on the early scenes with the twins and the sisters, I.2, II.1, II.2, III.1, and III.2, before the action expands into the marketplace. When the next set of actors joined, Cellan-Jones shifted to act IV scenes and V.1, which as the play's longest and most complicated scene proved the most oft-rehearsed scene in the play; he also left one day for the two-person scenes and Phoenix interiors. The third week focused primarily on I.1 and V.1, especially integrating the mimes with Aegeon and with the action of the conclusion.

During the last week, after some attention to the last three scenes of the play, every rehearsal was a run-through, including the technical run and the producer's run, with some extra attention to the scenes that would be taped the first studio day. The last 2½ weeks also involved compiling the camera script, so Cellan-Jones would frequently watch a bit of action, then stop the actors and for some minutes annotate his script with camera shots. That stop–and–start rhythm becomes tedious but is sometimes essential to working out the details of the action for the camera—another indication of how the camera can determine the process long before its red light goes on in the studio.

The balance of power in rehearsals for the BBC production of *The Comedy of Errors* was not director dominated, though the production itself was dominated by the director's ideas. Cellan-Jones planned and interpreted the overall action, wrote the camera script, and in editing selected the action he would use and the rhythm it would have. And of course he had made significant choices in casting. In shaping the characters and establishing delivery, blocking, and business, however, the actors had a large part.

Shared responsibility for interpretation can improve performance possibilities on the principle that the more creative heads there are the better. It does not, however, always make for tranquil rehearsals when "discussion" edges toward a tug-of-war of wills, the director wanting one sort of action, the actor another. In that situation, which occurred from time to time during *The Comedy of Errors* rehearsals and taping, more often than not Cellan-Jones adapted to the actor's point of view, sometimes out of respect for the suggestion, sometimes so as not to jeopardize the overall performance by taking a hard line on a single point. The art of negotiation at any level, national or personal, is ever a delicate one.

The rehearsal rhythm varied markedly between the all-male scenes and the male-female or all-female scenes. In general the men worked faster and focused more on action, quickly arriving at business and attitudes. More was settled earlier in these scenes. The women proved more meditative and reflexive, asking questions about motivation and attitude; pauses and discussions were longer with their scenes. Some of this difference in rehearsal rhythm stems from the difference in the characters; we see the impetus for the men's actions and responses, whereas the women must respond first, giving them a greater need for context. Also because the men's scenes are more frequently set in the street, they are often more active.

Most great leaps forward predictably occurred when the cast had memorized the lines, which for the principals was during the second full week (17–21 October). For instance, I.1, with all its background narrative and exposition about the twins and the family's separation, while a complicated scene to tape, proved fairly simple in rehearsal because Cellan-Jones had planned it carefully. In the scene's opening, Cellan-Jones wanted to establish the liveliness of Ephesian street life—the market, the street theatre, minstrels, beggars, the conglomerate of nuns, merchants, donkey and monkey—though none of this action could be rehearsed except the mimes, the focal element, until the supporting artists (extras) joined in the studio. Into this tumult comes the Duke, and the scene loses its raucous tone for the serious judicial determinations of state and the plight of the individual innocent of any crime save his Syracusan birth—a confrontation very important to Cellan-Jones.

Since it is a formal, public, processional, speech-centered scene, once the positions of the Duke and Aegeon were established, the actors' work in rehearsal focused on refining delivery and interaction. The complexity began with the need to unify Aegeon's speech and the mimes' movements. Several strands of the production had to have split-second timing to harmonize in I.1: Aegeon's speech, the mimes' enactment, and the music. The music, very lively melodies composed by Richard Holmes (who appears as the street band's harpsichordist in the production), was often used in *Comedy of Errors* to underscore or cover movement of entrance or exit (such as the Duke's) or wordless action (as when Antipholus of Ephesus sees his twin walk out of the Phoenix), to create atmosphere (as in the Syracusan's wooing of Luciana), and to bridge scenes. But in I.1 the music was an integral part of the action, carefully reflecting the mood of the speaker as well as the nature of the action described—the journey, the storm, the calm, the separation. In other words, Cellan-Jones wanted the band, like the mime troupe, to enact Aegeon's story.

Since all the timing was keyed to Cusack's delivery, at the eighth rehearsal (14 October), Cellan-Jones, Cusack, and Nick Chagrin, master of the mime troupe, sat down and carefully timed Aegeon's speech, Cellan-Jones deciding and setting with Cusack where the breaks and pauses needed to be in terms of both words and mime. Cellan-Jones gave Holmes the timings for the separate sections of speech so the music would exactly match delivery and action. Once delivery had dictated music length and the music was recorded ten days later (24–25 October), however, the music then determined action. The scene was rehearsed to a tape of the music so Cusack and the mimes would be used to the rhythm and pace. While doing the timing Cellan-Jones told Chagrin, who agreed, that the mime should be a bit of a send-up or parody of Aegeon, not at all sweet; it should have a sharp edge. What is life and death for Aegeon is for the mimes just another chance to perform.

Kitchen and Daltrey had thought carefully about the different experiences and responses of the twins, the two strangers and two residents in Ephesus. The Syracusans are chummy and expect banter, whereas the Ephesian master is hot tempered and prone to violence, a response the servant anticipates. When Antipholus of Syracuse contradicts Dromio of Ephesus, that Dromio will cringe, expecting a blow. The basis for that reaction appears in III.1, the first view of Antipholus of Ephesus; on his entrance Kitchen immediately cuffed the servant, and as the scene developed he also worked in another slap at the locked door of the Phoenix when the servant within says, "My name is Dromio." The offhand cuffings delighted Cellan-Jones every time he saw them. Adriana proved equally fiery and impatient as Suzanne Bertish chased a skittish Dromio around the dinner table, noisily resetting the dishes he had just collected. All such spontaneous additions in rehearsal pleased the director, whose cast offered him creative developments throughout rehearsals. When a scene would get bogged down, the actors worked options until a happy solution arose, as when Jo-anne Pearce, after weeks of alternatives, asked if the women could try starting IV.2 in tears, an approach that proved very effective and very funny.

At times the actors had a strong sense of character that altered Cellan-Jones's plans. For instance, Cellan-Jones had planned the Syracusans' meeting with the Courtesan as a fearful encounter and intended subsequent events to prompt them to draw swords and fight their way to the Abbey. But Kitchen was not interested in fighting; he might be seen buying a sword but did not want to draw it. In exploring other possibilities, the top of V.1 became an extended chase scene rather than a sword fight, and as a result IV.3's encounter with the Courtesan developed into an attempted seduction. Also, Cellan-Jones's discussions with Kitchen about speeches to camera in earlier scenes prompted Bertish to ask if Adriana might also speak to camera, so several asides were planned for her as well.

The mammoth V.1 necessitated constant clarification and careful planning in rehearsal; Cellan-Jones thought continually in terms of the split-screen shots he would use for the final confrontation of the twins. Early on, to underscore the confusion of identity, he asked Charles Gray, the Duke, to pause just after he calls the name in his line, "Antipholus, thou cam'st from Corinth first," so after his "Antipholus" the twins could both respond "Sir?"—a nice touch. Then Bertish saw the possibility for one last confusion of identities as the couples exit into the Abbey; she and Luciana cross to the Antipholi but stop in front of the wrong brothers, Adriana next to the Syracusan. Her quizzical look at the twins and a gesture from her husband send all laughing into the feast and add an effective grace note to the relationship: the women still cannot tell the brothers apart; the men must sort it out.

Wendy Hiller also offered some additions based on Emilia's character as Abbess in V.1. One day she completely altered delivery of her reentry line, "Most mighty duke, behold a man much wrong'd." In previous blocking, she had pushed the Syracusan pair ahead of her through the Abbey door to display them. In her reference (as is usual in playing the scene) the "man much wrong'd" was Antipholus of Syracuse. This day, however, Hiller entered first, delivered "Most mighty duke, behold a man much wrong'd" with a gesture at Aegeon, then beckoned forth the Syracusans to the shock of all present (a group response Cellan-Jones kept encouraging). Her questions of Cellan-Jones were always wonderful to behold: she would approach him with stately step, almost on tiptoe, and very quietly begin, "James? I was wondering if . . . ," and he would greet her with arms extended. During this rehearsal she gingerly approached and asked in a stage whisper if he could arrange for some sacred music to be heard as she came through the Abbey door; Cellan-Jones loved the idea and began providing a falsetto chant himself as they rehearsed, so the invisible choir became the joke for the sound track. Hiller completed the effect at the next rehearsal (27 October), when she solved Adriana's problem about crossing to knock at the door by asking if the door might open as if by magic and the Abbess appear without anyone's knocking, thus adapting the play's sense of witchcraft to more reconciliatory mysteries.

Cellan-Jones wanted a number of run-throughs of the play the last week of rehearsals to help Kitchen and Daltrey set the shifts between their twin characters and to let everyone get the rhythm of the action to build that all-important pace. The last run-through before going to the studio told the story of television production: Cellan-Jones encouraged energy and pace, watching the action with sharp eye, afterward honing moves for precision and being lavish with praise. The refinements of the preceding few days' work paid off. There were some nerves about going into the studio; nonetheless, everyone was humming and whistling the I.1 music as the production staff began pulling tape from the floor, stacking chairs, gathering rehearsal props, and emptying the warehouse that for a month had been Ephesus, while at Television Centre the real Ephesus was rapidly taking shape in studio 1.

Studio work begins a whole new set of rehearsals for the actors— camera rehearsals; although the actors know what the action is, these days in the studio are the first time that set, costumes, props, lighting, and sound are together, the first time the cameras see the action. Camera rehearsals are slow affairs, getting the camera angles, checking the shots, lighting, and sound, working on the cuts, changing the camera script as the director sees what it all looks like and how it works on the monitor.

The picture is the ultimate determinant of everything on the studio floor. Action that was fine in rehearsal suddenly causes trouble on the screen. For instance, in III.2 Cellan-Jones, watching the monitors, commented that Dromio ends up too close to Antipholus when he sits down; the camera angle affects perception. And if anyone sat to the right of Antipholus when Kitchen was seated at

the head of the table upstairs in the Phoenix, the actor had to
dodge the shadow of Kitchen's head. Pearce and Daltrey, both playing from that position, tended to continue regardless of shadow,
but Kitchen, very sensitive to the light and shadows, would shift his
head out of the way when he could (maneuvers evident even on the
finished tape if one watches for them). Kitchen had unexpectedly
gotten ill the previous evening, something between a cold and flu,
and despite remedies was not in good shape the first two days in
the studio. The rhythm of his performance was not affected, but he
looked very drawn during the taping of III.2.

Camera rehearsals took all afternoon, with Cellan-Jones simpli-
fying the camera script; he had built so many shots into the script
that he often found he could do without some of the quick cuts,
just as he sometimes found a shot he needed to add. It took the
entire evening recording session to tape the two scheduled scenes
upstairs at the Phoenix, II.1 and III.2. Take 2 of II.1 was quite
good, Cellan-Jones thought, but Daltrey and Bertish were not sure
their performances had been what they wanted and asked to do
another; designer Homfray, watching the monitor, was also sure he
had seen a screw visible in the door handle and dove downstairs to
adjust it.

The first two takes of III.2 ran into technical trouble, a camera
bobble on the very first pan, then flashes on the camera lens, which
stopped taping. The camera playing hide-and-seek through the
curtained door had been caught halfway out in one of the shots
during rehearsal, so everyone was aware how close the cutting
point was and breathed easier when past it. A word stumble and an
overturned goblet on the table ("Noah's flood" those present called
it) caused a short repeat, but everyone was settling into production
rhythm, which was what Cellan-Jones wanted the first day.

Working the next day on III.1, the scene in which Antipholus of
Ephesus discovers he is locked out of his house, provided a classic
example of what can happen during taping. Camera rehearsals had
gone well, Cellan-Jones pleased with the look of things and teasing Homfray that he wanted to see some tiny sailors crawling amid
the flags blowing on the rigging of the Lilliputian ship in the har-

bor perspective. Taping had been carefully planned; sound supervisor Chick Anthony was recording the dialogue at the door in duplex sound each time, so that Daltrey's voice would be available from either side of the door no matter how the scene was edited. Once taping began, however, an amazing assortment of glitches occurred. The first three takes broke off quickly; take 4 began but almost immediately there were flashes on camera 2, so it was swapped for camera 3, but camera 3 turned out to have a bad pedestal and that had to be changed. Take 5 was grand, the action lively, the exchange at the door rolling along, when engineering called up to say they had lost sound in the videotape engineering section where recording takes place. Everything in the studio was stopped while engineering sorted out the sound; shortly they called back, very sorry, to say they had had sound all along without knowing it, an indicator light had gone bonkers, carry on. Losing the rest of that good take put the day on a tighter schedule and set everyone a bit on edge.

When it was finally time to work on IV.2, the women were time conscious and pent up. They asked if they could signal the start of the scene, since both wanted real tears for the opening. The tears were fine; the only problem was the camera in the corner, which cast a huge shadow across Pearce's dress in one take before the situation was remedied. Though the action proceeded well, tensions surfaced on the studio floor and in the control room as time, performance, and technical aspects clashed.

Once the taping moved to exteriors as well as interiors, lighting director Dave Sydenham commented that he could not have lit a larger set, that he was using every instrument in the studio to light the piazza and the Phoenix. As the last part of the set, the arch between Porpentine and Phoenix, was put in place before the last three days of taping, he said he would refocus lights to cover that part of the floor. Cellan-Jones had told Sydenham and the cast he wanted the effect of full Mediterranean sunlight for the midday scenes in the square, but no one appreciated what that would mean during hours of camera rehearsals until they got to the floor in II.2 on day three, for the lighting succeeded in giving not only the brightness but also the heat of midday sun, since very little ventilation could get over the wraparound, virtually floor-to-ceiling cycloramic curtain.

A number of factors made day three a trying day in the studio: Kitchen was barely on the mend, the temperaments and tensions from the previous day had not improved overnight, the heat on the floor was intense, II.2, the "wafting" scene, was a long, meticulous scene to shoot, and the principals were very aware of the camera script, craning to see monitors and questioning moves ("Is there enough light on me here?" "Do you see me [that is, am I on camera] when I do this?"). To help alleviate the heat, Peter Hider asked that the lights be dimmed except when taping was actually in progress. The set and costumes looked vibrant and lovely under the lower light; the contrast was the more noticeable because Sydenham was using desaturation to wash out some of the intense color in the midday scenes.

Amid questions, complaints about the heat, which most performers stoically endured, and a scramble to cover the open back of the Phoenix hallway with a tapestry when Cellan-Jones added a shot that unexpectedly showed the opening into the scaffolding, the director worked and rethought his camera shots to make sure he got the action he wanted, cutting some, such as the planned shot of Adriana seeing the Syracusans from the Phoenix's window, adding more reaction shots before Adriana speaks, changing where cuts were taken. He carefully set up the opening shot as one of the whole square as it is painted on the backdrop of the mime cart, a shot into which he had Kitchen walk to force viewers to reorient perspective from illusion to reality. Boom shadows (the bane of taping, far more frequent than camera shadows in studio work) began to appear from time to time; Cellan-Jones would usually let a take run despite a shadow, especially in a scene such as II.2 for which there were several takes and therefore a number of cutting points.

The two other scenes for day three, the Dromios' mirror scene and IV.3, the Courtesan scene, were short but time-consuming with retakes. The mirror scene was simple in concept but difficult in execution, necessitating perfectly coordinated timing and movement between Daltrey and the actor playing his double. The moves with the hats and the finger to the eye had been planned and worked through in rehearsal, but the meticulousness of reflection acting only became obvious in the studio, where it required eleven takes with Peter Hider giving them a cadence to get the look just right.

The Courtesan scene, IV.3, was rescheduled from the last day to day three when Cellan-Jones and Hider realized they had a short day. It too endured some false starts and technical hitches (such as when a camera, running over a pea that had fallen from one of the market stalls, wobbled the picture) but had a few bright moments of its own. In selecting street people to block the Syracusans in the market so the Courtesan could appeal to Antipholus of Syracuse across the stall, Hider deftly picked a priest to back up against Antipholus amid all the talk of Satan and devils.

The day off was useful in resting the actors before tackling the two long scenes, I.1 and V.1. Much of I.1 worked as planned; the scene depended on Aegeon, and Cusack was solid in the studio. In the opening of I.1 Cellan-Jones combined action and camera movement in a huge curve, following the flame of the fire-eater up to the Phoenix, across the piazza as a mime did back flips and black-caped Nick Chagrin crossed to the mime cart, where the mimes posed on stage then suddenly released doves and tumbled back into the street to juggle, walk on stilts, and flirt with the "ladies" on the Porpentine balcony. The action and camera covered more than 270 degrees of the circular set. Given the music that would be dubbed over the action, Cellan-Jones had the exuberant opening he wanted.

Peter Hider suggested that for the Duke's entrance the camera first catch sight of the Duke's page, a midget dressed exactly like the Duke, then pull back and angle up as horse and procession enter—another illusion/reality effect. Cellan-Jones got extra mileage from the doves (several of which were still in the studio unretrieved some days later) when one perched on the mime cart; Cellan-Jones quickly told the cameraman to get a shot of it, a useful cutaway. He had more trouble getting the crowd to respond according to plan, as with the crowd blubbering, a response he had

been planning since he first rehearsed I.1. Finally he got the street
people crying as actively as he wanted for the shots of general
misery at Aegeon's sad tale, while those watching the monitors in
the control room roared at the effect.

Problems arose not only due to the length, complexity, and number of people and animals involved in the scene but because the
mime movement orchestrated for the crane shots during the second
taping sometimes came between Aegeon and the camera on the
first taping, an interference that had to be sorted out. Rehearsals
ran long, with only the first taping, the close-up on Aegeon and the
Duke, and the rehearsal of the second, the mimes, completed before dinner break. Cellan-Jones, pressured by time, gave the mime
troupe one take; they were very dissatisfied with their performance
in this, their big scene, and asked for just one more, but Cellan-
Jones told them it had looked better than they thought. What he
also meant was that, considering how little of that supplementary
action he planned to use, he could afford no more time. As it was,
getting the high shots took the production until 9:00 P.M., by which
time there was no chance of taping I.2 as planned, so they ran a
rough camera rehearsal of it and rescheduled the scene for day six,
the last studio day, now no longer the easy day they had hoped.

Day five was cooler in the studio since the action of V.1 was lit
for twilight, not midday, but it was a much longer scene. Principals
and extras were on their feet the entire day during the slow but
steady work of rehearsing and taping 360-degree coverage, shooting over and amid the crowd, and shifting as the action shifted.
Designer Don Homfray was most pleased by the shot from the
Abbey steps of the Duke's entrance through the far gateway and the
reverse shot on his exit because those completed the full circle view
of the set. To help the lighting changes, Homfray had also put
staples in the sea so the light would glint on them as off waves in
the moonlight, an effect Cellan-Jones admired. Sydenham floated
soft clouds and a moon across the cycloramic curtain and lit some
of the small windows in the miniature houses to complete the feeling of evening in Ephesus.

By 10:00 P.M. the scene was taped up to the Abbess's second
entrance, "Most mighty duke, behold a man much wrong'd," and

the first set of role exchanges between the twins. Day six, already scheduled with three scenes, would have to include the end of V.1 and all the split-screen shots as well. To accommodate the pressure and the need, the production staff arranged special morning recording time to pick up taping of I.2; then they finished rehearsing V.1 so it could be completed right after lunch. With a number of false starts, I.2 showed the aftereffects of the preceding long day on V.1 but finally worked after a camera cable was run through the market and camouflaged by sacks and baskets to facilitate Antipholus of Syracuse's last speech to camera. Cellan-Jones had planned another visually instructive opening shot for I.2, a close-up of the fortune-teller's table with its crystal ball and tarot cards. Cellan-Jones had the cards arranged so the Sun card with its illustration of twins was central. The fortune-teller then looked toward the port archway well before the actors entered; Cellan-Jones explained, "See, it's as if she sees them coming in her crystal ball."

Getting the rest of V.1 and the other necessary shots—the split screens plus the shots of action with Pinch at the Phoenix's window —took all afternoon. The split-screen shots are technical magic: one half of the screen is locked off and the action taped in the remaining portion; then when the second part is taped on the other half of the screen with sound from the first tape piped into the studio, the action from the earlier version is played simultaneously and presto, twins appear to be talking to each other on the monitor, an engaging and funny effect. In doing the Dromio and Antipholus split screens against the far gateway, Hider carefully arranged extras in the background close to the split line, explained where the split was, and told them under no circumstances to move. As a result, while the crowd noise is jubilant and Dromio or Antipholus quite responsive, the Ephesians in the background stand rigid and dour, obeying studio orders but adversely affecting the overall atmosphere of the shot.

The scene where the Ephesian Antipholus becomes Pinch's patient, IV.4, was rehearsed and taped after dinner with few hitches, Cellan-Jones quietly arranging to tape a camera rehearsal for this scene as well as IV.1 to increase his cutting points. Producer Shaun Sutton had arranged an extra hour's taping time that evening, which proved necessary when IV.1 was started just before 10:00 P.M. They rehearsed and finished taping the scene at 11:10, at which point Cellan-Jones had to abandon all the extra bits he had planned—the mime play (for which the mimes had been patiently waiting since day three), the mimes' orange stealing in the market, and the last little split screen of the Dromios' exit. There was no time. The last day was a tremendous and exhausting push for all concerned, but finishing was commendable. In production terms a bit of overtime is infinitely preferable to a day's overrun or having to remount a production, because the schedule rules studio work; meeting the deadline is of paramount importance to the BBC, and directors who run grossly over for artistic and aesthetic reasons or because of ill planning risk the wrath.

Afterward, relief at finishing was mixed with pleasure about the production. Actors could be heard commending the job Cellan-Jones had done, and the production camaraderie was, as usual, at its fullest just as it ended. Taping strangely combines elements of the first and last nights of a theatrical run, and the postproduction gathering had the air of both opening and closing nights. The performance was over, even though the production was far from completed.

Because the BBC schedulers wanted *The Comedy of Errors* to be the Christmas show that year, it therefore had to be ready for transmission on 24 December, so editing was scheduled immediately after taping, a slightly tighter schedule than was usual with the Shakespeare series. The last studio day was Wednesday, 9 November; editing began Tuesday, 15 November, and ran six days. Without a doubt editing is the most meticulous, painstaking part of production. Getting the finished product to look and sound the way the director wants it to takes time and patience. For instance, the first three hours of editing *The Comedy of Errors* were spent on the sequence from the credits to the Duke's entrance—before a line is ever delivered. Cellan-Jones's overriding concern in editing was pace; he wanted the show to move lickety-split and encouraged Peter Reason, the videotape editor, to nibble away at any pause in delivery, in the pickup of cues, or in action.

Editing I.1 was an exercise in building the composite of speech, mime action, and music. Listening to the music, Cellan-Jones explained to Reason, "It's a play about time, and so I've got those little bells in the music." Cellan-Jones had discovered in reviewing the tapes prior to editing (a process that makes editing far more efficient) that he lacked cutaways in this scene; he had set up the "blubbering" shots of the crowd but had no extra initial happy crowd shots in the piazza and not enough attentive, listening crowd shots. And there was little crowd noise (the last words the production manager yells before the tape runs is some variation on "absolute quiet!"). Cellan-Jones lamented that he should have gotten some wild tracks of crowd bustle and began making notes to overlay sound in the dubbing: "It needs noises, cheers, 'Hooray for the Duke,'" he said. In searching for cutaways, that dove on the mime cart became invaluable juxtaposed to a shot of two whores on the Porpentine balcony, and they found one shot of Luce meditative in a window of the Phoenix—not enough to suit Cellan-Jones, but all he had.

Throughout editing of I.1 the tape of Aegeon was used as the master tape with mime action used for drop-in shots. Cellan-Jones did not want an extended stretch of mime action, so he chose the best moments; much of the mime was consequently cut. Watching the scene develop, Cellan-Jones commented on Cusack's delivery, the naturalistic fumbles that endear him to audiences, as does his responsive face. By the end of the day, the videotape editor looked up and commented, "Well, that's ten minutes in the can."

By lunchtime the second day I.1 was completed. Cellan-Jones had selected which bits of crying response to use and put them in order, saving the best ones for last—first the Officer removing his glasses to wipe his eyes and then the donkey, which Cellan-Jones said he included only because Dromio had so many lines about being an ass. At the end of I.1 and also at the beginning of I.2 boom shadows appeared during the best takes, and Cellan-Jones was faced with the decision to choose either clean technical shots or performance. As most directors will, he chose performance; muttering about one shadow, he said he just had to buy the shadow since the shot was framed much better than the alternative.

The mirror scene turned out remarkably well in editing because of the editor's good eye in taking bits from different takes and his precise timing of cuts. Cellan-Jones, watching the sequence build, was pleased: "Yes, it's quite believable. . . . I know exactly what they [critics] will say: it's based on the Marx brothers—there was a mirror sequence in one of their films." That satisfaction with the sequence did not carry over into II.2, however, which Cellan-Jones did not think proved quite as lively in the studio as it had in rehearsal. Nonetheless, as Kitchen stepped into the shot of the mime cart at the start of the scene, Cellan-Jones chuckled and said, "I find it very funny, all these people talking to camera."

During the day the question arose of whether or not there should be an interval breaking up the broadcast of the production. Because *The Comedy of Errors* is such a short play, Cellan-Jones was still considering going straight through. If there were an interval it would have to come after act III, which production assistant Raquel Ebbutt had figured would be almost halfway through the running time. Also there were a number of comments about the bright color in the show. Reason, the videotape editor, added what a shame it was that the color did not show up as well on the VHS tapes or on American television.

On the third editing day they finished work on II.2 and nearly completed act III. Editing II.2 involved splicing two takes, deciding which was better in each case given the composition of the shots and the liveliness of the performance. For instance, in one take Bertish shifted position and blocked the other performers, but because the other take had different cutting points, it was not always easy to cover such problems.

In working on III.1, both Cellan-Jones and Reason commented on the troubled camera work—the number of zooms evident in supposedly steady shots, the bobbles, some framing problems, agreeing, "We got what we could out of it." Videotape editors are by nature a tight-lipped group, reserving judgment, circumspect and tactful when they do state their opinion, but sharp of eye and ear. They can seem like wizards in polishing the raw material of studio takes into a clean, crisp sequence. Cellan-Jones and Reason had the same feel for timing and similar technical acumen; they worked well together, as the close cutting and numerous sound edits of III.1 showed.

The very end of III.2, Angelo giving Antipholus of Syracuse the chain, began the fourth day of editing. An effective cannibalization of other takes for reaction shots, the edited scene is a composite of three takes, with a great deal of effort put into getting the head turns and gestures to match on cuts between takes. The gag of one twin at the Porpentine seeing the other leave the Phoenix followed III.2 and called for even finer cutting. Cellan-Jones had in mind a specific piece of music to use for this scene, but Kitchen's cross from the Phoenix to the market took too long for the music, a fact Cellan-Jones bemoaned, now having to find a longer bit of music to cover the action. In rehearsal and studio Cellan-Jones always knew what effect he had planned and how the pieces were to fit, but in the midst of studio taping, that information was not always precisely transmitted to the actors. Only editing made the pieces work.

An assortment of camera woes were discovered in IV.2, several large shadows on Luciana from the camera tucked in the corner near the window (and thus backlit if not carefully handled) and zooms at the start of shots, as if the shot was still being framed when the cut occurred. The vision mixer in the control room had taken particular care with cuts, watching the next shot, warning the cameraman if there was a problem prior to the cut, but she had no recourse if the shot changed after the cut. Editing around such happenstances took some doing.

In watching the takes Cellan-Jones momentarily considered cutting some of it, but judging the last take to be workable, he used it since that scene sets up the madness element of the next scene. There was not only madness in IV.4 but inescapable boom shadows, a result of working against the clock the last day. The videotape editor meanwhile worked to equalize sound levels, bumping the sound up a bit when an actor's voice was lowered, balancing volumes between speakers when necessary.

The story of editing V.1 was the search for cutaway shots; as Cellan-Jones finally said, there was "a desperate lack of coverage here." Where there were no cutaways and a shot was needed to cover a cut or a pause, it was invented and in one case even repeated. The chase scene in the market is a good example: the chase starts, the mimes join, Antipholus and Dromio collide in the market (there were actually two collisions; the second was cut in editing), then Cellan-Jones wanted some cutaways to extend the action. He had only some shots of the mimes leaving the wagon, so he included those next (even though by strict continuity the mimes had long since left the wagon), as if a second wave of mimes were joining the fracas, and used the close-ups of Nick Chagrin whistling directions to the mimes before returning to the shot of the Syracusans' escape into the Abbey, thus creating a long and noisy chase. The editor doubled the chase sound for effect, then tried the sequence with the "Jolly Music" playing, and it worked amazingly well; as Reason pointed out, the cuts even occurred on the downbeats, an effect he worked for where he could.

The cutaways available were few not only because of time pressure in the studio but because there were fewer takes of the separate sections of V.1. Editing of earlier scenes had benefited by having one or two shots added to the master from an otherwise less useful take. Cellan-Jones's only options in V.1 were from rehearsal footage taped as a back-up, but the shots were sometimes very rough (as is expected in camera rehearsal, the point of which is to work out the shots for actual taping).

Editing V.1 also included the most spectacular sound edits of the entire process. Reason had smoothly nibbled away at pauses, synchronized and created sound bridges in every scene, at one point after thirty minutes of painstaking work quipping, "There, a few seagulls over that and you'd never know the difference." While chastising Adriana, the Abbess had a line, "Thereof the raging fire of fever bred" in the middle of a nearly twenty-line speech. On one take Hiller said "raging fear of fever," on another "burning fire of fever"; all the right words were there, but on different takes. Cellan-Jones decided which take was better overall, and Reason patiently sliced the necessary word out of the other version and recorded it onto the sound track. The result is indiscernible, the trait that exemplifies effective editing.

Another major sound edit was even more challenging, since it involved shifting sound tracks between syllables of a word. Late in the action where the movements of the twins were shot twice for the split-screen effect, there was a difference between the two versions in the speed with which Antipholus of Ephesus took the long-awaited ducats from his twin and moved, declaring, "These ducats pawn I for my father here." The action required precise timing with the double, but since Kitchen taped Antipholus of Syracuse first, in that take the actor playing the Antipholus double could not predict Kitchen's exact movements as the Ephesian. Consequently, in one version Antipholus of Ephesus moved sooner than in the other, and the sound of the double's footsteps could be heard before Kitchen moved in the final split-screen shot. Reason edited out the footsteps by bridging the two sound tracks in the middle of the word "ducats" so deftly the result is completely natural.

The sixth and last editing day focused on the end of V.1, especially the split-screen shots. Reason said he could erase the hint of a line in the split-screen shots against the far arch by working with the 1-inch tape but not with the 2-inch tape used for the main editing. He did, however, adjust the lumens in most of the split-screen shots to match the color in the adjoining shots, since the split screens ended up brighter or paler, and once even half-and-half.

Cellan-Jones, who had to shoot every combination of angles to cover the twins at the end of the play, worked to get the interactions he wanted. Looking at the big split-screen shot in which the twins face each other, he said he would have framed it differently had he had the time. The only problem he ran into with these combinations, however, was a missing shot. After Antipholus of Ephesus declares, "I came from Corinth, my most gracious lord," there was no 2-shot of master and servant for Dromio to respond, "And I with him"; the only shot was the split screen of the Antipholi against the gateway in which Dromio is heard but not seen. Cellan-Jones therefore juggled with a reaction shot of the Syracusans to fill the gap. Cutting back and forth between brothers let him convincingly effect the transfer of necklace and ducats, the shots arranged from behind so all but the face of one twin is in shot. As the twins finally approach Emilia for an embrace, Luciana's back appeared briefly at the edge of the long shot on the only take. The moment was not marred, but it was not the ideal clean shot Cellan-Jones had wanted.

He was pleased with much of the end of the scene, though. Hiller gave Emilia's last line with full theatrical presence, while beside her Cusack's Aegeon gave a warm look and a nod, bringing the statement back to earth, a response Cellan-Jones thought was "wonderful." And the last intercut split screens of the Antipholi on the Abbey steps talking to the Dromios in the piazza looked "smashing," Cellan-Jones said, with the interactions and looks between the brothers engaging and successful. At the last close-up of Antipholus of Ephesus with a surly look, Cellan-Jones laughed appreciatively, "Nasty to the end, ol' Antipholus of Ephesus." They moved through the Dromios' handshake to the long shot of the mimes' bergomask and, completing the full circle of the visual action, to a high shot of the dance and map mixed to another quick shot of the parchment map of the Mediterranean that had opened the show (it was, in fact, the second draft of the map; the first one did not match the map on the floor in the dissolve and was promptly redrawn from the picture on the studio floor), and into the credits. Most of the hard work done, Cellan-Jones and Reason sat back to review the tape, second half first since that was the master reel on the machine, and as the action began, Cellan-Jones observed happily, "What a silly play this is."

As these production diaries demonstrate, Miller and Cellan-Jones have different methods of rehearsing and taping. Miller rehearsed predominantly for performance, whereas during rehearsal Cellan-Jones always conveyed a sense of display for the camera and getting the shots. The camera script was virtually unmentioned in Miller's rehearsals, whereas producing it played a major role for Cellan-Jones in the last weeks of rehearsal. In the studio, however, both directors naturally adapted their plans, adding or changing shots, discovering angles, refining moves. Editing posed challenges for both directors, for Miller in covering Troilus's eavesdropping scene at Diomedes' tent and for Cellan-Jones in finding coverage and cutaway shots for the large crowd scenes. While there are several workable methods of television production, it is always a matter of careful planning and foresight combined with inspiration, good taste, good sense, and a generous dab of good fortune.

10 *Titus Andronicus* in the Studio

The most crucial time for the BBC Shakespeare productions was the time in the studio, capturing the performances on tape. Watching the creative forces marshaled to make the hours in the studio count and seeing how those hours are spent can illuminate the dynamics of televising Shakespeare, especially when observing as efficient a studio director as Jane Howell.

To appreciate the degree of Jane Howell's control and planning, her support for and ambience with the actors and designers, the sense of a group effort she instills, one has to see her in action. In the studio taping of *Titus Andronicus* all these qualities were evident. Not only had most of the cast rehearsed *Titus* in 1984 before a strike delayed the production, thus forming a group bond, but in her earlier productions in the Shakespeare series Howell had also worked with many of the actors in the cast, Brian Protheroe, Trevor Peacock, Anna Calder-Marshall, and Derek Fuke, among others. And in this show as in the *Henry VI* tetralogy she had a company of supporting artists for the crowds, here playing both Goth warriors and Roman citizens and senators. She also had a unit set, her favorite for televised Shakespeare, designed for suggestivity and flexibility. The effect of a Roman amphitheatre was gained by the circular two-story walls (actually two-thirds of a circle in the studio). Within this arena, platform risers could be variously arranged to accommodate crowds or an emperor's chair on high, and when they were not used, a curtain, a table, or a colonnade could be set in to suggest different locales. Designed for quick change, the set proved very versatile; the most difficult set shift involved the double curtain hung for the forest scenes, and planning took care of that.

As versatile as was her set was Howell's recording time, which was available morning to night, from 11:00 to 1:00, 2:30 to 6:00, and 7:30 to 10:00 every day. Moreover, the taping schedule for 10–17 February had been carefully arranged to provide both for practical changes in the set and for Trevor Peacock's (Titus) schedule since he was performing in the RSC repertory and had to be on stage as Pete the Pipe in *Mother Courage* the evenings of 11 and 12 February. The forest scenes were scheduled first, since they involved the netting over the set, which could be hung as part of the initial preparation and struck overnight after taping. With almost a full day of camera rehearsals on Sunday, 10 February, all three forest scenes (V.1, the capture of Aaron, II.3, the killing of Bassianus, and II.4, the discovery of raped Lavinia) could be taped Monday 11 February. Tuesday covered IV.2 and II.1, Aaron's scenes with Tamora's sons, and IV.4, the Clown delivering pigeons to the Emperor, all scenes that did not call for Titus. On Wednesday, the day off, the crew set in the Andronici tomb, so that on Thursday work could begin with I.1. Thereafter, to help the actors, action was taped in story order: I.1 on Thursday; II.2 (off to hunt), III.1 (Titus cuts off his hand), and III.2 (the fly scene) on Friday; IV.1 (Lavinia names her assailants), IV.3 (arrows to the gods), and V.2 (Revenge visits Titus) on Saturday; and V.3 (the last banquet) on Sunday. Or such was the plan. Schedules usually get juggled a bit in the studio depending on circumstances, and in a production involving babies (for whom there are the strictest union time regulations: thirty minutes on, two hours off), Howell had made sure to get an extra day for taping, wisely as it turned out. In fact, she said her production manager's first task with the show was to beg, cajole, or coerce that extra day out of the powers-that-be.

More than just the taping order had been arranged, however. To enhance her interpretation of the action as young Lucius's dream or vision, she planned a series of careful blends between scenes; in editing she would mix the shots, bringing one up as the former faded, which meant these shots had to extend longer than for a regular cut. Once the action and camera were working harmoniously, she would simply give a note to cameraman or actor explaining the mood or shot or action she needed for the transition, as when she asked Brian Protheroe (Saturninus) at the end of scene thirteen (IV.4) to sink into himself as he sat on the throne, then to look down the gangway, because "I'm going to mix into the next scene with Lucius's entrance, and it's as if he's in your head and you can see him." Howell worked with velvet-gloved control in the studio; she knew what she needed to make the pieces fit, and she knew what she wanted for every piece.

On the studio floor during camera rehearsals her attitude was serious and intent; shot by shot she studied the monitor, then turned to change a movement, alter a camera angle or position, adjust the placement of background figures. It was a process of building pictures working in three dimensions. Throughout the meticulous repetitions of camera rehearsals, she carefully explained what she wanted: an actor needed to clear this far to frame someone behind him or he needed to be seated by the end of that line. And amid the stops, starts, resets, and reruns, she accompanied each adjustment with a sincere "thank you, Trevor, thank you, Brian, everyone; ready now, and again."

Because everyone understood the purpose of the scenes and taping rationale and because her instructions were uniformly clear, a sense of teamwork grew between actors and camera crew. When an actor got masked from the camera shot—as can happen when an actor is in the back of a group with four cameras working, especially an actor less experienced in television who may not always know where the shot is—Garth Tucker, camera supervisor, would sometimes gently move the actor during a break and explain the camera angle, since blocking for the camera is always a matter of inches. In rehearsing the complicated scenes, other actors might check their positions in a monitor hanging in the light grid and move slightly, a move that was not a matter of enlightened self-interest but doing what needed to be done. At other times an actor would turn to the cameraman and ask, "Is it better for you if I do this here or there?" so that each one tried to support and help the other, an ideal studio relationship not always so successfully achieved. Howell fostered trust between the actors and camera crew, and she would give actors leeway to alter moves: "Just tell the cameraman."

Such teamwork was essential to Howell's plan, for she divided the taping into large chunks, ten- or fifteen-minute segments, which is long for sustained takes in television. Such takes give actors a chance to sustain a performance for at least a scene or a large section of one, but they demand exceptional technical accuracy on the part of all concerned: lighting, sound, cameras, actors. She worked to achieve that accuracy right up to and during taping, sometimes giving ten minutes of detailed adjustments to blocking and camera moves just before the first take.

Yet even the best-laid plans and sincerest efforts can be tested by the imponderables of studio taping. The gremlins, as Howell called the problems that affect production, hit *Titus* the first day in the studio when the fire marshal declared that the supposedly fire-proofed netting hung three-fourths of the way around the studio was still flammable and could not be used. The props buyer, after lamenting man-made fibers that sneak into materials, arranged to have the netting struck during the dinner break, transported, and refireproofed overnight. The liner, a khaki-colored gauze, was left on the set as a back-up, but the effect of the forest was diminished without the texture of the netting. All three scheduled forest scenes got long, careful camera rehearsals. Of course, any camera re-hearsal involves extensive tinkering, repositioning, and explaining as the cameras meet the action and the director frames the shots, but first camera rehearsals are also a meticulous process of getting things going, of getting into the production.

The first camera rehearsal for *Titus* began Sunday at 2:00, and the entire afternoon session was spent on V.1, the capture of Aaron, running bits of action, checking camera angles, explaining moves to the supporting artists (the extras), and getting the look right. A director stays on the floor arranging shots, often shot by shot, during the first few run-throughs and then for the last camera rehearsal goes up to the control room to watch on the monitors. It was late afternoon and there had been several rehearsals be-fore they included the real baby in the scene and advised Hugh Quarshie (Aaron) how best to hold him so the baby could be seen.

After dinner, work began on the act II rape and murder scenes. Since Titus's sons must fall into a pit, a pile of tumbling mats were stacked to within three feet of the top step of the risers. Martius played the voice from the pit by hanging over the far side of the mats and speaking to the floor; then when it was time for him to reach for Quintus's hand he flipped over, slid down the mats under the steps, and pulled himself up enough to clear his arm, all in the space of Quintus's four lines. Despite everyone's hard work, a good bit of polishing was left for final rehearsals on Monday.

The second day opened with a happy ending to the netting crisis; the nets were successfully fireproofed and by 11:00 were again hanging in the studio, so Howell proceeded with one last meticulous camera rehearsal of V.1. Most of the lights, many with green and orange gels, flashed and flickered to contribute to the torch-lit gathering, a flicker achieved by bouncing the feed off the BBC radio signal. Make-up personnel had changed Lucius's scar from his right eye to his left after watching camera angles the previous day. Meanwhile Howell watched details, such as how fast the soldier could remove Aaron's belt, and worked to arrange more close-ups of Aaron on the ladder. She also positioned the Goths on the risers; first she stared at a monitor, studying the shot's composition, then turned onto the set to move a Goth up or back, right or left. Without fail she thanked the cast at each interruption, reset, or rerun. By 12:15 they added the torches and were ready for a full rehearsal on tape. In thinking through the scene since the preceding day, Howell had simplified Aaron's entrance and was worried about the animal skin wrapping the baby, which seemed to obscure the child. At 12:40 take 1 started, and the baby cried for the first time all day. Howell was generally pleased but said they would go for one more after lunch since a few moments needed tidying up.

They actually did four more takes of V.1 after lunch. The baby cried throughout most of take 2 from 2:30 to 2:40, and while Howell said that was useful for the opening and closing, she hoped for a better, that is, a quieter middle. Take 3 had barely begun at 2:47 when a camera had mechanical trouble, and another had to be substituted. Eight minutes later they began again only to encounter the baby wailing. Howell asked her production manager on the floor if any one of the three available babies was happy, since it was most unfair to ask the actors to play against that sound; one, he responded, had just been fed and obliged by snoozing through take 5, which incorporated some new camera shots as well. At 3:08 Howell, pleased, picked up a cutaway shot of Lucius to cover Aaron's climbing the ladder, which had seemed to make for a longish pause, then sent her congratulations to those on the studio floor and said, "Let's go on to the next as fast as we can."

The preparation for scene six (II.3) took over half an hour, and Howell finally started rehearsing before the technicians were entirely finished. Again she watched the floor monitor intently, then darted back to the actors, who were all dancing around dead Bassianus on the floor and using his anatomy for blocking ("move to his elbow"). By 4:45 Howell, aware of time pressure, wanted to "rehearse on tape," so they did, getting a boom in shot and several fluffed lines. Howell stopped take 2 immediately because she needed a longer pause for editing the fade-in and wanted to cue the start herself. Take 3 at 5:15 ran into a line fluff halfway through, so they started again; take 4 had the same problem, but they did a pick-up shot and ran to the end. Take 5 began with Tamora's second entrance but quickly caught a boom in shot, so restarted. Take 6 was a modified run to cover some snags but did not include Titus's part since Peacock had already left for the theatre. During dinner break the control room staff checked the videotapes of the afternoon's recording, once for fun running them at high speed so the action looked as melodramatic as *Birth of a Nation*.

Four more takes followed in the evening; one ran into camera trouble again, one quickly stopped, one had a line fluff, the last (at 7:50) went as far as they planned, though one spearhead had broken by then and fell off as Martius went into the pit. With the set under greenish light and smoke all day, the clearing seemed increasingly murky and disturbing as the action progressed. By mid-evening final rehearsals for ravished Lavinia's scene at the pit (II.4) began. At first there was no blood on her dress or her face; only her hair was a bit mussed. Watching the action, producer Shaun Sutton reminisced about the 1955 RSC production in which Olivier had been superb as Titus, but Vivien Leigh as Lavinia was neatly coiffed and calm on her entrance following the rape (the violence in that RSC production was highly stylized, with red ribbons for blood). During rehearsals Howell slowly began to modify Lavinia's appearance, smearing blood on her face and later having the gown ripped. Since Anna Calder-Marshall took a mouthful of blood make-up every rehearsal to mask her tongue, in the natural course of rehearsals her chin and her costume became quite convincingly bloodstained.

Later Calder-Marshall said playing Lavinia has an awful effect on an actress; "It puts you in touch with terrible things in yourself." During rehearsals she had always cried at the rape scene, but in the studio, she said, it was just too horrible; she was in a shock beyond tears. And the whole tongue treatment with the make-up surprised her; moreover, "It tastes terrible," she added.

By 9:25 they went for take 1, which Howell stopped immediately because the thrust of Lavinia to the camera needed to be quicker. After that false start the take went all the way through. Howell gave some notes while studio hands pumped more smoke in, so much that take 2 also had a false start while smoke cleared, Howell apologizing to the actors and asking them to concentrate meantime. As take 2 finally got under way, there was a loud crash off camera; something had fallen in the studio, so Howell stopped the take and started again. A boom got in shot during take 3; Howell moaned but ran it through, later adjusting Marcus's position on the steps because he was too low in frame. Ten o'clock, the scheduled end of taping, was looming close, and they still needed a powerful version of this scene. There might barely be time for one more take; tension mounted, and all eyes in the control room alternated between clock and monitors. At 9:54 take 4 began after a false start and finished at 9:59. Howell got one more wide shot and finally said "cut" as the second hand rose to 10:00. A full day in the studio, indeed. Howell and Sutton discussed editing the scene as the crew moved in to strike the nets.

Next day with the nets gone, the full two-level set was visible with its barred doors below and ramparts above and tunnel-like passageways leading to high arches that gave an impressive sense of depth and distance, the whole thing covered with a thin layer of gray Plasticine "brick" and "plaster." Beyond the set hung a painted cycloramic curtain showing more brick structures above the walls, giving the set an almost claustrophobic enclosure. Howell spent the morning's camera rehearsal working out the moves around the table in scene eleven (IV.2) with Tamora's sons and Aaron, setting up cuts to cover the action. The actors agreed on a spot to hear the trumpets, since the sound would be dubbed in later during editing. Meanwhile one of the braziers popped fire onto the scenery, causing a one-minute scuffle on the set. Howell's notes during the run-through were explanatory and precise: when to sit, when to clear, and why. After lunch they did one last run-through, with the real baby this time, which altered the timing significantly since all the moves of transfer and placement were far gentler and more careful than they had been earlier with the doll. The scene looked good as Howell made a few last-minute adjustments to the set and discussed how the last shot needed to be framed to mix with the next scene, because "I'm going to a close-up of the boy."

Take 1 started at 3:13, a false start when a camera appeared in the third shot. The take then ran through, catching a small boom shadow on Aaron's face and with the baby crying, though Quarshie was very good with the child, hushing him, rocking him, rubbing his tummy to quiet him, meanwhile never missing a line or breaking eye contact. Howell inquired about the baby situation, gave a few more notes on positions, and asked young Lucius to be less sarcastic with his remarks to Chiron and Demetrius, which needed to be simple and formal; the asides, Howell reminded him, show what he thinks. She also asked Quarshie to do his long aside as a chat to the camera. With these adjustments, take 2 proceeded at 3:35 with a line bobble and some baby trouble. By take 3 at 3:47 the baby was calm, just making a few sounds near the end. In the control room, Howell leaned back from the intense hunched posture she always had while watching the monitor and said, "That's the take. Now we're just looking for a few pick-ups," mostly worried about the baby being concealed when Aaron takes him. Howell told the production manager she would stop if baby Nicholas got at all upset, but she wanted to cover one shot.

After a last-minute technical hold, take 4 began at 4:10, and Quarshie again demonstrated his perception and concentration,

Howell's amphitheatre unit set for Titus Andronicus, *designed by Tony Burrough, with its archways, ramparts, and cycloramic curtain painted to suggest additional enclosing facades is fully visible in an early scene with rival brothers and masked Roman citizens. Bassianus (Nicholas Gecks,*

center) and Saturninus (Brian Protheroe, right, with sword); rear of shot, Aemilius (Walter Brown, left), Publius (Paul Kelly, partially hidden), and Marcus (Edward Hardwicke, behind Bassianus). © BBC

Covered with gauze and netting and eerily lit by lighting designer Sam Barclay, the unit set for Titus Andronicus *becomes the murky glade. Martius (Tom Hunsinger, left), Quintus (Crispin Redman), and Aaron (Hugh Quarshie, above).* © BBC

keeping eye contact while quickly righting a burning candle one of the other actors knocked over on the table. As the baby was laid on the table and Quarshie uncovered it, the moment came that everyone who had ever dealt with a male infant had been expecting—the baby promptly began to urinate. Quarshie's line came out a chortled "sweet blow-ow-ow-se" as he tried to stifle a laugh, and the other actors corpsed, eyes dancing, though everyone tried to play through it. Howell stopped the action, arranged a single shot to cover the moment, and proceeded until a thump in the studio occurred right over the transfer of the baby from nurse to Aaron, which was the one shot Howell needed. After juggling infant and sword and dagger all afternoon, in the last take Quarshie worked out for himself the natural place to switch the baby to his left arm

Smaller pieces were set in for some scenes of Titus Andronicus *to vary the unit set, as when sides of meat were hung as a backdrop for Titus's meeting with Tamora and her sons in disguise as Revenge, Murder, and Rape. Also visible are the bones in Titus's stump. Titus (Trevor Peacock, left), Chiron (Michael Crompton, partially hidden), Tamora (Eileen Atkins), and Demetrius (Neil McCaul).* © BBC

(there was only one good opportunity for this move in the action). In editing, much of what Howell used came from this last eventful take.

Late afternoon was spent on scene four (II.1, the plan for the rape), one long camera rehearsal with endless repetitions to establish the rhythm of the shots and another slow rehearsal for fine tuning. Close to dinner break they taped take 1, which had a bobbled line and a missed cut. Howell was concerned to keep power with the first shot as the camera pulled back. Take 2 went smoothly, ending at 6:01, a minute into dinner. The actors playing Tamora's sons explained that Neil McCaul (Demetrius) had not been in the cast the previous year when a strike delayed the taping of *Titus*, and though he had been blocked into the former plan, the brothers' relationship in all the scenes had changed during rehearsal. Howell later said the same, these boys had different dynamics, as was the case with the other new additions—young Lucius, Quintus, and the Clown. The actors also praised the power of the run-through the day before going into the studio; it was a remarkable performance, especially by Trevor Peacock (Titus), spellbinding and very exciting. That, of course, is the thrill of theatre, the build of an unbroken performance, which television taping with its divisions and repetitions can never have for an actor. And they also fondly remembered an improvisation in which they did part of a run-through Mafia-style, which seemed very appropriate and useful to them.

In scene thirteen (IV.4, Saturninus in state), as Howell explained that evening, she was deliberately parodying the Goth scene taped the day before, so she wanted the sense of repetition: the speaker on high and the crowd opposite on risers with a few important figures seated on stools between them. Howell was obviously attuned to the studio work, maintaining her unstinting intensity and attention with vigor and humor. During camera rehearsals she worked to get the Romans' reaction to the news of the Goths' presence, but since she had the same group of supporting artists· (extras) playing Romans as Goths, they gave the same singularly lifeless choral cry, perhaps a result of wearing masks. Howell was very precise about what she wanted, yet when asked by Eileen Atkins or another of the principals about a move, Howell invariably responded, "Whatever feels right," which was not indefiniteness on her part but trust and support of the artists to whom the parts now belonged.

Because the light was brighter in this scene (it was the first full "daytime" scene to be taped), the painted gray cycloramic curtain was more visible, and its vista of brick buildings, walls, windows, and doorways seemed to rise high over the second tier of the set as Saturninus surveyed it from his throne. It was nearly 9:00 when they went for a take. The cameras promptly shot into the lights because of the Clown's height, so the camera angle was adjusted while Howell asked for another knife: the one for rehearsal had looked like a razor, and this one like a butter knife. Two more takes and one sharp-tipped knife later, they reset for a last cover shot at past 9:30. Howell was feeling pressured because during dinner

Hugh Quarshie had asked if they could have one more go at scene four since he thought he could do it better, and Howell had promised they would try if there was time tonight. At 9:45 amid the reset for scene four she said she would not overrun but would go for one take of the scene, which started from the top at 9:50 and ended smoothly just after 9:59, a second day with a photo finish in the race with the clock.

The day off during the studio taping is never a day of rest for the production staff; they went right on with planning even though they did not work in the studio. By Thursday, facing four long studio days to finish, everyone looked drawn, gaunt about the eyes, especially Howell and Garth Tucker, the camera supervisor who headed the camera crew and did all the single-camera sequences. Anyone who doubts the stress of television work need only look in the faces of those responsible for a production during the middle of such a week's taping to know its ravages. In *Titus* the actors fared no better; Trevor Peacock could not sleep or eat the week of taping and often stayed up half the night, keyed up from studio work, while Anna Calder-Marshall went home and cried every night from the strain of being Lavinia, both actors suffering the burden of intensity.

Thursday was scheduled for the play's long opening ritualistic sequence, carefully broken into three segments for narrative and taping purposes. Howell rearranged the action to tell the story more clearly for television, she said, visually presenting the tension between the Emperor's sons before Titus enters. To expedite taping, however, the intermediate section, scene two, the burial in the dark, ghoulish Andronici tomb, was treated first because the slatted-roofed colonnade and the hanging mummified bodies could be set in position during the day off. It is far easier to strike such set pieces than to ready them. There was morning recording time from 11:00 to 12:15, so rehearsals for this single-camera sequence began in earnest.

By 11:50 they had recorded two takes and gotten clearance to reset for the rest of the scene, where the formal, processional nature of the play's opening becomes readily apparent: take out the dead Emperor, bring on the victorious general and his captives, have rival groups vie in the open, name a new emperor, bury more dead, exit for a wedding and return, then all march out. And the rituals clearly involved blood: the marking of Alarbus as sacrifice and the Andronici brothers' return with blood-ringed eyes and bloodstained fingers, a procedure based not on Roman practice but African ritual painting. By 3:20 scene one was rehearsed and ready to be taped. Take 1 was decent, but Howell wanted to try for a better, though takes 2 and 3 each caught a camera in shot on Lucius's reentry from the tomb. Between the takes the action seemed covered, though, so at 4:30 rehearsal for the long conclusion of the scene began, with no taping possible until evening. This intricate, heavily populated segment required painstaking rehearsal and careful positioning on several levels of the set, and as she worked on scene three after the dinner break, Howell decided to postpone that evening's taping because after such long rehearsals everyone would be too tired and frayed. So they ran the scene several times to perfect it so they could tape the next morning. By 8:45 the fatigue was apparent; problems kept cropping up and were slowly solved. As it neared 10:00 Howell turned to Brian Protheroe after Saturninus's self-indulgent outbursts at scene's end and said, "You are a silly prat, Brian, and it's lovely," then sent everyone home.

Even before the official start time of 11:00 the next morning Howell was running camera shots with the crew and refining moves from the previous night; morning recording time was extended until 1:30 to get the scene taped. After a refresher runthrough, at 12:10 Howell opted for a rehearsal on tape and told the cast, "I want it like last night when you were hysterical and tired. You were wonderful last night." At 12:24 they started take 1, ending at 12:46, after which Howell gave copious camera and blocking notes. At 1:04 they started take 2, and though there were a few line fluffs and a boom in shot, every note Howell had given was expedited on that second take.

Because the morning session was later than the usual schedule, the afternoon work with scene eight (III.1, Titus cuts off his hand) did not begin until 3:00. Even in rehearsal this scene was very powerful, given Titus's and Lavinia's suffering, and to protect the actors Howell and production manager Tony Garrick repeatedly asked the studio to keep very quiet. Most of Howell's as well as fight arranger Malcolm Ranson's effort in rehearsing this scene focused on the hand chopping. By 5:10 they were ready to tape the almost twenty-minute scene, and Howell gave last details, asking Titus's blindfolded sons to look back toward him when they hear his voice and telling Hugh Quarshie to show less of the severed hand. Howell reminded those on the floor that she wanted to get in two takes before the dinner break.

Take 1 began and caught a boom in shot, so they restarted, production manager Tony Garrick giving the tribunes their march cadence. The pressure the actors felt in this intense scene showed in the number of missed words, and the take also had two camera shadows and a boom in shot, not to mention Lavinia's tongue at one point. At 5:42 when the scene ended they immediately requested taping time beyond the 6:00 dinner break. Take 2 began at 5:52. The hand cutting was even more gruesome this take as Titus bent out of shot and then came up with a ravaged look, but there were still missed words and booms in shot. The long, developing shots used for this scene meant any problem negated a long sequence of action, and Howell said she needed so many pick-up shots for either of these takes that they would have to run the whole scene after dinner, a move Trevor Peacock sanctioned because he felt he had not yet given the performance he wanted.

On take 3 in the evening session Peacock was strong, but a boom got in shot early, so Howell stopped them. The next take caught a line fluff early on, so they stopped and restarted, Peacock maintaining total concentration between takes and Howell trying to protect him by advising her production manager on the floor not to let anyone, even make-up or wardrobe personnel, near him. At 7:55 take 5 began and proceeded with almost no problems except for a few words. Howell sat back contemplating, "There's some wonderful stuff in that. Let us go on," a decision she maintained even though Peacock was still concerned.

In rehearsing scene nine (III.2, supper at Titus's), the cast wanted to rehearse with a fly but were told, "We're saving the flies for takes." But they were not saved for long, since taping began at

9:26. The third take ended at 9:59, leaving scene five, also scheduled, unrehearsed and untaped.

Saturday's work began with scene ten (IV.1, writing in the sand), for which another colonnade had been set up. After several camera rehearsals, recording began at 12:30 and stopped as Lavinia struggled to turn the pages of the book with stumps and mouth. During take 2 Anna Calder-Marshall figured out how to maneuver the book, grabbing the cover and letting the pages fall rather than trying to turn them with her mouth. By 1:02 three takes were recorded, with the last a good performance in which textual slips were deemed acceptable.

After lunch they recorded nine variations of Lavinia and young Lucius running through the colonnade, a sequence that precedes scene ten in the final tape. Then, to gain some extra time, at 3:30 they began rehearsing scene twelve (arrows to the gods) during the scene shift, looking at camera angles amid much pounding and with lights going up and down in the background. Howell built detail to enhance the worried whispers of the scene, at one point asking young Lucius to look anxiously at Marcus to prompt Titus's "To it, boy." Recording did not begin until 5:12, but because the scene was not long and resets were quickly managed, they got three takes in before dinner, overcoming a boom and a camera in shot. Just before dinner Howell checked the Revenge, Murder, and Rape make-up, which was based on the rock group Kiss, for scene fifteen that evening, asking for a few adjustments so they would look starker.

All evening was spent on the scene in which Revenge visits Titus, which was taped in two parts. The poles and sides of meat had been set in during the dinner break, so Howell began work immediately, encouraging Tamora's sons to keep an edge of hysterical fear and pornographic excitement and asking Peacock to be less neat with his papers. Time pressure again drove the work, for Howell knew the technical demands of the scene's end would eat up time. By 8:30 she gave word to get ready to record the first part of the scene. Take 1 caught a camera cable in the high angle shots but ran to the end. The second take ran into instant shadowing and the cable in shot again, so was stopped and restarted. When it ended at

9:17, Howell glanced at the clock and remarked, "I don't care about mistakes; go on."

Her decision was wise, since the reset for the end of the scene proved complicated and time-consuming. The action was a ritual butchering and called for Chiron and Demetrius to be flown upside down, suspended from cables attached to body harnesses and also hooked up with pumps and tubes of red make-up under their costumes so their slit throats would appear to gush blood. For the actors' health, they delayed flying them until the last rehearsal so they would not be upside down any longer than necessary, and Malcolm Ranson carefully talked Titus through the cuts without the blood, practicing the off-camera knife swap between the cuts so the second cut would be done with a bloody knife. It proved trickier than expected to light Titus so near the hanging bodies, too, and adjustments ensued.

Ten o'clock passed during the preparations, so the scene was recorded in overtime, but they had foreseen this eventuality early and made the necessary arrangements with engineering. Taping finally finished on the one possible take at 10:40, the actors having been flown for over twenty minutes. A number of false starts held up taping, and a combination of the late hour, the scene's action, and the cumulative fatigue from taping gave Peacock a zombied aura that enhanced the scene's eeriness. As Titus approached the boys with the knife, Tamora's gagged sons increased their anxious noises, and as he cut, the pump turned on with a loud whirring later dubbed over. The actors playing Chiron and Demetrius afterward said not all the cries and whimpers were acting: hanging upside down, trussed up for killing, gagged, with plugs in their ears and noses to keep the blood from flowing in, they could scarcely breathe. As it was, word had it the next day, the blood make-up ran over one actor's contacts and ruined them, so they had to be replaced. Once recording stopped, the dangling actors were quickly lowered to the waiting Malcolm Ranson, who monitored them to insure their physical stability before they left the studio.

The atmosphere in the studio the last day of a long, intense taping stint is difficult to describe, but as the end nears, the staff and actors radiate their enjoyment of the taping process and the dramatic product. The tension does not entirely disappear, but it alters to a celebration of production, especially with the televised Shakespeares. Everyone reflects on previous shows or on bringing this one to fulfillment, and people smile for the first time in days. There is a full day's work to be done, but an exuberance greets the task, perhaps the more so with *Titus* since it was the last of the Shakespeare series, so an extra sense of accomplishment permeated the air.

In the lighting gallery Sam Barclay, the lighting director, reminisced about the eleven Shakespeare productions he had lit during the series, from *Measure* to *Titus*, and how much he had enjoyed working on the more obscure shows such as *Timon of Athens* and *Pericles* because he did not know those plays beforehand. In surveying the monitors, he also commented that the challenge of lighting a unit set such as *Titus*'s is to vary it, giving as many different moods and effects as possible (he also worked with the unit set in Howell's *Henry VI–Richard III* sequence). Early on in the series, he continued, only four lighting directors were assigned to the Shakespeares; it was a very exclusive assignment, though later, he added wistfully, the assignment was opened up. But the BBC did use many of its best people in the series, as the awards for lighting won by Barclay, John Summers, and Dennis Channon testify. Listening to these memories, another engineer commented that the Shakespeares he had enjoyed most were *King Lear* and *Othello* because of their special energy in the studio, and others agreed.

When not downstairs in the make-up rooms, the make-up designer and crew usually sat at the back of the lighting gallery to evaluate the effect of the make-up by watching the various monitors there. As the studio was abuzz with preparations for scene five (II.2, the hunting scene postponed earlier in the week), the make-up personnel talked of how wonderful the Shakespeares had been because productions of Shakespeare and Dickens offer the most challenges for make-up and are the most fun to work on. As they spoke, a rerun of *Bonanza* was on an auxiliary monitor in the gallery, one of the BBC's morning broadcasts, and the make-up crew laughed at how clean and antiseptic Hoss and the other characters looked and said how much they would like to work on a western and show the Americans a few things.

Then it was time to prepare Lavinia and Titus for rehearsal, so make-up designer Cecile Hay-Arthur and her assistant went downstairs to fit the stumps. Even Anna Calder-Marshall and Trevor Peacock were cheerful as they offered their hands for the binding process, which began with a powdering and a white cotton glove, over which one or two heavy rubber cones—the stumps complete with real bones from a butcher shop—were forced, held in place by two stretch bandages and four splints each so the wrist would not move. Within thirty minutes, Peacock said, the hand would have no feeling at all; the preceding night his arm had been numb to the elbow. He had an easier time in acting with the stump than did Calder-Marshall, he added, because he could compensate for the extra length by the way he held his other arm, but Calder-Marshall had no options even though the costumes were designed to drape and hide forearm length.

As this work proceeded, the pot on the burner in the corner simmered, the ever-ready gelatinous blood for the show, and in a basket on the floor were piled the two heads and a hand from III.1, the heads excellent, recognizable models of the actors, complete with somewhat pinched, agonized expressions and credibly heavy, as was the hand, which Hay-Arthur explained had chicken bones in it to help Lavinia pick it up with her mouth as scripted.

Meanwhile rehearsal and taping of scene five was completed, and scene sixteen (Lucius's return to Rome with Aaron) began efficiently. When the baby cried in rehearsal, Howell calmed him, talking to him and holding her script over his face to shade his eyes as she gave notes to actors and cameramen. Work on scene seventeen followed immediately. As with the play's first scene, Howell had divided the last long scene (V.3) into three parts and three separate television scenes, all scheduled for this last day in the studio. The banquet section was complicated by the fact that, as with the butchering scene the evening before, only one take was possible: the table would probably break apart when upended; moreover, there were no extra costumes if an actor got bloodstained. The word was "go for it." Consequently, preparations and rehearsal were meticulous. Ranson worked on all the stabbings so the knives would be at the proper angles and aimed at the right places and so the victims would fall convincingly (a picture in the BBC *Titus* script captures Saturninus collapsing very effectively under Lucius's blows). They mimed the eating and table overturning in the early rehearsals, though they did cut and serve meat pie in the last camera rehearsal so Peacock could practice serving the portions and carrying the platter one-handed.

Before the recording the studio floor was a flurry of technicians; then at 5:22 they started to tape. There was a false start because of the smoke (getting the right level of smoke was a continual problem because of the studio ventilation: if it was on, the smoke speedily dissipated; if off, everyone roasted and choked). The take restarted and proceeded flawlessly, a wonderful performance. They reviewed the tape to make sure everything was right and set up a cut-in of Titus and Lavinia watching the banquet. By 5:40 that part of the scene was finished.

At dinner that evening everyone was elated; Anna Calder-Marshall and Trevor Peacock came to the canteen for the first time, and Peacock ate his first full meal of the week; all he had to do in the evening recording session was play a corpse. The production staff bought champagne and shared it around, and praise was lavished on Howell, who was not present. Once back in the studio, work on the last scene was nonetheless disciplined; the first camera rehearsal of scene eighteen ended before 8:00. By 8:40 Howell told the studio to get ready to record, but instead she went up to the control room and fine-tuned one more camera rehearsal from there, commenting in passing that the point of the shot of Lucius on the throne with the Goths now on guard in the background is that these are the people he has befriended and who have come in to trample Rome, staging that gives testimony to the eloquence of her camera script. Lucius, she added, is a perfectly horrid character, a case of the worst man winning.

At 9:00 take 1 began, a false start with line fluffs almost immediately. It then ran to its end with a few snags evident. Howell gave notes and, sensing that Aaron wanted to go closer to Lucius at the end of their confrontation, passed word to Quarshie that he need only tell the cameraman what move he would make. Meanwhile costume designer Colin Lavers put a breastplate under Peacock's robe so his breathing would not show since dead Titus was in the foreground of many shots. Take 2 started at 9:24, a good one. Howell wanted one more to cover the speeches at the top of the scene; take 3 caught a huge swallow from "dead" Titus on a close-up, and Lucius announced Aaron's doom almost casually rather than with the fire and anger of the earlier takes. Howell recorded the sound of the group's shout on a wild sound track and got a cut-in of young Lucius to cover Titus's swallow. Then at 9:55 on the last evening, the taping of *Titus* was declared finished, the BBC Shakespeare series reached its end, and the staff, cast, and crew straightened up and headed for a postproduction party in the Shakespeare offices upstairs after an intense but gratifyingly productive week in the studio.

Conclusion

Now does my project gather to a head.
—The Tempest

Televising Shakespeare poses the fundamental issue of what an audience watches and responds to, Shakespeare or television. Now a cultural icon, Shakespeare has long since left the teeming crowd at the Globe and ascended the heights; his words, pedagogically encrusted, are ensconced as part of high culture, to be preserved, studied, and appreciated by the elite. That is the view toward most classic theatre, in fact; not everyone attends, but it is so valuable a cultural commodity that state subsidies and grants from businesses support it. (As a member of the King's Men, Shakespeare enjoyed state subsidy as well—that relationship is almost as old as drama—but his Globe audiences were not all lords and courtiers.) According to many viewers and critics, television, unlike Shakespeare, rarely even catches a glimpse of the heights, much less contemplates an ascent. Television, after all, is popular culture. Thus the distrust and outright antagonism between high culture and popular culture, which Herbert Gans has described at length in his work on that subject, are rehearsed again in attitudes toward the BBC Shakespeare series.

The elite and the masses, as they are characterized, have different tastes, different orientations, and the preference of one is often viewed askance by the other. The common feeling, Gans observes, is that popular culture debases whatever it takes from high culture;[1] this assumption noticeably manifests itself in some reviews and critiques of the Shakespeare series. Hamlet expresses a related view in discussing theatre and public response with the Players at Elsinore: "For the play, I remember, pleas'd not the million; 'twas caviary to the general"; laments about the popular reception of the Shakespeare series in essence echo his view.

The cause of the tension between the two cultures stems from their basic attitudes toward art. As Gans explains: "High culture is creator-oriented and its aesthetics and its principles of criticism are based on this orientation. . . . The popular arts are, on the whole, user-oriented, and exist to satisfy audience values and wishes."[2] In his own time, Shakespeare often bridged these demands, providing fine art that was crowd pleasing and crowd-pleasing art that was fine. The desire for such bridging continues to prompt productions of his works, whether for live audience or for camera. How to combine modern technology, the popular medium of television, and a set of 400-year-old classic plays written predominantly in verse, how to bridge popular culture and high culture, was the BBC's challenge with the Shakespeare series. It is part of the ongoing effort to find a Globe for the modern world.

The 1944 film of Henry V, now a classic, offered Laurence Olivier a great performance vehicle, challenged his artistry, and gave him technical capabilities the stage could not; it also let him reach a mass audience, the moviegoers rather than the theatre-goers, an audience vast as the vasty fields of France. He chose a popular medium and meant the film to be popular, a factor that influenced a number of his aesthetic decisions, especially regarding the way he cut the script and worked for a positive tone. Cedric Messina envisioned much the same sort of audience and sought the same appeal for the BBC Shakespeare series; by producing the entire canon for television, the BBC would insure that millions of viewers would have access to plays they otherwise might never see, millions could discover the power and beauty of Shakespeare's works. In fact, before the close of the Shakespeare series the press reported its potential audience as exceeding 150 million viewers worldwide. For classic drama in the age of rock music and professional sports (like the Globe next door to the bear-baiting pit), that is a very respectable number; Messina should be pleased.

Of course, the very scope of the BBC's endeavor meant the series could not be shaped as carefully as a single film could be, since it involved thirty-seven separate works rather than one, nor was the series meant to have a uniform shape. Though it perhaps began with an assumption of consistent and accepted production attitudes, artistic creativity and the nature of the material soon prompted the series to become an exploration of televising Shakespeare—how Shakespeare's words and dramatic situations could grace the medium and how the medium could enhance the effect of Shakespeare's action and characters.

For subject matter, Shakespeare gave television all any medium could ask for—political intrigues and reunions of long-separated family members, questions of life's ultimate meaning and witty repartee, the slaughter of innocents and the peal of wedding bells; duels, murders, ambushes, bandit attacks, chases, battles, rebellions; carnal, bloody, and unnatural acts, accidental judgments and casual slaughters; storms, shipwrecks, man-eating bears, ghosts and headless corpses, rapes and self-mutilations; twins and transvestites and bed-tricks; spirits and fairies and visions; kings and commoners; young love, confirmed lechery, fidelity, greed, reconciliation, betrayal, buffoonery, jealousy, humor, pride, ambition, manipulation, malice, and magnanimity; unswerving justice and unstrained mercy, the thrill of victory and the agony of defeat; things dying and things newborn. From soliloquies to armies at war, rhetorical flourishes to puns, Shakespeare provides an unequaled range of drama. For its part, television offered the plays technology to do much that the stage can do and much that it cannot, given cameras and microphones, the ability to record and select words and action and to use optical effects in presenting them. In the course of the series, much of television's technical potential was brought to bear on the productions: voice-overs, split-screen shots, sudden invisibility, slow motion, and other effects of editing—montage, fades, wipes, sound bridges. Not every play demanded the full arsenal, but technical effects proved useful for a host of productions.

The inevitable comparison of television with theatre crops up in directors' and actors' comments about the series as it has persistently cropped up throughout this commentary. Shakespeare's works were born and bred in the theatre; they bear its stamp and share its nature. In much of the Shakespeare series, television proved its compatibility with theatre. Producing the plays for television does not deny their theatrical power nor vie with it; rather it pays tribute to it. Film was still maturing when it reached out to encompass Shakespeare and classic novels, almost like a rite of passage; television has done much the same. The BBC has now televised the entire canon for the first time some fifty years after it first televised scenes from a Shakespeare play and after decades of producing contemporary and classic plays and adapting fiction to the small screen—and creating the standard for such productions in doing so. It offered television in the service of Shakespeare and thereby provided some beautiful and effective productions.

As the series itself demonstrates, a dual and collaborative awareness shaped the televised canon, an awareness of the theatrical nature of the material and an awareness of the television medium in which it was being performed. That some of the productions may seem limited by the medium, unexciting visually or as performance, is a concern of less import than the fact that so many of the productions create an engaging world for the action through intricate detail or insightful stylization and that so many deliver powerful performances and challenging interpretations. Because the productions have the extended life of videotape, much of their value still remains to be determined, but as Hippolyta might say, all the story of the Shakespeare series told over, and all the plays transfigur'd so together, "more witnesseth than fancy's images, / And grows to something of great constancy, / But, howsoever, strange and admirable."

Appendixes

Taping and Transmission Dates for
the BBC *Shakespeare Plays*

TAPING DATES

(Cedric Messina, producer)

Romeo and Juliet	31 January–5 February 1978
Richard II	12–17 April 1978
Measure for Measure	17–22 May 1978
As You Like It	30 May–16 June 1978
Julius Caesar	26–31 July 1978
Henry VIII	27 November 1978–7 January 1979
1 Henry IV	7–12 March 1979
2 Henry IV	11–16 April 1979
Twelfth Night	16–21 May 1979
Henry V	18–25 June 1979
The Tempest	23–28 July 1979
Hamlet	31 January–8 February 1980

(Jonathan Miller, producer)

Antony and Cleopatra	5–10 March 1980
The Winter's Tale	9–15 April 1980
The Merchant of Venice	15–21 May 1980
The Taming of the Shrew	18–24 June 1980
All's Well That Ends Well	23–29 July 1980
Timon of Athens	28 January–3 February 1981
Othello	9–17 March 1981
A Midsummer Night's Dream	19–25 May 1981
Troilus and Cressida	28 July–5 August 1981
1 Henry VI	13–19 October 1981
2 Henry VI	17–23 December 1981

(Shaun Sutton, producer)

3 Henry VI	10–17 February 1982
King Lear	26 March–2 April 1982
Richard III	31 March–6 April 1982
Macbeth	22–28 June 1982
Cymbeline	29 July–5 August 1982
The Merry Wives of Windsor	1–8 November 1982
Coriolanus	18–26 April 1983
Pericles	21–28 June 1983
The Two Gentlemen of Verona	25–31 July 1983
The Comedy of Errors	3–9 November 1983
King John	1–7 February 1984
Love's Labour's Lost	30 June–6 July 1984
Much Ado About Nothing	15–21 August 1984
Titus Andronicus	10–17 February 1985

TRANSMISSION DATES

	British	American
Romeo and Juliet	3 December 1978	14 March 1979
Richard II	10 December 1978	28 March 1979 (repeated 19 March 1980)
As You Like It	17 December 1978	28 February 1979
Julius Caesar	11 February 1979	14 February 1979
Measure for Measure	18 February 1979	11 April 1979
Henry VIII	25 February 1979 (repeated 22 June 1981)	25 April 1979
1 Henry IV	9 December 1979	26 March 1980
2 Henry IV	16 December 1979	9 April 1980
Henry V	23 December 1979 (repeated 23 April 1980)	23 April 1980
Twelfth Night	6 January 1980 (repeated 29 June 1981)	27 February 1980
The Tempest	27 February 1980	7 May 1980

Hamlet	25 May 1980	10 November 1980 (repeated 31 May 1982)
The Taming of the Shrew	23 October 1980	26 January 1981
The Merchant of Venice	17 December 1980	23 February 1981
All's Well That Ends Well	4 January 1981	18 May 1981
The Winter's Tale	8 February 1981	8 June 1981
Timon of Athens	16 April 1981	14 December 1981
Antony and Cleopatra	8 May 1981	20 April 1981
Othello	4 October 1981	12 October 1981
Troilus and Cressida	7 November 1981	17 May 1982
A Midsummer Night's Dream	13 December 1981	19 April 1982
King Lear	19 September 1982	18 October 1982
The Merry Wives of Windsor	28 December 1982	31 January 1983
1 Henry VI	2 January 1983	27 March 1983 and 3 April 1983
2 Henry VI	9 January 1983	10 April 1983 and 17 April 1983
3 Henry VI	16 January 1983	24 April 1983 and 1 May 1983
Richard III	23 January 1983	2 May 1983
Cymbeline	10 July 1983	20 December 1982
Macbeth	5 November 1983	17 October 1983
The Comedy of Errors	24 December 1983	20 February 1984
The Two Gentlemen of Verona	27 December 1983	23 April 1984
Coriolanus	21 April 1984	26 March 1984
King John	24 November 1984	11 January 1985
Pericles	8 December 1984	11 June 1984
Much Ado About Nothing	22 December 1984	30 October 1984
Love's Labour's Lost	5 January 1985	31 May 1985
Titus Andronicus	27 April 1985	19 April 1985

BBC Productions of Shakespeare before the Series

As You Like It (scenes)	5 February 1937
Henry V (scenes)	5 February 1937
Julius Caesar (scenes)	11 February 1937
Much Ado About Nothing (scenes)	11 February 1937
A Midsummer Night's Dream (scenes)	18 February 1937
Twelfth Night (scenes)	20 February 1937
The Merry Wives of Windsor (letter scene)	12 March 1937
Twelfth Night (one scene)	12 March 1937
Macbeth (scenes)	25 March 1937
Richard III (scenes)	9 April 1937
A Midsummer Night's Dream (scenes)	23 April 1937
Twelfth Night (scenes)	14 May 1937
Pyramus and Thisbe	14 July 1937 (repeated 23 July 1937)
Romeo and Juliet	16 August 1937 (repeated 18 August 1937)
Measure for Measure	25 October 1937
Cymbeline (outside broadcast)*	29 November 1937
Macbeth (scenes from the Old Vic production)	3 December 1937
Othello	14 December 1937 (repeated 18 December 1937)
Pyramus and Thisbe	28 January 1938
Julius Caesar	24 July 1938 (repeated 27 July 1938)
Twelfth Night (outside broadcast)	2 January 1939
The Tempest	5 February 1939 (repeated 8 February 1939)

Katherine and Petruchio
    (David Garrick's version
    of *Shrew*)
	12 April 1939
	    (repeated 22 April 1939)

As You Like It	14 July 1946
A Midsummer Night's Dream (outside broadcast)	24 July 1946

The Merchant of Venice	1 July 1947
A Midsummer Night's Dream	
Part 1	28 July 1947
Part 2	29 July 1947
Romeo and Juliet	5 October 1947
Hamlet	
Part 1	7 December 1947 (repeated 9 December 1947)
Part 2	14 December 1947 (repeated 16 December 1947)

King Lear	
Part 1	22 August 1948 (repeated 26 August 1948)
Part 2	29 August 1948 (repeated 2 September 1948)

The Merchant of Venice (trial scene)	24 January 1949
Macbeth	20 February 1949 (repeated 24 February 1949)

Twelfth Night (adaptation by Robert Atkins)	6 January 1950

Othello
    (French adaptation by Georges
    Neveux of last scene)
	8 March 1950

Othello	23 April 1950 (repeated 27 April 1950)

Richard II	29 October 1950
	    (repeated 2 and 7 November
	    1950)

A Midsummer Night's Dream
(children's program; adaptation
by Robert and Ian Atkins)
Part 1   26 November 1950
Part 2   3 December 1950

Julius Caesar   25 February 1951
                                     (repeated 1 March 1951)
A Midsummer Night's Dream   17 April 1951
(children's program; adaptation   (repeated 22 April 1951)
by Robert and Ian Atkins)
Henry V   22 April 1951
                                     (repeated 26 April 1951)
The Tempest   10 May 1951
(children's program)

King John   20 January 1952
                                     (repeated 24 January 1952)
The Taming of the Shrew   20 April 1952
(adaptation by Barbara Nixon)   (repeated 24 April 1952)
The Merry Wives of Windsor   16 November 1952
                                     (repeated 20 November 1952)

As You Like It   15 March 1953
                                     (repeated 19 March 1953)
Henry V   19 May 1953
Romeo and Juliet   22 May 1953
(adaptation by Dallas Bower)   (repeated in two parts, 23 and
                                     25 August 1955)

The Comedy of Errors   16 May 1954
(adaptation by Lionel Harris and   (repeated 20 May 1954)
Robert McNab)
Othello   20 June 1954
(excerpts)
Troilus and Cressida   19 September 1954
(adaptation by George Rylands)   (repeated 23 September 1954)

The Merchant of Venice   13 March 1955
                                     (repeated 17 March 1955)

Julius Caesar	5 September 1955
(scenes from the Michael	
Benthall production)	
The Merry Wives of Windsor	2 October 1955
(outside broadcast)	
Othello	15 December 1955
	(repeated 14 June 1956)

The Tempest	14 October 1956
Cymbeline	30 October 1956
(excerpt from the Old Vic	
production)	

The Merry Wives of Windsor	
(excerpts for Schools)**	15 January 1957
Twelfth Night	10 March 1957
(for Schools)	
Life of Henry V	29 December 1957
(Television World Theatre)	

Macbeth	31 January 1958
(for Schools)	
A Midsummer Night's Dream	9 November 1958
(adaptation by Eric Crozier)	

Life and Death of Sir John Falstaff	
(adaptation by Ronald Eyre;	
for Schools)	
Part 1	20 January 1959
Part 2	27 January 1959
Part 3	3 February 1959
Part 4	10 February 1959
Part 5	17 February 1959
Part 6	24 February 1959
Part 7	3 March 1959
Julius Caesar	5 May 1959
(adaptation by Stuart Burge)	

An Age of Kings

Part 1: The Hollow Crown	*Richard II*	28 April 1960 (repeated 7 January 1962)
Part 2: The Deposing of the King	*Richard II*	12 May 1960 (repeated 14 January 1962)
Part 3: Rebellion from the North	*1 Henry IV*	26 May 1960 (repeated 21 January 1962)
Part 4: The Road to Shrewsbury	*1 Henry IV*	9 June 1960 (repeated 28 January 1962)
Part 5: The New Conspiracy	*2 Henry IV*	23 June 1960 (repeated 4 February 1962)
Part 6: Uneasy Lies the Head	*2 Henry IV*	7 July 1960 (repeated 11 February 1962)
Part 7: Signs of War	*Henry V*	21 July 1960 (repeated 18 February 1962)
Part 8: The Band of Brothers	*Henry V*	4 August 1960 (repeated 25 February 1962)
Part 9: The Red Rose and the White	*1 Henry VI*	25 August 1960 (repeated 4 March 1962)
Part 10: The Fall of a Protector	*2 Henry VI*	8 September 1960 (repeated 11 March 1962)
Part 11: The Rabble from Kent	*2 Henry VI*	22 September 1960 (repeated 18 March 1962)
Part 12: The Morning's War	*3 Henry VI*	6 October 1960 (repeated 25 March 1962)
Part 13: The Sun in Splendour	*3 Henry VI*	20 October 1960 (repeated 1 April 1962)

| Part 14: The Dangerous Brother | *Richard III* | 3 November 1960 (repeated 8 April 1962) |
| Part 15: The Boar Hunt | *Richard III* | 17 November 1960 (repeated 15 April 1962) |

Julius Caesar
(for Schools)

Part 1		8 November 1960 (each part repeated a day later)
Part 2		15 November 1960
Part 3		22 November 1960
Part 4		29 November 1960

| *The Winter's Tale* | | 20 April 1962 |
| *Henry V* (for Schools) | | 26 September 1962 |

As You Like It
(from Michael Elliott's stage version)   22 March 1963 (repeated 5 August 1964)

The Spread of the Eagle

Part 1: The Hero	*Coriolanus*	3 May 1963
Part 2: The Voices	*Coriolanus*	10 May 1963
Part 3: The Outcast	*Coriolanus*	17 May 1963
Part 4: The Colossus	*Julius Caesar*	24 May 1963
Part 5: The Fifteenth	*Julius Caesar*	31 May 1963
Part 6: The Revenge	*Julius Caesar*	7 June 1963
Part 7: The Serpent	*Antony and Cleopatra*	14 June 1963
Part 8: The Alliance	*Antony and Cleopatra*	21 June 1963
Part 9: The Monument	*Antony and Cleopatra*	28 June 1963

| *The Comedy of Errors* (outside broadcast; Aldwych Theatre) | | 1 January 1964 |
| *Hamlet at Elsinore* (outside broadcast; recorded at Kronberg Castle, Elsinore, Denmark) | | 19 April 1964 (repeated 24 January 1965) |

Julius Caesar (for Schools)	23 April 1964	
Macbeth (for Schools)	1 October 1964	

Macbeth (for Schools)	5 April 1965	
The Wars of the Roses (outside broadcast from Royal Shakespeare Theatre, Stratford-upon-Avon)		
Part 1: *Henry VI*	8 April 1965	
Part 2: *Edward IV*	15 April 1965	
Part 3: *Richard III*	22 April 1965	

Repeated in 11 Parts:		
Part 1: The Inheritance	*Henry VI*	6 January 1966
Part 2: Margaret of Anjou	*Henry VI*	13 January 1966
Part 3: The Lord Protector	*Henry VI*	20 January 1966
Part 4: The Council Board	*Edward IV*	27 January 1966
Part 5: The Fearful King	*Edward IV*	3 February 1966
Part 6: The Kingmaker	*Edward IV*	10 February 1966
Part 7: Edward of York	*Edward IV*	17 February 1966
Part 8: The Prophetess	*Richard III*	24 February 1966
Part 9: Richard of Gloucester	*Richard III*	3 March 1966
Part 10: Richard the King	*Richard III*	10 March 1966
Part 11: Henry Tudor	*Richard III*	17 March 1966
Coriolanus (outside broadcast; Festival Theatre, Chichester)	23 May 1965	
Love's Labour's Lost (outside broadcast; Theatre Royal, Bristol)	6 June 1965	

Julius Caesar (outside broadcast; Ashcroft Theatre)	23 April 1966	

Troilus and Cressida   25 September 1966
  (outside broadcast; National
  Youth Theatre at Belgrade
  Theatre, Coventry)
Macbeth
  (adaptation by Michael Simpson;
  for Schools)
  Part 1   11 October 1966
                         (repeated 12 October 1966 and
                         11 and 12 November 1969)
  Part 2   18 October 1966
                         (repeated 19 October 1966 and
                         18 and 26 November 1969)
  Part 3   25 October 1966
                         (repeated 26 October 1966 and
                         25 November and 3 December
                         1969)
  Part 4   8 November 1966
                         (repeated 9 November 1966 and
                         2 and 10 December 1969)

Much Ado About Nothing   5 February 1967
  (Franco Zeffirelli's National
  Theatre production)
Romeo and Juliet   3 December 1967
  (Play of the Month)

The Tempest   12 May 1968
  (Play of the Month)
All's Well That Ends Well   3 June 1968
  (adaptation by John Barton;   (repeated 19 February 1970)
  RSC)

Julius Caesar   13 April 1969
  (Play of the Month)   (repeated 5 July 1970)

Richard II   30 July 1970
  (Prospect Theatre)   (repeated 20 January 1971)

Macbeth (Play of the Month)	20 September 1970 (repeated 20 June 1971)
A Midsummer Night's Dream (outside broadcast; Play of the Month)	26 September 1971 (repeated 7 August 1973)
Hamlet (based on Robert Chetwyn's production; Prospect Theatre; purchased program)	23 September 1972
Twelfth Night (outside broadcast)	14 May 1974
Much Ado About Nothing (New York Shakespeare Festival production)	14 September 1974
King Lear (Play of the Month)	23 March 1975 (repeated 9 March 1977)
Love's Labour's Lost (Play of the Month)	14 December 1975

*"Outside broadcast" is a BBC term meaning filmed on location.
** "For Schools" denotes excerpts broadcast as educational programming during the school day.

Notes

CHAPTER 1

1. Messina, Preface, p. 8.
2. Fenwick, "Transatlantic Row," p. 25.
3. Esslin, "Drama and the Media in Britain," pp. 105–6.
4. Day-Lewis, "Giving Shakespeare the Works."
5. *BBC-TV Facts and Figures 1984.*
6. Messina, Preface, pp. 7–8.
7. Information courtesy of BBC Television Script Unit. See appendix 2 for a complete list of BBC Shakespeare television transmissions prior to the series.
8. Figures in pounds from Irwin, "A Date with Bard's Birds," p. 10. Figures in dollars from Gelatt, "The Beeb's Bard," p. 48. About all the expense figures, Fraser Lowden—who as production associate for the series kept track of budgets—said that "considering the fluctuation in exchange rates and everpresent inflation, all figures are a nonsense," but that these are "accurate enough." Letter to author, 28 July 1986.
9. Donovan, "The Bard's in the Black."
10. Roberts, interview with author, 11 June 1985.
11. Noakes and Lowden, interview with author, 23 June 1980.
12. Venza, interview with author, 12 June 1985.
13. Walker, interview with author, 18 June 1985.
14. Krajci, interview with author, 14 June 1985.
15. Perry, "Perryscope."
16. Shallcross, interview with author, 2 July 1985.
17. Fenwick, "The Production," in *BBC-TV Shakespeare: Romeo and Juliet,* p. 21.
18. Messina, Preface, p. 9.
19. Ibid., p. 8.
20. For instance, see his interview comments in Andrews, "Cedric Messina."
21. Coburn, "Shakespeare Comes to the Colonies," p. B2.
22. "BBC Scrap £¼m[illion] *Much Ado.*"
23. Griffin-Beale, "All's Well," p. 10.
24. Irwin, "A Date with Bard's Birds," p. 11.
25. Banham, "BBC Television's Dull Shakespeares," pp. 32, 34–35.
26. Andrews, "Cedric Messina," p. 137.
27. Messina, Preface, p. 9.

28. Fenwick, "Transatlantic Row," p. 27.

29. Fenwick, "The Production," in *BBC-TV Shakespeare: 1 Henry IV and 2 Henry IV*, passim.

30. Homfray, interview with author, 11 October 1983.

31. Fenwick, "The Production," in *BBC-TV Shakespeare: Hamlet*, p. 18.

32. Ibid., p. 17.

33. "Wilders Interview at MLA," p. 9.

34. See also Fenwick, "The Production," in *BBC-TV Shakespeare: Antony and Cleopatra*, p. 17.

35. Hallinan, "Jonathan Miller," p. 134.

36. Fenwick, "The Production," in *BBC-TV Shakespeare: Julius Caesar*, p. 22.

37. Fenwick, "The Production," in *BBC-TV Shakespeare: The Merchant of Venice*, p. 17.

38. Fenwick, "The Production," in *BBC-TV Shakespeare: The Winter's Tale*, p. 17.

39. Day-Lewis, "History in an Adventure Playground."

40. Fenwick, "The Production," in *BBC-TV Shakespeare: King Lear*, p. 19.

41. Fenwick, "To Be or Not to Be a Producer."

42. Ibid.

43. Smith, "Shakespeare: 'Being Done as Bard Intended,' " p. 1.

44. Maher, "Shaun Sutton," p. 190.

45. Ibid., p. 192.

46. Ibid., p. 190.

47. "Exit Bard, Mayhem Stage Right." See also Peter Waymark, "Russia and the War . . . More Murder in *Titus*," *Times* (London), 27 April 1985, p. 19, for another account of the same statement.

48. See appendix 1 for a complete list of taping and transmission dates for the series.

49. "Four New Girls for the Bard."

50. Hallinan, interview with author, 19 June 1986.

51. "Miss Johnson Stays Mum."

52. Fiddick, "BBC Shakespeare Greets U.S."

53. Venza, interview with author, 12 June 1985.

54. Thaler, letter to WNET/Thirteen, New York, 13 February 1981.

55. Holocaust and Executive Committee of the Committee to Bring Nazi War Criminals to Justice in the United States, telegram to WNET/Thirteen, New York, 16 February 1981.

56. See Schoenbach, WNET/Thirteen, New York, memorandum dated 11 February 1981, which quotes full Anti-Defamation League statement. Part of this statement also appears in Unger, "On TV."

57. Schappes, letter to the editor.

58. Weil and Kotlowitz, WNET memorandum about *The Merchant of Venice*, WNET/Thirteen, New York, 12 February 1981.

59. See Unger, "On TV," and Carmody, "Wait There's More."

60. The countries listed in the 1983 BBC Television Publicity press materials for the sixth season are Australia, Austria, Bahrein, Belgium, Canada, Chile, China, Colombia, Dubai, France, Greece, Hong Kong, Hungary, India, Iraq, Ireland, Italy, Japan, Jordan, Kenya, Korea, Lebanon, Panama, Peru, the Philippines, Poland, Portugal, Qatar, Rumania, Saudi Arabia, Singapore, Taiwan, Thailand, Trinidad and Tobago, Turkey, Venezuela, and West Germany. In 1987 BBC Marketing lists sixteen more countries as having purchased the series: the Bahamas, Barbados, Bhutan, Bulgaria, Czechoslovakia, Egypt, Holland, Honduras, Jamaica, Malaysia, Mexico, New Zealand, Puerto Rico, Spain, Sri Lanka, and Yugoslavia, although Bahrein, China, Hong Kong, Panama, and Venezuela are no longer on the list.

61. Moshinsky, interview with author, 8 July 1986.

62. Poole, letter to author, 6 October 1985. All quoted material comes from this letter and telephone interview with author, 2 July 1986.

63. Occasionally a reviewer would use a *Perspective* as a prologue to the review of a production, citing a salient point as focus. A number of reviewers complained when the *Perspective* and the production were out of step, and at least once a reviewer used the *Perspective* as a stick to beat the production with (*Times* (London), 8 February 1981, using Stephen Spender's remarks about *The Winter's Tale*). The technique of this single-camera operation also garnered some negative criticism. Julian Barnes of the *London Observer* asked, "Is there any presenter of this theoretically useful intro-slot who hasn't ended up, however careful his or her script, looking either a wally or a patsy?" and catalogued bad memories, including poet P. J. Kavanaugh trying to talk about *Pericles* "against a Force Nine gale off the Cornish coast." "Poet in a Force Nine Gale."

64. Andrews, interview with author, 20 June 1986.

65. A task force was established to recommend postsecondary uses of the series. From this group evolved the franchise telecourse devised by the University of California at San Diego and the Coast Community College district, which produced composite adult study guides and instructor materials for the first two seasons, until their funding stopped. The Bay Area Community College Television Consortium picked up the study guide program and continued it without funding for the remaining seasons, producing twenty-five higher-education study guides on individual plays, published by Kendall/Hunt.

66. Hallinan, interview with author, 19 June 1986. Subsequent quotations are from this interview.

67. From Tel-Ed educational materials, viewer's guide for first *Shakespeare Hour* season.

68. During the first season of *The Shakespeare Hour*, the theme of love was illustrated by *A Midsummer Night's Dream, Twelfth Night, All's Well That Ends Well, Measure for Measure,* and *King Lear,* with minidocumentaries on such topics as the role of the fool in drama and society. An early sketch of the two subsequent seasons included *Richard II* (or *Richard III*), *1 Henry IV, The Taming of the Shrew, Macbeth,* and *Julius Caesar* on the theme of power, and *The Merchant of Venice, Hamlet, The Winter's Tale, The Tempest,* and *Othello* on the theme of revenge.

69. Andrews, interview with author, 20 June 1986.

70. Hallinan, interview with author, 19 June 1986.

71. Smith, "Good Night, Sweet Series," p. 38.

72. Rich, "Peaks and Valleys," pp. 1, 5.

73. "Today" and Phillips, "Love's Labour."

74. James, "The Fantastic Voyage."

75. Last, " 'Shakespeare' Creates Boxed-In Feeling."

76. Nicholson, "A Precious Stone."

77. Reynolds, "*The Tempest*: BBC 2."

78. Ibid.

79. Dunkley, review of *Romeo and Juliet.*

80. Day-Lewis, "History in an Adventure Playground."

81. Venza, interview with author, 12 June 1985.

82. Maslin, "TV: *Caesar.*"

83. Day-Lewis, "Years of the Bard."

84. Rissik, "BBC Shakespeare," p. 28.

85. Phillips, "Love's Labour."

86. Shallcross, interview with author, 2 July 1985.

CHAPTER 2

1. Fenwick, "Transatlantic Row," p. 27.

2. Venza, interview with author, 12 June 1985.

3. Ibid.

4. Ibid.

5. Downey, interview with author, 13 June 1985. Additional material on this subject also from Downey, telephone interview with author, 11 November 1984.

6. Downey, interview with author, 13 June 1985.

7. Hogg, interview with author, 12 October 1983.

8. Venza, interview with author, 12 June 1985.

9. Drew, "The Oscars' Best."

10. Brown, "A Good Pedigree."
11. Reynolds, "*The Tempest*: BBC 2."
12. Fiske and Hartley, *Reading Television*, pp. 123–24.
13. Slim, review of *King John*.
14. "From Rags to Riches" and Davies, "Preposterous Plots."
15. Moshinsky, interview with author, 8 July 1986.
16. James, "Dance of Gold."
17. Clark, "A Modern Shakespeare Controversy."
18. McNally, review of *A Midsummer Night's Dream*.
19. Wells, "The History of the Whole Contention."
20. Irwin, "A Date with Bard's Birds," p. 10.
21. Shulman, "Beauty and the Bard."
22. "Four New Girls for the Bard."

CHAPTER 3

1. Barton, *Playing Shakespeare*, p. 185.
2. McLuhan, *Understanding Media*, p. 312.
3. Fiske and Hartley, *Reading Television*, p. 124.
4. Ibid., p. 117.
5. J. Goody and I. Watt, "The Consequences of Literacy," in *Language and Social Context*, ed. P. P. Giglioli (Harmondsworth, Middlesex, England: Penguin, 1972), pp. 311–57, quoted in Fiske and Hartley, *Reading Television*, p. 122.
6. See Shallcross, "The Text," in *BBC-TV Shakespeare: Julius Caesar*, p. 30, and *Richard II*, p. 29.
7. *BBC-TV Shakespeare: The Comedy of Errors*, p. 51, marginal note.
8. See the following for a comparison of the number of scenes in the standard text and the number of scenes in the BBC television series (prologues/choruses included) for each play (listed in order of taping):

	Text	BBC
Romeo and Juliet	25	42
Richard II	19	23
Measure for Measure	17	28
As You Like It	22	28
Julius Caesar	18	22
Henry VIII	18	38
1 Henry IV	19	21
2 Henry IV	19	22
Twelfth Night	18	27
Henry V	29	30

The Tempest	10	11
Hamlet	20	20*
Antony and Cleopatra	42	31
The Winter's Tale	15	15*
The Merchant of Venice	20	20
The Taming of the Shrew	2/12	0/11**
All's Well That Ends Well	23	28
Timon of Athens	17	11
Othello	15	12
A Midsummer Night's Dream	9	19
Troilus and Cressida	25	24
1 Henry VI	27	31
2 Henry VI	24	30
3 Henry VI	18	35
Richard III	25	35
King Lear	26	20
Macbeth	27	29
Cymbeline	27	39
The Merry Wives of Windsor	23	23***
Coriolanus	29	39
Pericles	27	32
The Two Gentlemen of Verona	20	23
The Comedy of Errors	11	11
King John	16	16
Love's Labour's Lost	9	18†
Much Ado About Nothing	17	18#
Titus Andronicus	14	18†

* 2 scenes run together; 1 scene divided
** induction listed first
*** order juggled
† possibly more; script ambiguous
# 1 scene divided by tape break, as if passage of time

9. André Bazir, *What Is Cinema?*, vol. 1., trans. Hugh Gray (Berkeley: University of California Press, 1967), p. 24, quoted in Cook, "Two Lears," p. 180.

10. Fenwick, "The Production," in *BBC-TV Shakespeare: Measure for Measure*, p. 25.

11. Fenwick, "The Production," in *BBC-TV Shakespeare: The Tempest*, p. 19.

12. R. Alan Kimbrough argues that "the obviously fake ... becomes only a distraction when it is subjected to the clarity of the camera." Styliza-

tion can work, but "when the fake pretends to be real the danger is far greater." "Olivier's *Lear*," p. 117.

13. Wilders, "Adjusting the Set."

14. Fenwick, "The Production," in *BBC-TV Shakespeare: Romeo and Juliet*, pp. 20–21.

15. Fenwick, "The Production," in *BBC-TV Shakespeare: Richard II*, p. 19.

16. Fenwick, "The Production," in *BBC-TV Shakespeare: Julius Caesar*, p. 20.

17. Ibid.

18. Dommett, "*Macbeth* at the Other Place."

19. Kretzmer, "The Mail TV Critic."

20. Fenwick, "The Production," in *BBC-TV Shakespeare: Hamlet*, p. 18.

21. Hallinan, "Jonathan Miller," p. 134.

22. Ibid., pp. 134, 136.

23. Ibid., p. 137.

24. Ibid.

25. "Interview with Jonathan Miller."

CHAPTER 4

1. Miller, interview with author, 11 August 1981.

2. Ibid.

3. Jonathan Miller, author's notes from his informal talk with acting company of Alabama Shakespeare Festival, Anniston, Alabama, 29 July 1984.

4. Miller, interview with author, 11 August 1981.

5. Fenwick, "To Be or Not to Be a Producer."

6. Miller, "The Afterlife of Art."

7. Hallinan, "Jonathan Miller," pp. 136–37.

8. Fenwick, "To Be or Not to Be a Producer."

9. Miller, interview with Mary Maher, 20 December 1983.

10. Fenwick, "The Production," in *BBC-TV Shakespeare: The Taming of the Shrew*, pp. 20–21.

11. See Fenwick, "The Production," in *BBC-TV Shakespeare: Othello*, p. 26.

12. Ibid.

13. Miller, interview with Mary Maher, 20 December 1983.

14. Fenwick, "The Production," in *BBC-TV Shakespeare: Othello*, p. 19.

15. *"King Lear"* (program note).

16. Miller, interview with Mary Maher, 20 December 1983.

17. Fenwick, "The Production," in *BBC-TV Shakespeare: King Lear*, p. 29.

18. Ibid., p. 25.

19. Ibid., p. 27.

20. Davies, "Spying on Greatness."

21. Fenwick, "The Production," in *BBC-TV Shakespeare: King Lear*, p. 21

22. Ibid., pp. 27–28.

23. Cowie, "Olivier, at 75, Returns to *Lear*," p. H1.

24. Kroll and Dallas, "Return of the Prodigal King."

25. Cook, "Two Lears," p. 186.

26. Fenwick, "The Production," in *BBC-TV Shakespeare: Troilus and Cressida*, p. 28.

27. Miller, *Subsequent Performances*, p. 121 (caption).

28. Ibid., pp. 101, 109.

29. Hughes, "How the Fat Knight Got a Fresh Face," p. 41.

30. Miller, *Subsequent Performances*, p. 65.

CHAPTER 5

1. Moshinsky, interview with author, 8 July 1986.

2. Moshinsky, "A Medium Fit."

3. Moshinsky, interview with author, 8 July 1986.

4. Fenwick, "The Production," in *BBC-TV Shakespeare: All's Well That Ends Well*, p. 26.

5. Ibid., p. 27.

6. Ibid., p. 25.

7. Ibid., pp. 27–28.

8. Moskinsky, interview with author, 8 July 1986.

9. Ibid.

10. Janson, *History of Art*, p. 448.

11. Moshinsky, "A Medium Fit."

12. Moshinsky, interview with author, 8 July 1986.

CHAPTER 6

1. Fenwick, "The Production," in *BBC-TV Shakespeare: The Winter's Tale*, p. 18.

2. Howell, interview with author, 11 July 1985.

3. Billington, "Shaping a Gory Classic."

4. "Notes on Production."

5. Howell, interview with author, 11 July 1985.

6. Fenwick, "The Production," in *BBC-TV Shakespeare: The Winter's Tale*, p. 27.

7. Howell, interview with author, 11 July 1985.

8. Fenwick, "The Production," in *BBC-TV Shakespeare: Richard III*, p. 27.

9. Howell, interview with author, 11 July 1985.

10. "Notes on Production."

11. Ibid.

12. Howell, interview with author, 17 February 1985.

13. Fenwick, "The Production," in *BBC-TV Shakespeare: Richard III*, p. 28.

14. Howell, interview with author, 11 July 1985.

15. Fenwick, "The Production," in *BBC-TV Shakespeare: 3 Henry VI*, p. 23.

16. Ibid., p. 24.

17. Howell, interview with author, 11 July 1985.

CHAPTER 7

1. Fenwick, "The Production," in *BBC-TV Shakespeare: Henry VIII*, p. 22.

2. Ibid.

3. Ibid., p. 19.

4. Ibid., p. 27.

5. Fenwick, "The Production," in *BBC-TV Shakespeare: As You Like It*, p. 20.

6. Ibid., pp. 21–23.

7. Ibid., p. 22.

8. Fenwick, "The Production," in *BBC-TV Shakespeare: The Merry Wives of Windsor*, pp. 18–20.

9. Ibid., pp. 25–26.

10. Ibid., p. 28.

11. Fenwick, "The Production," in *BBC-TV Shakespeare: Pericles*, p. 21.

12. Ibid., p. 17.

13. Ibid., p. 27.

14. Fenwick, "The Production," in *BBC-TV Shakespeare: Measure for Measure*, p. 19.

15. Ibid., p. 25.

16. Ibid., p. 24.

17. Ibid., p. 25.

18. Fenwick, "The Production," in *BBC-TV Shakespeare: Richard II*, p. 20.

19. Fenwick, "The Production," in *BBC-TV Shakespeare: Henry V*, p. 20.

20. Fenwick, "The Production," in *BBC-TV Shakespeare: 1 Henry IV*, p. 20.

21. Ibid., p. 21.

22. Fenwick, "The Production," in *BBC-TV Shakespeare: King John*, pp. 21–22.

23. Fenwick, "The Production," in *BBC-TV Shakespeare: Much Ado About Nothing*, p. 20.

24. Fenwick, "The Production," in *BBC-TV Shakespeare: The Merchant of Venice*, p. 20.

25. Ibid., p. 18.

26. Ibid., p. 19.

27. Fenwick, "The Production," in *BBC-TV Shakespeare: Macbeth*, p. 21.

28. Fenwick, "The Production," in *BBC-TV Shakespeare: Hamlet*, p. 28.

29. Ibid., p. 18.

30. Fenwick, "The Production," in *BBC-TV Shakespeare: Othello*, p. 20.

31. Fenwick, "The Production," in *BBC-TV Shakespeare: Two Gentlemen of Verona*, p. 26.

32. Ibid., p. 26.

33. Hordern, interview, 1982.

34. Fenwick, "The Production," in *BBC-TV Shakespeare: Richard II*, p. 25.

35. Nelligan, interview, 1979.

36. Fenwick, "The Production," in *BBC-TV Shakespeare: Richard II*, p. 25.

37. Rossiter, interview, 1984.

38. Hordern, interview, 1982.

39. Lindsay, interview, 1984.

40. Fenwick, "The Production," in *BBC-TV Shakespeare: Henry VIII*, p. 25.

41. Fenwick, "The Production," in *BBC-TV Shakespeare: Coriolanus*, p. 23.

42. Moshinsky, "A Medium Fit," p. 10.

CHAPTER 8

1. Miller, interview with author, 11 August 1981.
2. Miller, "The Afterlife of Art."

CHAPTER 9

1. Hale and "W.H.B.," reviews of *The Comedy of Errors*.
2. Cellan-Jones, interview with Henry Fenwick, 27 October 1983.
3. Homfray, interview with author, 11 October 1983.
4. Masefield, "William Shakespeare."

CONCLUSION

1. Gans, *Popular Culture*, p. 19.
2. Ibid., p. 62.

Bibliography

PRIMARY MATERIALS

The BBC published individual scripts of the *Shakespeare Plays* series between 1978 and 1986. Scripts of plays in the first season (*Romeo and Juliet, Richard II, Measure for Measure, As You Like It, Julius Caesar,* and *Henry VIII*) were also published in the United States by Mayflower Books, New York. Each script includes an essay on the play by series literary advisor John Wilders; an essay on the production by Henry Fenwick based on interviews with director, actors, and designers; annotations of camera scenes and of textual cuts and changes; and a glossary. Specific dates of publication for the scripts are:

1978   *Romeo and Juliet, Richard II, As You Like It*
1979   *Measure for Measure, Julius Caesar, Henry VIII, Twelfth Night, 1 Henry IV, 2 Henry IV, Henry V*
1980   *The Tempest, Hamlet, Taming of the Shrew, The Merchant of Venice*
1981   *Antony and Cleopatra, The Winter's Tale, All's Well That Ends Well, Timon of Athens, Othello, A Midsummer Night's Dream, Troilus and Cressida*
1983   *1 Henry VI, 2 Henry VI, 3 Henry VI, Richard III, King Lear, Macbeth, Cymbeline, The Merry Wives of Windsor*
1984   *Coriolanus, Pericles, The Two Gentlemen of Verona, The Comedy of Errors*
1986   *King John, Love's Labour's Lost, Much Ado About Nothing, Titus Andronicus*

Other publications stemming from the BBC Shakespeare series include Roger Sales, ed., *Shakespeare in Perspective,* 2 vols. (London: Ariel Books/BBC, 1982, 1985). Both volumes are transcripts of the BBC educational programming for television (focused on the play) and radio (focused on performance) in conjunction with the series. See also Edward Quinn, ed., *The Shakespeare Hour: A Companion to the PBS-TV Series* (New York: Signet, 1985) for a series of interpretive essays, with study questions and bibliography, on productions chosen for the first season of PBS's *Shakespeare Hour* on the theme of love: *A Midsummer Night's Dream, Twelfth Night, All's Well That Ends Well, Measure for Measure,* and *King Lear.*

REVIEWS

In Britain the BBC Shakespeare series productions were regularly reviewed in the London *Evening News, Evening Standard, Express, Financial Times, Mail, Mirror, Morning Star, Observer, Telegraph,* and *Times*
as well as in the *Manchester Guardian* on the day of or a few days following each broadcast.

In the United States the BBC Shakespeare series productions were regu-
larly reviewed in the *Christian Science Monitor, Los Angeles Times, New
York Daily News, New York Times, Shakespeare on Film Newsletter,
Shakespeare Quarterly, Variety,* and *Women's Wear Daily* and by the Na-
tional Catholic News Service. Some reviews can also be found in other
newspapers, including the *Boston Globe, Cleveland Plain Dealer, Dallas
Morning News, Detroit News, Los Angeles Herald Examiner, Milwaukee
Journal, Minneapolis Tribune, New Orleans States-Item, New York Post,
Philadelphia Inquirer, San Antonio Express, San Francisco Chronicle, Se-
attle Times, Times-Picayune, USA Today,* and *Village Voice,* and coverage
also appeared in *Newsweek, Time,* and *TV Guide* and occasionally in
Playboy and *Vogue.*

WORKS CITED

Andrews, John. "Cedric Messina Discusses the Shakespeare Plays."
    Shakespeare Quarterly 30 (1979): 134–37.
————. Interview with author, 20 June 1986.
Banham, Martin. "BBC Television's Dull Shakespeares." *Critical Quar-
    terly* 22 (1980): 31–40.
Barnes, Julian. "Poet in a Force Nine Gale." *London Observer,* 16 De-
    cember 1984, p. 20.
Barton, John. *Playing Shakespeare.* London: Methuen, 1984.
"BBC Scrap £¼m[illion] Much Ado." *London Daily Telegraph,* 29 March
    1979, p. 15.
BBC-TV Facts and Figures 1984. London: BBC Information Services,
    1984.
Billington, Michael. "Shaping a Gory Classic for TV." Review of *Titus
    Andronicus. New York Times,* 14 April 1985, p. H29.
Brown, Ben. "A Good Pedigree Can't Save Poor Play." Review of *Timon of
    Athens. Detroit News,* 14 December 1981, p. B1.
Carmody, John. "Wait There's More." *Washington Post,* 13 February
    1981, p. C11.
Cellan-Jones, James. Interview with Henry Fenwick, 27 October 1983.

Clark, Kenneth R. "A Modern Shakespeare Controversy." *Boston Globe*, 19 April 1982, p. 37.

Coburn, Randy Sue. "Shakespeare Comes to the Colonies." *Washington Star*, 25 January 1979, pp. B1–B2.

Cook, Hardy M. "Two Lears for Television." *Literature/Film Quarterly* 14, no. 4 (1986): 179–86.

Cowie, Peter. "Olivier, at 75, Returns to *Lear*." *New York Times*, 1 May 1983, pp. H1, H25.

Davies, Russell. "Preposterous Plots on the Channel Islands." Review of 2 *Henry VI*. *Times* (London), 16 January 1983, p. 52.

———. "Spying on Greatness." Review of *King Lear*. *Times* (London), 26 September 1982, p. 31.

Day-Lewis, Sean. "Giving Shakespeare the Works." *London Daily Telegraph*, 11 December 1978, p. 10.

———. "History in an Adventure Playground." Review of *Richard III*. *London Daily Telegraph*, 24 January 1983, p. 11.

———. "Years of the Bard." *London Daily Telegraph*, 5 March 1979, p. 11.

Dommett, Sue. "*Macbeth* at The Other Place 1976: A Commentary." Master's thesis, Shakespeare Institute, University of Birmingham, 1977. In the collection at the Shakespeare Centre Library, Stratford-upon-Avon, England.

Donovan, Paul. "The Bard's in the Black." *London Daily Mail*, 18 September 1982, p. 17.

Downey, Roger. Interview with author, 13 June 1985.

———. Telephone interview with author, 11 November 1984.

Drew, Mike. "The Oscars' Best, Worst and Itchiest." Review of *Measure for Measure*. *Milwaukee Journal*, 11 April 1979, Accent, p. 7.

Dunkley, Chris. Review of *Romeo and Juliet*. *London Financial Times*, 6 December 1978, p. 19.

Esslin, Martin. "Drama and the Media in Britain." *Modern Drama* 28, no. 1 (1985): 99–109.

"Exit Bard, Mayhem Stage Right." *Liverpool Daily Post*, 27 April 1985, p. 13.

Fenwick, Henry. "The Production." Essays in *The BBC-TV Shakespeare*, scripts of the BBC Shakespeare Plays. London: BBC, 1978–86.

———. "To Be or Not to Be a Producer." *Radio Times*, 18–24 October 1980, pp. 90ff.

———. "Transatlantic Row Breaks over the BBC's Most Ambitious Drama Series." *London Telegraph Sunday Magazine*, 24 September 1978, pp. 22–31.

Fiddick, Peter. "The Avon Catalogue." *Manchester Guardian*, 1 December 1978, p. 8.

————. "BBC Shakespeare Greets U.S. with a Black Farce." *Manchester Guardian*, 26 January 1979, p. 1.

Fiske, John, and John Hartley. *Reading Television*. London: Methuen, 1978.

"Four New Girls for the Bard." Photograph. *London Daily Mail*, 7 October 1980, p. 15.

"From Rags to Riches." *London Express*, 17 February 1979, p. 26.

Gans, Herbert J. *Popular Culture and High Culture: An Analysis and Evaluation of Taste*. New York: Basic Books, 1975.

Gelatt, Roland. "The Beeb's Bard." *Saturday Review*, 17 February 1979, pp. 45–48.

Griffin-Beale, Christopher. "All's Well That Ends Well for BBC Bardathon." *Broadcast*, 8 February 1982, pp. 10–11.

Hale, Lionel. Review of *The Comedy of Errors*. *News Chronicle* (England), 13 April 1938. In the collection at the Shakespeare Centre Library, Stratford-upon-Avon, England.

Hallinan, Tim. Interview with author. 19 June 1986.

————. "Jonathan Miller on the Shakespeare Plays." *Shakespeare Quarterly* 32 (1981): 134–43.

Hogg, Ian. Interview with author. 12 October 1983.

Holocaust and Executive Committee of the Committee to Bring Nazi War Criminals to Justice in the United States. Telegram to WNET/Thirteen, New York, 16 February 1981.

Homfray, Don. Interview with author, 11 October 1983.

Hordern, Michael. Interview comments in Stone/Hallinan press materials for *King Lear*.

Howell, Jane. Interviews with author, 17 February, 1985, 11 July 1985.

Hughes, David. "How the Fat Knight Got a Fresh Face." *Times* (London), 26 October 1980, p. 41.

"Interview with Jonathan Miller." Recording in Tel-Ed educational materials for *The Taming of the Shrew*, 1981.

Irwin, Ken. "A Date with Bard's Birds." *London Daily Mirror*, 2 December 1978, pp. 10–11.

James, Clive. "Dance of Gold." Review of *A Midsummer Night's Dream*. *London Observer*, 20 December 1981, p. 32.

————. "The Fantastic Voyage." Review of *Romeo and Juliet*. *London Observer*, 10 December 1978, p. 20.

Janson, H. W. *History of Art*. Englewood Cliffs, N.J.: Prentice-Hall and New York: Harry N. Abrams, 1962.

Kimbrough, R. Alan. "Olivier's *Lear* and the Limits of Video." In *Shakespeare on Television: An Anthology of Essays and Reviews*, edited by J. C. Bulman and H. R. Coursen, pp. 115–22. Hanover, N.H.: University Press of New England, 1988.

"*King Lear*" (program note). National Film Theatre (London) *July Programme*, July 1985, p. 31.

Krajci, John. Interview with author, 14 June 1985.

Kretzmer, Herbert. "The Mail TV Critic." Review of Royal Shakespeare Company's *Macbeth*. *London Daily Mail*, 5 January 1979. Excerpted in *Shakespeare on Television: An Anthology of Essays and Reviews*, edited by J. C. Bulman and H. R. Coursen, p. 249. Hanover N.H.: University Press of New England, 1988.

Kroll, Jack, with Rita Dallas. "Return of the Prodigal King." Review of *King Lear*. *Newsweek*, 8 November 1982, p. 105.

Last, Richard. " 'Shakespeare' Creates Boxed-In Feeling." *London Daily Telegraph*, 11 December 1978, p. 11.

Lindsay, Robert. Interview comments in Stone/Hallinan press materials for *Much Ado About Nothing*.

Lowden, Fraser. Interview with author, 23 June 1980.

_____. Letter to author, 28 July 1986.

McLuhan, Marshall. *Understanding Media: The Extensions of Man*. New York: Signet, 1964.

McNally, Owen. Review of *A Midsummer Night's Dream*. *Hartford Courant*, 24 April 1982, p. B5.

Maher, Mary Z. "Shaun Sutton at the End of the Series: 'The Shakespeare Plays.' " *Literature/Film Quarterly* 14, no. 4 (1986): 188–94.

Masefield, John. "William Shakespeare." Quoted in Royal Shakespeare Company's *The Comedy of Errors* program, 11 September 1962.

Maslin, Janet. "TV: *Caesar* Tailored to Small Screen." *New York Times*, 14 February 1979, p. C22.

Messina, Cedric. Preface to *The BBC-TV Shakespeare: As You Like It*, pp. 6–10. New York: Mayflower Books, 1978.

Miller, Jonathan. "The Afterlife of Art." Address at Alabama Shakespeare Festival, Anniston, Ala., 28 July 1984.

_____. Interview with author, 11 August 1981.

_____. Interview with Mary Maher, 20 December 1983.

_____. *Subsequent Performances*. London: Faber, 1986.

"Miss Johnson Stays Mum." *London Evening Standard*, 31 January 1979, p. 15.

Moshinsky, Elijah. Interview with author, 8 July 1986.

_____. "A Medium Fit for the Bard." *Manchester Guardian*, 26 July 1984, p. 10.

Nelligan, Kate. Interview comments in Stone/Hallinan press materials for *Measure for Measure*.

Newcomb, Horace. "Toward a Television Aesthetic." *Television: The Critical View*, 3d ed., edited by Horace Newcomb, pp. 478–94. New York: Oxford University Press, 1982.

Nicholson, Christopher. "A Precious Stone Called Culture." Review of *Richard II. London Daily Mail,* 11 December 1978, p. 23.

Noakes, Trevor. Interview with author, 23 June 1980.

"Notes on Production." Stone/Hallinan press materials for *Henry VI* plays.

Perry, James A. "Perryscope: The Man behind TV's 'Shakespeare Plays.'" *New Orleans States-Item,* 11 April 1979, p. B2.

Phillips, Mike. "Love's Labour Was All but Lost." Review of *Romeo and Juliet. London Daily Mail,* 4 December 1978, p. 27.

Poole, Victor. Letter to author, 6 October 1985.

————. Telephone interview with author, 2 July 1986.

Reynolds, Stanley. "*The Tempest*: BBC 2." *London Times,* 28 February 1980, p. 9.

Rich, Frank. "Peaks and Valleys in Papp's Marathon." *New York Times,* 5 February 1989, sec. 2, pp. 1, 5.

Rissik, Andrew. "BBC Shakespeare: Much to Be Desired." *Literary Review* (February 1985): 28–29.

Roberts, Bruce. Interview with author, 11 June 1985.

Rossiter, Leonard. Interview comments in Stone/Hallinan press materials for *King John.*

Schappes, Morris U. Letter to the editor. *New York Times,* 4 February 1981, p. A22.

Schoenbach, Jill. WNET/Thirteen, New York, memorandum about Anti-Defamation League statement. 11 February 1981.

Shallcross, Alan. Interview with author, 2 July 1985.

————. "The Text." Essays in *The BBC-TV Shakespeare,* scripts of the BBC Shakespeare Plays. London: BBC, 1978. 1978 scripts.

Shulman, Milton. "Beauty and the Bard." *Times Sunday Magazine* (London), 3 December 1978, pp. 48ff.

Slim, John. Review of *King John. Birmingham* (England) *Post,* 26 November 1984, p. 16.

Smith, Cecil. "Good Night, Sweet Series, Parting is Such . . . Or Is It?" *Los Angeles Times,* 26 May 1985, Calendar, pp. 38–39.

————. "Shakespeare: 'Being Done as Bard Intended.'" *Los Angeles Times,* 26 June 1981, Part 6, pp. 1, 17.

Thaler, Abraham. Letter to WNET/Thirteen, New York, 13 February 1981.

"Today." Television column. *London Mirror,* 3 December 1978, p. 27.

Unger, Arthur. "On TV." *Christian Science Monitor,* 13 February 1981, p. 19.

Venza, Jac. Interview with author, 12 June 1985.

"W. H. B." Review of *The Comedy of Errors. Birmingham* (England) *Ga-*

zette, 13 April 1938. In the collection at the Shakespeare Centre Library, Stratford-upon-Avon, England.

Walker, Sheila. Interview with author, 18 June 1985.

Weil, Suzanne, and Robert Kotlowitz. Memorandum about *The Merchant of Venice*, WNET/Thirteen, New York, 12 February 1981.

Wells, Stanley. "The History of the Whole Contention." Review of *Henry VI/Richard III* tetralogy. *Times Literary Supplement*, 4 February 1983, p. 105.

Wilders, John. "Adjusting the Set." *Times Higher Education Supplement* (London), 10 July 1981, p. 13.

"Wilders Interview at MLA." *Shakespeare on Film Newsletter*, December 1979, pp. 3ff.

OTHER RELATED WORKS

Berry, Ralph. *Changing Styles in Shakespeare*. George Allen & Unwin, 1981.

——. *On Directing Shakespeare: Interviews with Contemporary Directors*. New York: Barnes and Noble, 1977.

Bulman, J. C., and H. R. Coursen, eds. *Shakespeare on Television: An Anthology of Essays and Reviews*. Hanover, N.H.: University Press of New England, 1988.

Cook, Judith. *Shakespeare's Players*. London: Harrap, 1983.

David, Richard. *Shakespeare in the Theatre*. Cambridge: Cambridge University Press, 1978.

Drakakis, John, ed. *Alternative Shakespeares*. London: Methuen, 1985.

Elam, Keir. *The Semiotics of Theatre and Drama*. London: Methuen, 1980.

Jorgens, Jack J. *Shakespeare on Film*. Bloomington: Indiana University Press, 1977.

Kitchin, Laurence. "Shakespeare on the Screen." *Shakespeare Survey* 18 (1965): 70–74.

MacCann, Richard Dyer. *Film: A Montage of Theories*. New York: Dutton, 1966.

McQuail, Denis, ed. *Sociology of Mass Communication*. Baltimore: Penguin, 1972. Especially "The Television Audience: A Revised Perspective," "The Television and Radio Audience in Britain," and "Commitment and Career in the BBC."

Marc, David. "Understanding Television." *Atlantic Monthly*, August 1984, pp. 33–44.

Miller, Jonathan. "Shakespeare and the Modern Director." In *William*

Shakespeare: His World, His Work, His Influences, edited by John Andrews. 3 vols. New York: Scribner, 1985. 3:815–22.

Newcomb, Horace, ed. *Television: The Critical View*. 3d ed. New York: Oxford University Press, 1982.

Pearson, Jacqueline. "Shadows on the Shadow Box: The BBC Shakespeare." *Critical Quarterly* 21, no. 1 (1979): 67–70.

Ravage, John W. *Television: The Director's Viewpoint*. Boulder: Westview, 1978.

Styan, J. L. *The Shakespeare Revolution*. Cambridge: Cambridge University Press, 1977.

Sutton, Shaun. *The Largest Theatre in the World: Thirty Years of Television Drama*. London: BBC, 1982.

Trewin, J. C. *Going to Shakespeare*. London: Allen & Unwin, 1978.

Wilders, John. "Shakespeare on the Small Screen." *Shakespeare Jahrbuch* 117 (1982): 56–62.

Williams, Raymond. *Television: Technology and Cultural Form*. London: Fontana/Collins, 1974.

Zitner, Sheldon P. "Wooden O's in Plastic Boxes: Shakespeare and Television." *University of Toronto Quarterly* 51 (1981): 1–12.

Index